COGNAC

Nicholas Faith

COGNAC

Hamish Hamilton · London

Photographs by Michel Guillard

Design by Craig Dodd

Maps drawn by Richard Natkiel
(Sketches from *La Vigne* by Bertall)

Post-cards supplied by Christian Genet

First published in Great Britain 1986
by Hamish Hamilton Ltd
Garden House 57–59 Long Acre London WC2E 9JZ

Copyright © 1986 by Nicholas Faith

British Library Cataloguing in Publication Data
Faith, Nicholas
    Cognac.
    1. Brandy—History
    I. Title
    641.2'53   TP599
    ISBN 0-241-11831-X

Typeset by MS Filmsetting Limited, Frome, Somerset
Printed in Great Britain by
Jolly & Barber Ltd, Rugby

CONTENTS

Acknowledgements

My old friend Michael Longhurst first suggested that I should write a book about cognac. At times since then I cursed him because of the troubles his idea caused me: but these feelings are more than counterbalanced by my gratitude to him and to his delightful wife Marie-Christine for their support and hospitality.

The book was originally edited by Julian Jeffs, whose tactful needling induced me to return to my researches and produce a far more complete and satisfactory second draft. In particular he gently propelled me back to my sources to explain more fully the art and science of distillation as practised in the Charente. My publisher, Christopher Sinclair-Stevenson, gave me much-appreciated support for a properly illustrated book. My friend, Michel Guillard, has captured the unique atmosphere of the Charentes in his photographs while his wife Catherine organised the other illustrations with her usual charm and efficiency.

As other strangers have discovered, it is a hospitable region and I owe a great debt of gratitude to large numbers of Cognacais. My biggest debts are to Alain Braastad of Delamain, who could have written a far more complete history than I have and who read the manuscript with an appreciative critical eye. The historical sections also owe a great deal to Gérard and Marie-Geneviève Jouannet and to the *Annales* which he edits (and she organizes), amazingly the first systematic attempt to investigate Cognac's rich history.

I owe a particular debt to the small group who helped me disentangle the technicalities of cognac, notably Francis Gay-Bellile at the Station Viticole, Maurice Fillioux and Michel Caumeil at Hennessy, Pierre Frugier at Martell, Jacques Rouvière at Bisquit and Robert Leauté at Rémy Martin. At the Bureau National de Cognac, a model professional organisation, Gérard Sturm and Madeleine Caverne provided me with unstinting help.

It is impossible to name everyone else who helped me in Cognac, but, possibly invidiously, can I single out Pauline Reverchon, Colin and Fiona Campbell, Jacques Hine, Hugues Echasseriaux, Alain Royer, Jean-François Gauthier-Auriol and that indomitable veteran, Maurice Hennessy.

Introduction · The Uniqueness of Cognac

In winter you can tell you are in cognac country as soon as you turn off the main Bordeaux–Paris road at Barbezieux. The landscape does not change at all dramatically; it is more rounded, perhaps a little more hilly, than between Bordeaux and Barbezieux, and there are an increasing number of vines. But then the major impact has nothing to do with the sense of sight. It has to do with the sense of smell. At night during the distillation season from December to March the whole atmosphere is suffused with an unmistakable aroma, a warmth that is almost palpable: brown, rich, grapey. It emanates from dozens of otherwise unremarkable groups of farm buildings, distinguished by the lights burning as the new brandy is distilled.

Cognac emerges from the gleaming copper vats in thin, transparent trickles, tasting harsh and oily, raw yet recognizably the product of the vine. If anything, it resembles *grappa*; but what to the Italians is a saleable spirit is merely an intermediate product to the Cognacais. Before they consider the product ready for market it has to be matured in special oak casks. Most of the spirits, described by the more poetically minded locals as 'sleeping beauties', are destined to be awakened within a few years and sold off as relatively ordinary cognac, but a small percentage is left to sleep for much longer. Every year expert palates sample them and eliminate – or, rather, set aside for immediate sale – those deemed incapable of further improvement. As the survivors from this rigorous selection process mature, so their alcoholic strength diminishes and within forty or fifty years, is down to 40° – the strength at which cognacs, old and new, are sold to the drinker. These truly aristocratic brandies are then transferred to great glass jars (demi-johns, known as *bonbonnes*), each holding about 25 litres of the precious fluid and stored, even more reverently, in the innermost recesses of their owners' cellars – the aptly named *paradis* familiar to every visitor to Cognac.

Hennessy has the most famous *paradis* in Cognac itself, but an even more impressive collection is hidden away in the ancient crypts of the medieval church of Châteauneuf, a little town a few miles away. The crypts are used by the region's major wholesaler, Messrs Alfred Tesseron. For over fifty years three generations of the family have supplied even the most fastidious of the cognac houses with at least a proportion of the brandies they require for their finest, oldest blends. The Tesserons naturally avoid competing with their wholesale customers by selling cognac directly to the public, but they do have a few retail clients, like the Ritz and the Savoy hotels in London. The Tesserons' two *paradis* contain over 1,000 *bonbonnes* dating back to the early nineteenth century. I was privileged to taste a sample of the 1853 vintage.

The world of cognac is governed by certain immutable rituals. Even when pouring the 1853, the firm's general manager swilled out the empty glass with a little of the cognac and dashed the precious liquid to the floor to ensure that the glass was free from impurities. Astonishingly, my first impresion of the cognac was of its youth and freshness. Anyone whose idea of the lifespan of an alcoholic beverage is derived from wines is instinctively prepared for the telltale signs of old age, for old wines are inevitably faded, brown, their bouquet and taste an evanescent experience. Old cognacs often retain their youthful virility, their attack. It seems absurd: the brandy was

*Opposite: M Guy
Tesseron: he prefers the
1906*

*Left: Bonbonnes at the
Tesserons*

*Overleaf: The
Hennessys' Chateau at
St Brice – only a couple
of miles from the centre
of Cognac*

made when Queen Victoria was young, and the grapes came from vines planted, some of them, before the French Revolution. Yet it was no historical relic, but vibrantly alive. But then the perfect balance of such a venerable brandy is compounded of a series of paradoxes: the spirit is old in age but youthful in every other respect; it is rich but not sweet; deep in taste though relatively light, a translucent chestnut, in colour. Its taste is quite simply the essence of grapiness, without any hint of the over-ripeness that mars lesser liquids.

But the secret of a great cognac lies in its 'nose', its bouquet. In the words of Robert Delamain, scholar and cognac merchant, what one looks for in a cognac is 'above all a scent, a precious scent that exists nowhere else in nature, not in any flower, not in any herb; a soft aroma that engulfs you in successive waves; a scent that you examine, you explore, in order to uncover other agreeable, if indefinable, aromas'.[1] The warmth and delicacy Delamain is describing linger on and on after the glass has been emptied. In the wine tasters' vocabulary the crucial attribute is that the brandy is 'long'. At the end of the last century (when the 1853 was being transferred from oak to its appointed *bonbonnes*) Professor Ravaz claimed: 'The bouquet of a good *eau-de-vie* from the Grande Champagne lasts for a week or more.'[2] He was not exaggerating. In the distilleries themselves the aroma lingers on throughout the eight or nine months in every year when the stills themselves are empty.

Only after tasting a cognac of that age and quality can you appreciate the truly miraculous nature of the whole enterprise and begin to understand how it is that the name of a small town in western France has become synonymous with the finest distilled liquor in the world. As a result, Cognac is by far the best-known town in France, Paris only excepted; yet even today Cognac has only 30,000 inhabitants, and when it first rose to fame in the eighteenth century fewer than 5,000 people sheltered behind its walls. Whatever the town's size, the reputation of its brandy would have been a prodigious achievement, for anyone with access to grapes and the simplest of distillation apparatus can make brandy of a sort. But only the Cognacais can make cognac, a drink with qualities that are enhanced by age until it becomes the very essence of the grapes from which it was distilled.

The success of the Cognacais is due to a multitude of factors – a combination of geography, geology and history. They had the perfect soil, the right climate – and the ability to market their products to appreciative customers the world over. At first sight nothing about Cognac, a small town in the middle of an agreeable, albeit unremarkable landscape, is special. On more detailed investigation almost everything about the region is out of the ordinary. The most obvious distinction is geological, as it is for most of the *terroirs* producing France's finest wines and spirits. But whereas the soils and subsoils of Bordeaux and Burgundy, if unusual, are not unique, the Cognac region includes formations found nowhere else. In Delamain's words:

So far as the super-Cretaceous period is concerned, it appears in the Charentais in so specially characteristic a form that in the international language of geology these terrains are referred to by their Charentais names: Angoumois (from Angoulême), Coniacien (from Cognac) and Campanien (referring to the Champagne country of the Charente).[3]

These last three formations are especially rich in chalk, and they produce the best cognacs. But, as a modern expert has pointed out, geology by itself provides an inadequate explanation:

To confine yourself to the chemical make-up of the soil narrows and falsifies the problem. The physical nature of the earth appears to have a much greater importance: the most appreciated qualities derive from chalky soils composed of especially delicate and porous chalk lying on a similar type of chalk subsoil. Because it is so porous the subsoil accumulates rain water, which it releases gradually as it is required, like a humidifier.[4]

[1] Robert Delamain, *Histoire du Cognac*, Paris, Stock, 1935.
[2] Louis Ravaz and Albert Vivier, *Le Pays du Cognac*, Angoulême, 1900.
[3] Op. cit. [4] Ibid.

Cognac's geography, and thus its weather, are equally special, though they are less easy to pinpoint than its geological peculiarities. Cognac is at the very border of the geographical divide that separates northern from southern France – the northern 'Langue d'Oil' from the southern 'Langue d'Oc'. In the later Middle Ages the linguistic boundary passed through Saintes, due west of Cognac, and Matha, a few miles north of the town. The change is not as dramatic as that in the Rhône valley, where you are suddenly aware of the influence of the Mediterranean, but it is nevertheless abrupt enough to emphasize that you are in a different world.

Travellers have long been aware of the change. In Robert Delamain's words:

For sailors from the whole of northern Europe, the coast of France below the Loire estuary was the region where, for the first time, they felt they were in the blessed South, where the heat of the sun makes life easier, where fruits ripen and wine flows. The Bay of Bourgneuf, and the Coast of Saintonge sheltering behind its islands, were for them the first sunny shores they came across.[1]

Cognac itself still retains some of the elements of a sleepy southern town, closing at midday, drowsing in the hot summer sun. Its inhabitants, however businesslike, lack any northern brusqueness.

For the town is at the heart of a very special border region, a rough oblong bounded on the north by the Loire, between the Bay of Biscay and the mountains of the Massif Centrale. The French themselves would call it Aquitaine, but the region I am trying to define is rather more restricted, since it peters out to the south of Bordeaux, its special softness lost in the heat of the Basque country. The whole area is remarkable for its gentleness. There are no abrupt slopes, no cliffs, no obvious drama in the landscape at all. Often it appears dull to the uninstructed eye until one begins to appreciate its subtleties. Its most obvious characteristic is its weather, like the landscape gentle, temperate, but more emollient than further north. Everything is softer, lighter, gentler, and Cognac epitomizes those qualities.

Naturally the River Charente, which bisects the area, is a gentle river: 'the most beautiful stream in all my kingdom,' said King Henry IV nearly four hundred years ago. They call it *molle*, the soft sweet Charente, which twists and turns on its leisurely way to the sea. Bordered by willows and poplars, troubled only by fishermen (and the town's ever-energetic oarsmen), the Charente is an almost absurdly picturesque river. Echoing its breadth, its alluvial basin is broad, and the slopes above, like the river, are spacious and gentle. It is on these slopes that the grapes for the best cognac are grown.

The heart of the region is a rectangle within the oblong, which naturally embodies the climatic advantages enjoyed by the region as a whole. It is near enough to the coast for the winters to be mild. To the east it is bounded by the first foot-hills of the Massif Central, and as the country gets less rounded the weather becomes a little harsher, the brandies become less mellow. Cognac itself enjoys the best of both worlds. The climate reinforces the initial advantages provided by the geological make-up of the soil. Because Cognac is so northerly a vineyard, the long summer days encourage grapes to ripen slowly and regularly, giving them the right balance of fruit and acidity required for distillation purposes. But the sunlight is never harsh, the 'micro-climate' unique. Even the most transient visitor notices the filtered light, its unique luminosity – more intense sunlight would result in over-ripe grapes with too much sugar. In his delightful book on Cognac, Cyril Ray quotes a variety of authors, including the novelist Jacques Chardonne, the map-maker

[1] Ibid.

Overleaf: Burie: tranquillity incarnate

15

Louis Larmat and Louis Ravaz, all of whom use the word '*doux*' or '*douce*' to describe the region, its weather and above all the light – which Jacques de Lacretelle describes as 'tamisée' – filtered.

The weather has another contribution to make after the grapes have been fermented into wine and then distilled, but only those who live in Cognac appreciate fully how this quality of diffused intensity extends even to the rain. The Charente region is wetter than many other parts of France, but, in the words of Professor Ravaz, the rain falls 'often, but in small amounts . . . sometimes it is only a persistent mist which provides the earth with only a little moisture, but which keeps the atmosphere saturated with humidity and prevents any evaporation.'[1] Ravaz's description sounds remarkably like that of a Scotch mist. Both cognac and malt whisky require long periods of maturation in oak casks and their special qualities emerge only if the casks are kept in a damp, cool atmosphere.

The individual components of the cognac formula could, in theory, have been reproduced elsewhere, but the result is unique. In the words of Professor Ravaz, who did more than anyone else to rebuild the cognac vineyard after the phylloxera disaster:

The same variety of grape can be grown anywhere and in the same way as in the Charente: distillation can be carried out anywhere else as at Cognac and in the same stills; the brandy can be stored in identical casks as those we employ in our region; it can be cared for as well, or maybe even better. But the same combination of weather and terrain cannot be found anywhere else. As far as the soil is concerned, it is not enough that it should belong to the same geological formations; it must have the same physical and chemical composition. And no one has ever found such a duplicate. In addition, the climate of the region must be identical to that of the Charente, and that is almost inconceivable. There is therefore very little chance that all the elements which influence the nature of the product should be found together in any region apart from the Charente; and thus *no other region can produce cognac*. The slightest difference in the climate, the soil, and so on is enough to change completely the nature of the brandy; and that is as it should be because there are, even in the Charente, a few spots (small ones, it is true) which produce mediocre brandy. All the trials which have been made all over the place to produce cognac with the same varieties and the Charentais methods have resulted only in failure. And this lack of success could have been foreseen if people had only remembered this one principle: that the nature of products is dependent on a combination of conditions which occurs only rarely.[2]

Even Professor Ravaz omits one crucial element in the creation of Cognac – the unique qualities of the people themselves. The combination that he outlines provide only the potential for making Cognac and ignores the very different qualities needed to spread its fame throughout the world. For the potential could be realized only through a very special type of man, combining two superficially incompatible qualities. The making and storage of the spirit demands painstaking patience, a quality usually associated with peasantry in general and especially marked in a country with such a troubled past as that of the Charente. In Maurice Burès words: 'Scarred for a long time by incessant wars, the Charentais became reserved, introverted, discreet.'[3] But this combination was precisely the opposite of the open outlook required if cognac was to be marketed the world over. It was always destined chiefly for sale abroad, for, unlike Northerners, the Charentais did not need spirits to keep themselves warm in winter and have always drunk sparingly of their own product.

[1] Ravaz and Vivier, op. cit.

[2] Ibid.

[3] Maurice Burès, 'Le type saintongeais', *La Science Sociale*, vol. 23, Paris, 1908.

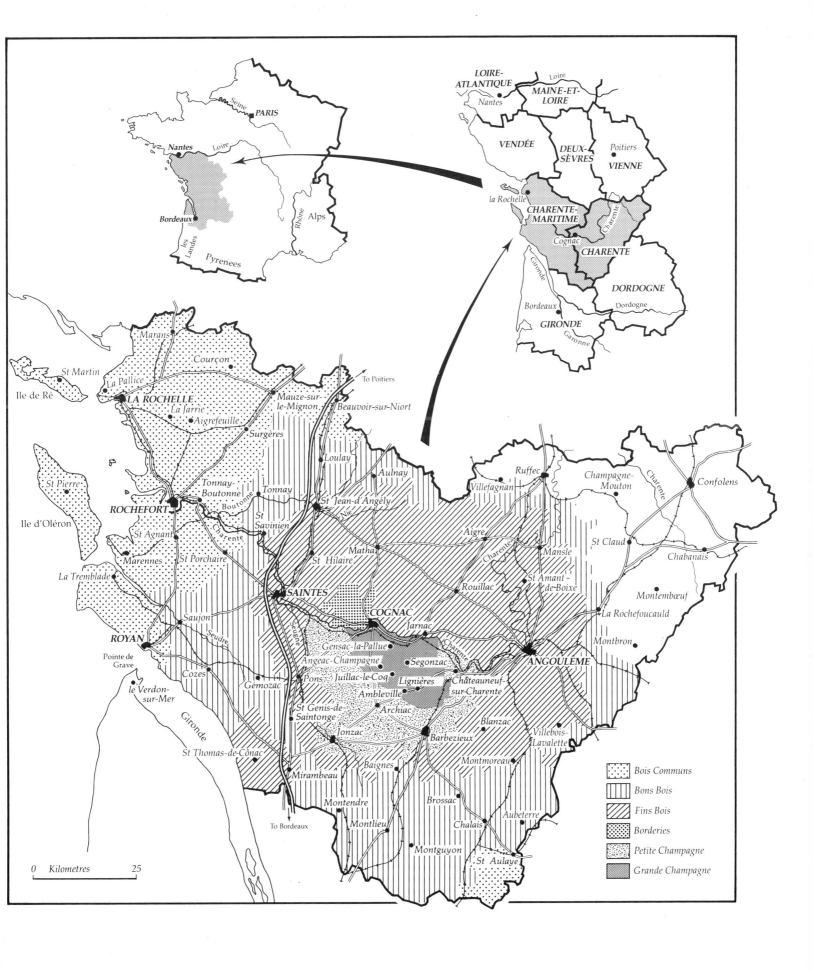

LOIRE-ATLANTIQUE
MAINE-ET-LOIRE
Loire
Nantes
VENDÉE
DEUX-SÈVRES
Poitiers
VIENNE
la Rochelle
CHARENTE-MARITIME
Cognac
Charente
CHARENTE
Gironde
Bordeaux
Garonne
GIRONDE
DORDOGNE
Dordogne

Seine
PARIS
Nantes
Loire
Bordeaux
Rhône
Alps
les Landes
Pyrenees

Marans
Courçon
St Martin
La Pallice
Ile de Ré
LA ROCHELLE
La Jarrie
Aigrefeuille
Mauze-sur-le-Mignon
Beauvoir-sur-Niort
To Poitiers
Surgères
Loulay
Aulnay
St Pierre
Villefagnan
Ruffec
Champagne-Mouton
Charente
Confolens
Tonnay-Boutonne
Tonnay
St Jean-d'Angély
Ile d'Oléron
ROCHEFORT
Boutonne
St Savinien
Niort
Aigre
Charente
Mansle
St Claud
Chabanais
St Agnant
Charente
Mathas
St Hilaire
Rouillac
St Amant-de-Boixe
Marennes
St Porchaire
Montembœuf
La Tremblade
SAINTES
COGNAC
La Rochefoucauld
Saujon
Seugne
Jarnac
Charente
Montbron
ROYAN
Seudre
Gensac-la-Pallue
Angeac-Champagne
Segonzac
ANGOULEME
Pointe de Grave
Cozes
Pons
Juillac-le-Coq
Lignières
Châteauneuf-sur-Charente
le Verdon-sur-Mer
Gémozac
Ambleville
Archiac
Gironde
St Genis-de-Saintonge
Blanzac
Villebois-Lavalette
St Thomas-de-Cônac
Jonzac
Baignes
Barbezieux
Montmoreau
Mirambeau
Brossac
Montendre
Aubeterre
Montlieu
Chalais
To Bordeaux
Montguyon
St Aulaye

0   Kilometres   25

Bois Communs
Bons Bois
Fins Bois
Borderies
Petite Champagne
Grande Champagne

Their instinctive unwillingness to allow anyone to intrude on the intensely private life of the family is symbolized by the classic face of the Cognac countryside with its dour stone walls interrupted only by stout, permanently shut wooden doors that enclose spacious cobbled farmyards surrounded by fermentation vats, still rooms, storehouses. Outsiders find the blank stone walls sad and menacing; the inhabitants find them deeply reassuring. *Cagouillards*, snails, they are nicknamed, shut in their fortresses. This collective introversion, this native defensiveness, is not confined to the countryside but extends to the small country towns – like Cognac itself.

Yet, miraculously, the inhabitants have managed to combine the two qualities. The fusion was best expressed by the region's most distinguished native, the late Jean Monnet, the 'founder of Europe'. He was the son of one of Cognac's leading merchants, and he remembers how every evening 'at dusk, when we lit the lamps, we had to shut every shutter. "They can see us," my mother would say, so greatly did she share the anxiety, the fear of being seen, of exposure which is so marked a trait of of the Charentais character.'[1] The paradox was that in the household of the Monnets, as in those of many other merchants, guests were not exclusively aged aunts or squabbling cousins but also included buyers from all over the world. As a result, the little world of Cognac provided the young Jean Monnet with 'an enormously wide field of observation and a very lively exchange of ideas. I learned there, or springing from there, more than I could have done from a specialized education.'[2] This combination of a patient peasant obsession with detail and an international outlook is as unusual, and as important, as Cognac's geology and geography.

Cognac is the fusion of many factors, so there is no simple or obvious way to arrange a book on the subject. By training I am an historian and therefore naturally begin with the historical circumstances that created the Cognac we know today before providing a detailed description of the making of the spirit and an analysis of the remarkable changes seen in the twentieth century. But I start with history also because Cognac is in a sense a new-found-land, opened up by successive generations of explorers who gradually uncovered its unique qualities. And a final reason for starting with the past: Cognac's uniqueness is not confined to its geology and its geography; it extends also to its inhabitants and their history.

[1] Jean Monnet, *Mémoires*, Paris, Fayard, 1976.
[2] Ibid.

THE CREATION OF COGNAC

1 · From Salt … to Wine …

The traveller is made aware of Cognac's most famous product even before he or she reaches the town, for the roads all around are lined with endless placards bearing the names of famous brands and rather rougher signs promoting the innumerable individuals who sell their own cognac (and the local apéritif, Pineau des Charentes) directly to the public. But the main road from Saintes to Angoulême merely skirts the old town, visible only as you cross the bridge over the Charente, so the casual visitor is tempted to believe that the town centres on the Place François Ier at the top of the hill. In fact, this unremarkable junction is the centre of the new town that grew up outside the town's walls only in the nineteenth century. The new town is agreeable enough, with telltale signs of prosperity such as a plethora of *pâtissiers* and bookshops. Otherwise it is indistinguishable from a hundred others throughout France.

The historic heart of Cognac lies in the old town which clusters behind the Château de Cognac in a semicircle on the steep banks of the Charente. Many of the buildings in this picturesque and still unspoilt huddle date, like the Château itself, from the sixteenth century; others are up to a couple of centuries younger. But all of them – houses, offices and warehouses – have been blackened into uniformity by the activities of *Torula compniacensis richon*, the famous fungus that thrives (as who would not) in the rich, damp air of warehouses full of casks of maturing brandy. The buildings are still much as they were originally built, for the Hennessys, who have bought many of the businesses formerly housed in them, have resisted the temptation to indulge in wholesale reconstruction in the name of efficiency. They have spruced up the interiors but have otherwise allowed their premises to remain an agreeable warren.

The Hennessy writ stops at the street that forms an approximate centre to the semi-circle, the rue Saulnier (Street of the Salt Harbour), named after the commodity that first made Cognac an important commercial centre. It is still cobbled, its most recent feature a gutter running down the centre of the street, installed in the sixteenth century to improve the sanitation arrangements. Half-way up the street on the right is the Maison de la Gabelle, an imposing double-fronted structure, recognizable from the amiably battered and grotesque gargoyles on each side of the door. It is now rather dilapidated and is used, like every other spare building in the old town, as a brandy warehouse. Originally it was far more important, for the *gabelle* was the tax on salt in the days when it was a basic necessity for preserving meat and fish for consumption during the winter, a tax that formed an important element in the revenues of many impecunious monarchs.

Further up the street is a rather less imposing building, formerly the offices of the cognac business owned by the Gauthier family, which still lives in the house. It is a typical example of the sort of accommodation that for hundreds of years housed firms and the families that owned them. Like its neighbour, it is double-fronted, the two halves separated by a covered corridor leading from the street to the yard behind the house. On the ground floor one side was devoted to work; in the front was a general office, behind a private office for the firm's partners. The dining room was on the other side of the corridor, below the living-room, the *grande chambre*, and the

Opposite: The Rue Saulnier – with the latest in central drainage

bedrooms. The horses were stabled behind the house, and, despite its compactness, the other corner of the yard housed a still, which fell into disuse only after the First World War.

The street, the Maison de la Gabelle, the continuing presence of the Gauthiers, all emphasize the leisurely continuity of the world of Cognac, the thread of international commercial awareness, despite wars and civil commotions, that marks this apparently sleepy little town, making it more like a major sea port, such as Bordeaux, than the typical French country town it appears at first sight. Indeed, the major shifts have been relative, as Cognac's fortunes have varied in relation to those of larger and apparently better placed centres of trade nearer the coast, changes that have occured as salt gave way to wine and was in turn replaced by brandy.

As a town Cognac dates back over two thousand years and was probably named after a pre-Roman chieftain called Comnos or Conos.[1] It is surprising how many different spellings can be found for so apparently simple a name. In Latin, the name was variously Compniacum, Compinacum, Compnacum and Coniacum. More recent variants include Coingnac, Compniac, Cougnac, Congnac, Coegnac and as late as the eighteenth century, when the town was already world-famous, Coignac or Cogniac.[2]

Its importance was originally geographical. In the words of a modern geographer, Cognac had 'the advantage of being a crossroads on the river axis of the Charente linking Limousin and the sea, near the threshold of Poitou and the estuary of the Gironde. On the site of a sheltered stretch of the Charente in the chalky soils between the broad pastures of Jarnac and Merpins, it was first a fortified town, a religious centre, a stopping point.'[3] Its geographical importance was recognized as early as the eleventh century, when it was first fortified. The Cognac we know today started to emerge when northern sailors rediscovered the quality of the region's salt. Very *conservatif* they found it, suited especially to preserving fish and meat. Indeed, its qualities became famous throughout northern Europe as the Flemish, the Scandinavians and the Germans from the Hanseatic ports all spread its fame; the Hanseatic merchants even set up special fishery stations in Norway to use the salt. In theory Cognac should have been at a definite disadvantage as against towns nearer the sea. But it was on a tidal river at the limit of sea-going navigation, and from the twelfth century on it enjoyed two crucial advantages: it had a *monopole saulnier,* the right to insist that every cargo of salt passing along the river had to be trans-shipped in the town; and because it was in the western part of the Angoumois its merchants had only to pay a *quint,* a single tax of 20 per cent on the salt they traded, whereas their unhappy brethren in Saintonge and Aunis nearer the coast had to pay the *quart de sel,* a levy of 25 per cent due whenever the salt changed hands.

Unfortunately, the town enjoyed no such advantage when the balance of trade shifted in the second half of the twelfth century. In 1152 Eleanor of Aquitaine, heiress to the whole region, married Prince Henry of England, who mounted the throne two years later as Henry II and ruled a vast Anglo-French Empire for the next thirty-four years. The marriage led to an amazing change in English drinking habits, as virtually the whole population took to drinking the wines from the new dominions and made their fortunes until the English finally departed three

[1] The —ac ending is common in the area, and historians have always assumed that such towns were originally someone's home. Recent researches suggest that this is not necessarily so, although no one has yet queried the derivation so far as Cognac is concerned.
[2] Today, although there is an agreed spelling of the name, it can be pronounced in two ways, for many inhabitants use a long 'o', as in 'cone'.
[3] M. Lartaut, in *Norois*, Paris, 1963.

*A former inhabitant of
the Rue Saulnier?*

centuries later. Not surprisingly, 'Aliénor' remains a heroine of regional history, a heavily romanticized legend still fondly recalled in many an after-dinner speech. But the importance of the alliance has rather blinded historians to three other crucial developments: new ports, new boats and new social relationships.

The most famous new port was La Rochelle on the coast, but more important for Cognac was the development of Tonnay-Charente on the river itself, only a few miles inland. The new type of ship, the *cogue,* was first developed by the Flamands. Each displaced over 1,000 tons, and they thus were far more efficient than the much smaller vessels they replaced, which held only one tenth as much. The *cogues* could sail as far upriver as Tonnay, where they were loaded with wine shipped along the Boutonne, the Sèvre, the Seudre or the Charente itself in much smaller barges – the famous *gabares* used by the Cognacais to transport casks of brandy until the 1930s.

Almost inevitably, these changes ensured that the pattern of feudal relationships normal throughout France was broken, and a new legal framework emerged; the Roles or Judgments of Oléron, named after the island just off the coast, formed the basis for maritime law affecting shipwrecks and other nautical problems throughout western Europe. But the changes worked right throughout the whole region. In Robert Delamain's words:

These two products, salt and wine, which foreigners sought out in the ports of the coast of the Saintonge, created in the rural mass of the Charentais basin a mentality adjusted to commercial practices, a mentality which was highly unusual at a time when the whole economy elsewhere was confined within the limits of the *seigneurie,* in which lords and peasants alike were forced to find within the domaine the wherewithal to clothe and feed themselves.[1]

[1] Op. cit.

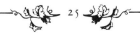

2 · . . . to Brandywijn

Bordeaux and La Rochelle became rival suppliers to the English trade. Bordeaux concentrated on its famous light red wine, claret, but the wines shipped from further north were mostly white. And whereas the merchants of Bordeaux jealously preserved their monopoly, and thus effectively shut out from the international trade the 'Haut Pays' upriver, the whole of the Charente basin, extending 50 miles inland, benefited from the demands of the English market.

As late as the sixteenth century, when the English had been chased from France for a century or more, we find the expression *vin de Cognac*. Although it was not as important or as expensive as *vin de Ritsel* (wine from La Rochelle), Cognac itself retained some of the importance it had acquired earlier from the salt trade. Nearer the sea the vines had spread over land also suitable for grain, but the Cognac region was different. In his last study of the area the late, great Professor Enjalbert compared Cognac with the area around Reims, now famous for champagne. In both regions the word champagne was used originally to describe a landscape similar to the original Campania north of Rome, a fair, fertile, rolling countryside. It was unfortunate for the Cognacais that the wine makers round Reims were the first to use the word as a brand name and thus to confuse generations of brandy drinkers. In both regions the vine was originally largely confined to the hills, while grain remained dominant in the more fertile 'Champagne' valleys and the slopes above them. Around Cognac vines were first planted instead of the *bois* (woods), which had only partially been cleared for growing grain and which later proved a natural source of the wood required for distillation. The vines then spread to the Champagnes – the chalky hillsides round Châteauneuf that overlooked the Charente valley itself – which had continued to grow cereals throughout the Middle Ages. In 1576 a local historian, Corlieu,[1] emphasized that the 'Grandes Champagnes de Segonzac' produced great quantities of fine wines which were shipped downriver all over the world. A century later these slopes emerged also as the source of the best wine for distillation purposes.

In earlier centuries Cognac and its surrounding countryside had owed its special position not to geographical advantages but to royal favour. The town had been granted its first charter early in the thirteenth century by the heir of 'Aliénor', the hapless King John ('Jean Sans Terre' to the French), and soon afterwards his widow reunited the town with its natural hinterland, the Angoumois, the county of Angoulême. Early in the fourteenth century Cognac was separated from the feudal lordships that still normally ruled rural France, whereas Jarnac, a few miles further upriver and its main potential rival, was dominated by its feudal lords until the Revolution of 1789. In consequence, and much to the resentment of its inhabitants, Jarnac has generally played very much a secondary role. King John had set off the train of events that ensured that the famous brandy would be called cognac and not 'jarnac'.

The Charente was reconquered by the French far sooner than Bordeaux, the last redoubt of the English occupation, abandoned only in the mid-fifteenth century. In the short term this created

[1] J. Corlieu, *Receuil en forme d'histoire*, Marseille, Jeanne Laffitte, 1976.

problems for the locals, since they lost their most important market and their region remained a battleground through the later years of the Hundred Years' War. But in the longer run it was the Bordelais who suffered worse from their dependence on a single outlet. The alternative buyers of the Charente's wines, who filled the gap left by the English, were from the same northern countries which had earlier taken their salt from the Cognacais. They provided a far greater continuity than had the English; and whereas the Bordelais never became a force in the French market, the Charentais, once reunited with their fellow countrymen, managed to sell their wines also at home.

Three centuries after King John, a lucky accident ensured that Cognac was again singled out for royal favour. Francis I, the very model of a Renaissance monarch, was born in the town in 1492 and naturally showed his gratitude to his birthplace after he ascended the throne of France twenty-three years later, by immediately exempting the inhabitants from all of the many taxes, forced loans and other levies imposed on the rest of the county of Angoulême to sustain the French army in its numerous wars. The citation emphasized how loyal the town, very much on the frontier of two provinces, had been through many assaults and sieges by the country's enemies.

Francis I's attachment to Cognac ensured that the town retained its privileges – and its inhabitants their feeling of being special, part of a wider world – during the tumultuous century that followed his death. In 1544 there was a revolt, brutally suppressed by the royal forces, against the *gabelle,* the dreaded salt tax. The Angoumois then became one of the heartlands of French Protestantism and thus, inevitably, a major battleground in the religious wars that dominated the last half of the sixteenth century; one of the crucial battles was in Jarnac itself. The Protestants, and their ethic, took root and provided a further boost to the inhabitants' commercial-mindedness.

The upheavals continued during the first half of the seventeenth century, culminating in the Fronde, the Civil War between the feudal barons and the young King Louis XIV, who inherited his throne as a mere baby in 1643. Again Cognac was involved. Again it was lucky. It staunchly held out on behalf of the king against the assaults of one of the leading Frondeurs, the Duc de la Rochefoucauld, and was duly rewarded for its loyalty. The mayor was ennobled; the inhabitants were exempted from taxes for twenty years and were granted the right to hold four fairs a year, each to last three days. These provided an unequalled meeting place for the local farmers and merchants. As the century wore on, the fair-goers began increasingly to bargain, not over wine, but over a new product, *eau-de-vie*.

The introduction of brandy was due almost entirely to the Dutch. The inhabitants of the northern Netherlands freed themselves from the Spanish yoke in the 1570s and almost immediately dominated European trade; their supremacy lasted for over a century and affected every supplier who came into contact with them. Inevitably the Charentais had to follow their demands for the new product, brandy. Historians have always assumed that the change-over was due to two factors, transport economics and a decline in the quality of wines provided by the Charentais. Neither explanation is entirely accurate. A distilled spirit, eight or nine times more concentrated than wine, was obviously far cheaper to ship and could simply be cut with water by the buyer to provide the equivalent amount of liquid. But the original trade involved the shipment of wine, not brandy, to the Netherlands as raw material for some of the many distilleries built there in the late sixteenth century. These were originally called *wijnbranders* (literally, 'wine

COGNAC — Tours du Vieux Pont

Aux Tours de France, Cognac

COGNAC — *Maison de la Nourrice de François-Ier*

burners') and the product therefore *brandywijn* or *brandvin* ('burnt wine'). Although these 'burners' used a wide variety of raw materials, wine was officially favoured: the Dutch government discouraged the use of the obvious alternative, grain. Even before 1600 there were complaints that the distilleries tended to make corn far too expensive for the poor, a concern that formed a recurring theme in the story of brandy. In the early eighteenth century the French government discouraged the planting of vines in order to provide enough grain to feed the population.

The pattern changed only slowly as the French gradually absorbed the techniques and the equipment pioneered by the Dutch, for distillation, like drainage, was a Dutch speciality. (The French used Dutch engineers to drain the marshes of the Aunis early in the seventeenth century.) The Dutch imported copper from Sweden, built the stills, bought the raw material (which they transported in their own ships) and then marketed the final product. It took a century for the French to shift the *brandywijn* business nearer home.

The Dutch were dominant because they were by far the biggest buyers both of wine and, later, of *brandywijn*. They needed the spirit to compensate for the impurities in the water carried by their

Rue Saulnier: Remains of ancient riches

sailors during long spells at sea, and there was an increasing demand for spirits both at home and from the markets they supplied throughout northern Europe. But their original dominance extended to every aspect of the distillation business. At first the Dutch established their own stills on the Charente, buying only the basic wine from the locals. When the French first started to distil their wines themselves they imported the complete stills from Holland, and when they began to make their own they used the same Swedish copper as the Dutch. Even at the end of the

seventeenth century stills imported from the Netherlands were 20 per cent more expensive than their locally made equivalents, and in the eighteenth century, although the French could make all the components required to build their stills, many of the distillers were ignorant enough to be cheated by their suppliers (who sold the bits by weight and simply added extra ones when weighing them).

Predictably, the quantities and strengths of the *brandywijns* were both expressed in Dutch. The *velte* (amounting to just over 7 litres) was a basic measurement of quantity, and the *barrique* (the contents of a cask) was reckoned not in French *pintes* but in *veltes*.[1] Similarly, the strength of the spirit was expressed in relation to standard Dutch gin (*preuve d'Hollande*), about 49 per cent alcohol.[2] The basic spirit, much scorned by connoisseurs, was 'three–six', double *preuve d'Hollande*, because three parts of water were mixed with six of alcohol. 'Three–seven' was even stronger because seven parts of alcohol were used instead of six, while 'three–five' was slightly weaker.

Despite the Dutch dominance, the French started to sell their own *eaux-de-vie* at an early stage. There is a reference to a *barrique d'eau ardente* shipped from Bordeaux in 1517, but the first records of sales of *eau-de-vie* come from La Rochelle, the most important sea port between Bordeaux and Nantes. In 1549 *quatre barriques d'eau-de-vie bonne et marchande* ('four barriques of *eau-de-vie*, wholesome and fit for sale') were traded, and in 1571 a certain Jehan Serazin was described as a *marchand et faizeur d'eau-de-vie* ('merchant and producer of *eau-de-vie*'). By the end of the century the trade was important enough for it to be monopolized, a favourite means for impecunious French monarchs to raise money throughout the ages. In 1604 one Isaac Bernard paid an unknown sum for a monopoly of the production and export of all the *eaux-de-vie* made in the provinces of Tours, Poitou, Languedoc and Guyenne – effectively the whole of western France.[3] Inevitably, this extremely wide grant was largely ignored by the Flemish as well as by native merchants, who dodged it by carrying brandies by road as well as by sea. Nevertheless, the monopoly was confirmed four years later, and it was not until 1610 that Bernard had to surrender it. This was largely because of the opposition of the powerful merchants of Nantes, although the list of merchants who had broken the monopoly was a long one – showing just how widespread the trade had already become.

In Cognac itself the names included one Jacques Roux, a Protestant who lived on until the middle of the seventeenth century and who occupies a special place in the history of the cognac trade. In 1737 his great-great-granddaughter, Rachel Lallemend, married Jean Martell, and thus provided the young hopeful with a secure position within the merchant hierarchy of the town. So there is an uninterrupted line from Jacques Roux to Jean Martell's direct descendants, the Firino–Martells, who run Cognac's largest business to this day. They are not unique: Phillipe Augier, who in 1643 founded the oldest Cognac firm still in existence, got his start in life by marrying the daughter of a rich banker and paper merchant from Angoulême: and Marie Ranson, the descendant of another protestor, married James Delamain in 1763.

Cognac's long commercial tradition proved crucial in establishing its brandies on the

[1] Both *barrique* and *pinte* varied greatly in size, although in time the cognac *barrique* was standardized as 27 *veltes*, about 205 litres.
[2] *Preuve de Londres* (London gin) was about 58 per cent, that of Cognac about 60 per cent alcohol.
[3] Pierre Martin-Civat, 'La monopole des eaux-de-vie sous Henri IV', *100ᵉ Congrès Nationale des Sociétés Savantes*, Paris, 1975.

European market, for they were not the first to be produced in France. *Chimistes–apothicaires* in all the major French towns were also distillers, and in commercial terms the pioneers came from Armagnac, a couple of hundred miles to the south-west. The Armagnacais enjoyed the same natural advantages as their northern competitors: they had ample stretches of marginal scrubland suitable for vines; they had plenty of wood to fuel the *brûleries*; and they could transport the resulting spirit, largely by river, to the well established port of Bayonne. But they lacked Cognac's long commercial tradition and thus the merchant class required to act as middle-men between the local growers and distillers (who later combined the two functions) and the foreign buyers.

Even in Cognac the Roux, the Augiers and their colleagues were brokers buying not on their own account but on commission (often at the fairs so thoughtfully provided by Francis I) for buyers in La Rochelle, for the area was merely providing raw material which was processed elsewhere – and by foreigners at that. Typical was an agreement recorded in 1624 between two Dutchmen living in the Charente to build a distillery at Tonnay-Charente to distil wines shipped downriver. Despite the wars – La Rochelle was beseiged for years in the 1620s – a close-knit merchant class was being established, foreshadowing the more permanent group which emerged a couple of centuries later upriver in Cognac. But even the Rochellais were not independent, for they in turn depended on orders from Holland. These were not confined to brandy: both merchants and brokers were dealing in may other local products as well, especially the paper for which the region was already famous. The merchant brokers enabled mill owners and vineyard proprietors alike to sell their products; and in both instances they acted as what we would call 'freight forwarders' assembling small lots to be transported in bulk. In return they sold imported implements – and Dutch stills.

The Cognacais were also still dealing in the region's wine. According to the received version of the history of Cognac, the local growers became greedy and planted inferior, high-yielding varieties which produced wines that were unsuitable for export and therefore had to be distilled. This is a gross over-simplification, since the trade in the rival products, wine and brandy, coexisted for over a century. The major source of information on this subject is one Father Arcère, who wrote a history of La Rochelle published in 1753. In it he states: 'The wine from the region of Aunis was once highly regarded; if in time it has lost its former reputation, this misfortune must be attributed to the poor choice of varieties used; these plants have impaired the quality of the fruit while increasing its yield.' It was largely the Balzac and the Folle, later called the Folle Blanche, which provided 'quantity but not quality'.

The reverend father was writing a century and a half after the brandy trade had grown up, and even then he admitted that in some vineyards (notably those with clerical and therefore, to him anyway, careful owners) the wines were still as good as ever. Certainly, there were no signs of decadence when the brandy business first emerged. A medical textbook written by the Prince de Conti's doctor in 1603 claims: 'The wines of Aunis and Anjou, which are white, excel all others in goodness', and an agricultural handbook published a quarter of a century later echoes the same point.

It was largely a matter of horses for courses. Just as vines had formerly been concentrated on the uplands as against the river valleys, so wines suitable for drinking continued to be produced wherever they could command a premium price, as they could in the Borderies. This name covers a small rectangle due north of Cognac which owed its name to the *bordes*, the *métairies,* smallholdings cultivated by sharecroppers who were tenants of the outside investors who had invaded the area in the late sixteenth century. The sweet white wines produced in the Borderies from the Colombard grape were much prized by the Dutch until the second half of the eighteenth century. After an appalling frost in 1766 they lost their market to competitors from Sauternes and Barsac and switched to producing wines for distillation into cognacs which are still very special – and as highly regarded as the wines once were.

But the Borderies were the only real exception to the rule that, by the end of the seventeenth century, brandy was triumphant. As the province's Intendant wrote to Louis XIV in 1698:

Wine is the major product of the Angoumois, but the most important vineyards are in the Cognac district. The red wines find an outlet in Poitou and the Limousin. Very little is sold to foreigners, who do not find them stout enough to stand the journey. But when the white wines are converted into brandy, which is their normal fate, the English and Danish fleets come to look for them, in peacetime anyway, at the ports of the Charente and drink them up, to the great advantage of the province.[1]

By then politics had led to major shift in customers. The Dutch had developed a major export trade selling their spirits to the Baltic countries, where they much preferred brandy to the native *aquae vitae* distilled from grain. But in the early 1670s the French had invaded the Low Countries, and the two countries were at war for most of the rest of the century. Imports of French wine for 'burning' or 'distilling' (a term which was increasingly used during the latter half of the century) were soon banned, and as the wars intensified the English started to take over as major customers, a change that was to make the reputation of the region's major product.

[1] Quoted in Delamain, op. cit.

3 · 'Coniack Brandy' and How to Distil It

For the Dutch merchants and their local agents *brandywijn* was just one product among many. In the 150 years after Isaac Bernard's vain attempt to establish a monopoly it was transformed into a unique spirit: 'cognac' or, as it was more usually termed, 'coniack brandy'. The timing was perfect: the Cognacais started distilling when the art was emerging from medieval alchemy and had become a subject of universal technical and scientific interest. So brandy became a widespread restorative: it was the universal remedy carried by every traveller. As Auguste Hennessy remarked in 1849: 'The fact is that the public originally took to drinking brandy and water for medical reasons, and, having found it both pleasant and effective, they are likely to continue.'[1] Brandy and water was a classic stimulant in Britain and – as *fine à l'eau* – in France as well.

But cognac appealed to a different market; indeed, its emergence as the superior form of a routine drink would have been impossible without the existence of a market sufficiently rich and fashion-conscious to pay a premium price. Fortunately for Cognac, in the last forty years of the seventeenth century the drinkers of the café society of Restoration London developed a marked taste for luxury beverages. 'Coniack brandy' was only one of a group of drinks – including sherry, port and fine claret – first developed for this unprecedented group of customers.

The virtues of Cognac's brandies had been noted as early as 1617, when a bill of sale at La Rochelle mentioned brandy that was guaranteed to be from Cognac: five years later we find brandies from Cognac paying $9\frac{1}{2}$ livres in tax as against $8\frac{1}{2}$ for those from Bordeaux and between 7 and $7\frac{1}{2}$ for those from Spain or the South of France. In 1678 'coniack brandy' was first mentioned in the *London Gazette*, the official English journal. The wars between Britain and France that occupied much of the next thirty years did not prevent cognac's rise to fame – indeed, the scarcity bred of wartime difficulties seems merely to have enhanced the drink's attractions for a fashion-conscious market.

Cognac was only one of a group of such drinks. The names of the four greatest *châteaux* of Bordeaux emerged first in the auctions held in the first decade of the eighteenth century, during the War of the Spanish Succession. French ships were seized as 'prizes' and their contents auctioned (a procedure so routine that it smells of collusion between the two sides). The small ads in the *London Gazette* also recorded less frequent sales of brandies, and in January 1706[2] an advertisement proclaimed that thirty-four 'Pieces of Old Coniack Brandy' were available for sale at the port of Southampton. Clearly, this was no ordinary brandy: none of the other spirits advertised was 'old', and all the others were sold in London. The distinction is equally clear in other advertisements. 'Bordeaux and Nants' brandy was 9 shillings a gallon, 1 shilling less than 'Old Cogneac, fit for drams' – implying that it alone could be drunk neat. 'Bordeaux brandy'

---

[1] Quoted in Charles Tovey, *British and Foreign Spirits*, London, Whittaker, 1864.
[2] Britain was still employing the old calendar under which the year started on 25 March. By our reckoning it was January 1707.

THE CREATION OF COGNAC

clearly had rather a bad reputation: one lot of 'Entre-Deux-Mers brandy' is described as having 'a much better flavour and Proof than generally Bordeaux is'.

But our clearest picture of the emerging cognac market comes from a series of advertisements placed by two rival suppliers in the City of London, William Cowper, 'wine cooper' of Crooked Lane, and Major Thomas Bird, who owned a warehouse in Pudding Lane. They were getting their supplies from the same sources, ships supposedly seized as prizes and located either at Leith, the port of Edinburgh, or in Guernsey; they agreed on the difference in price between 'coniack' and other brandies but on precious little else. Cowper undercut the major by 1 shilling a gallon and even offered better terms to bigger buyers. The major hit back: 'Some others in Print,' he thundered, 'pretend to sell neat brandy they call French at a cheaper rate. To prevent the abuse in fetching theirs for his, he gives a printed receipt therewith of the Price and Quantity' – but only if you bought a gallon. He then reduced his prices:

Major Bird having had great encouragement from the Sale of true neat French Brandy, clean and full proof, and being desirous of selling the best at a moderate Profit, doth according to his promise advertize that the market price of good Brandy is much lower than when he last advertized his price: therefore he will now sell the best old Cognac at 9s. 6d. a gallon ...

– 6 pence a gallon less than his previous price, though still 6 pence dearer than his rival's. The Major's charge removed Cowper from the scene, and he continued to advertise his cognacs for four years at steadily increasing prices. By September 1711 he had apparently exhausted his stocks, and because none was available on the market except for 'one small parcel and that sold from 16s. to 17s. a gallon by reason of the Duty of 7s. a gallon laid by the late Parliament and not any hopes of having more till a peace', he was reduced to selling brandy from Portugal (which paid much less duty) at a mere 12 shillings a gallon.

Peace, when it came two years later, did not bring any reduction of the discrimination against French drinks, but the market for cognac was now secure. It was not only the British buyers who distinguished between cognac and lesser brandies. There were at least two local witnesses to the rise of cognac: Jean Gervais, a local magistrate who wrote a much quoted description of the area in the 1720s, and Étienne Munier, a well-known engineer whose description, written half a century later, remains our basic source of information about cognac in the later eighteenth century. 'The brandy from Cognac is accepted as the best in the world,' wrote Gervais. 'The region of Cognac is famous for its brandies,' echoed Munier, adding, 'The quality of Cognac's brandies being superior to all others, they will always be preferred if the price is the same.'

These local opinions were confirmed by authorities based in Paris, where cognac, unlike the wines of Bordeaux (but like those of Burgundy and Champagne) found a ready market.[1] In the first three-quarters of the century, before the publication of Diderot's *Encyclopédie* (which was also highly complimentary), the standard source of information on scientific matters was the *Dictionnaire universel du commerce,* written by Jacques Savary and published after his death by his brother, Abbé Philémon Louis Savary. The original, published in 1723, did not include any separate entry for cognac, but the *Supplément* published seven years later contained a complete analysis of the subject, including the simple encomium: 'Brandy from Cognac is better and more highly regarded than any other.'

[1] Burgundy and champagne could be transported to Paris directly by river. Cognac had to be carted overland to Châtellerault, then down the Vienne and Loire rivers to Orléans, the *entrepôt* for Paris.

None of the sources defines Cognac at all exactly. But trade was inevitably localized at the time, dependent on the nearest river port, which often gave its name to the products shipped through it, so it is highly unlikely that the wines used for cognac brandy could have come from as far afield as Angoulême to the east or Saintes or La Rochelle to the west. All three were bigger than Cognac itself, and the documents would have named them, as they did brandy from 'Nants'. So the original brandies which made Cognac famous clearly came from the 'Champagne' areas to the south and south-east of the town and, probably, from the Bois to the north and north-east. Munier did at least define Champagne: for him the name encompassed 'a mere seven or eight parishes, to wit, Angeac, Segonzac, etc., where the earth is soft and powdery, destined preferably for the cultivation of white grapes.'

This intense localization was a major novelty. Until the drinkers of Restoration London had defined the precise qualities they were seeking, vines had been planted where the wine could be marketed and not because the soil or the climate was particularly suitable. Even in the eighteenth century we cannot say how much brandy labelled as 'cognac' actually came from other areas. But logically it *should* have come from a catchment area within, at most, 20 miles round the town, thus excluding much of the present area allowed to call its brandies 'cognac'.

The actual distillation was a matter of routine. Distillation is a simple enough process, based on the fact that alcohol vaporizes at a lower temperature than water. So when a fermented liquor (wine, or the sort of 'mashes' used to produce malt whisky) is heated, the alcohol vaporizes, is trapped in a pipe leading from the top of the still and is then cooled. Of course, there are an infinite number of practical problems involved: the shape and size of the vessel, the metal from which it should be constructed, the type and quality of the liquor to be distilled, the shape of the

How it all began: an historic stone still

Right and overleaf: Mr Merlet tending his still at Roissac

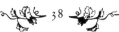

pipe conducting the spirit to the cooler, the moment at which the liquor is acceptable – and the cut-off point after which it is either too weak or too full of impurities (or both). But all these points were matters of trial and error, mostly solved by the end of the seventeenth century. Then, as now, the wines were made into a *brouillis,* a half-strength spirit, in a first distillation before the second (*la bonne chauffe*) produces the real stuff. It has always been a matter of pride to the Cognacais that their brandies are produced by a double distillation process. The only other spirits traditionally made in this way are the Calvados of the Pays d'Auge in Normandy and Scotland's malt whiskies. Other, lesser spirits (like most Calvados or Armagnac) are made from a single *chauffe*.

This distinction has led to one of Cognac's most enduring, most widespread and most misleading legends: that the secret of double distillation was a happy accident, the product of the musings of a local soldier-poet, the Chevalier de la Croix Maron. He wrote a long poem called *La Muse Catholique*, which ran into two editions, published in 1607 and 1614 respectively. In a preface to the first edition, dedicated, as usual, to a great local lady, he remarks how he has been distracted from his Muse by 'a thousand different notions on as many different subjects ... I have distilled the springtime of my spirits' – the pun is the same in both English and French. He then proceeds to dilate a little on this conceit. Unbelievably, a whole school of thought has been erected on this idle notion, this short, allusive, whimsical play on words. The fullest account of the idea was published only a few years ago by the late Pierre Martin-Civat, a local antiquarian. This provoked a savagely effective exposé from Alain Braastad, a grandson of Robert Delamain, who shares his grandfather's historic interests. But this had little effect. The Bureau National, Cognac's official ruling body, still publicizes the idea that the Chevalier discovered the secret of cognac, and the legend is even enshrined in the standard work on the legal definition of cognac.[1]

For many people in Cognac still believe not so much in the idea itself but in the need for some romantic origin for Cognac's fame. This point of view is best represented by Mademoiselle Pauline Reverchon, the distinguished lady who has made the town's museum an essential stop for any visitor interested in Cognac – the town, the drink, and the people who grew the grapes and distilled the spirit.[2] Despite, or perhaps because of, her love of the Cognacais and their achievements, even Mlle Reverchon believes that people need a romantic story to consume with their cognac.

But the legend of the almost mystical origin of cognac's double distillation process threatens the very basis of its reputation, because it is the precise opposite of the truth. During the century when cognac was making its name, its reputation did indeed rely on the fact that it was distilled twice. But at the time, lesser spirits were distilled not once (as the legend assumes) but several times. The truth was that only the grapes grown around Cognac were capable of producing a superior, drinkable spirit after only two *chauffes*. Raw materials – not just grapes – from everywhere else in France had to be distilled again and again to remove their noxious impurities. In the process, of course, they became nearly 'rectified'; they lost the qualities inherent in the raw material. Only the grapes from Cognac produced spirit which, because it had been distilled no more than twice, retained the flavour of the original grape.

The Cognacais realized and exploited their advantages immediately. They did not need to

[1] Marguerite Landrau, *Le Cognac devant la loi*, Cognac, L'Ile d'Or, 1981.
[2] The museum is free and is open every day except Tuesday from 14.30 to 17.30 between 1 October and 31 May, and from 10.00 to 12.00 and from 14.30 to 18.00 between 1 June and 30 September.

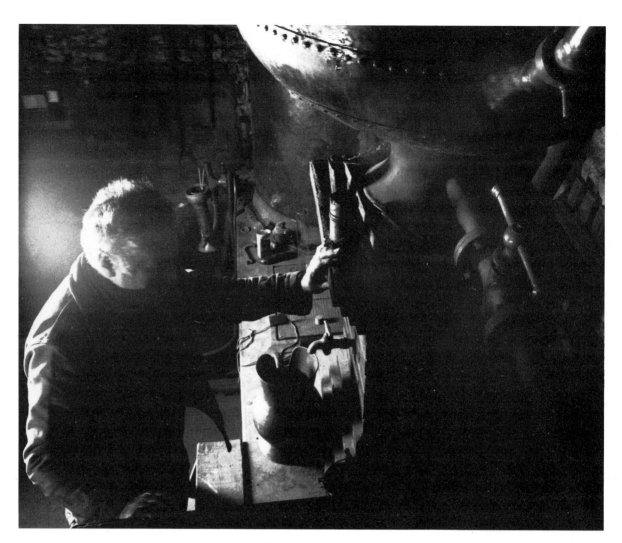

devise any new apparatus; they merely followed the best of existing technology. They were lucky because they were perfecting their product during a century when a great many people interested in science – aristocratic amateurs as well as professional technicians – were compiling books on the subject. None of them advanced contemporary understanding of the chemistry of the distillation process; they merely helped the ordinary distiller to improve his product.

The Cognacais did not mind: they were practical folk, not chemists. They made no impact on the art or science of distillation – indeed, are not mentioned at all in Professor Forbe's standard work on the subject.[1] In 1766 the Royal Agricultural Society of Limoges offered a prize for the best treatise on the subject, but even then the criteria were strictly practical: 'on the best way to distil wines taking into account quantity, quality and saving of costs'. Apart from this one show of intellectual initiative they relied on their incomparable raw materials. Reasonably enough, the Cognacais have not felt the need to change the formula which made them rich and famous, so the distillation of cognac, by and large, remains just as it was in the eighteenth century – in fact, I have been able to include their methods and equipment in chapter 10, in which I describe today's distillation techniques.

[1] A. Forbes, *History of Distillation*, Leiden, 1970.

Despite their superficial modernity and practicality, the Cognacais relied on medieval, almost Aristotelian chemistry, discursing learnedly on phlegms and vapours. A typical, and highly influential, authority was Jean François Demachy, by training a pharmacist, who became director of the central dispensary of the French army. A practical fellow, he believed that 'habit and the experience of the *Bouilleurs* is more useful than would be the rules and tables' established by mere theorists. He reserved a special scorn for his contemporary Lavoisier, the father of modern chemistry. But even Etienne Munier, the great eighteenth century authority on cognac, agreed with Demachy: 'In the silence of the study one can discuss theories,' he wrote , 'but only in practice can one become an artist.

Demachy's work, his three-part *L'Art du distillateur d'eaux fortes* (which was even translated into German), is described by Forbes as a mere 'compilation of facts on the distilling trade'. This is unfair, for it provides a unique, encyclopaedic view of the problems facing distillers in the eighteenth century. These had not greatly changed for a century or more, if only because there had been no great advances in the science of chemistry during that time. Christopher Glaser, chemist to Louis XIV, had frequently advised what he called 'cohibition', which Forbes defines as distilling 'several times, each time adding the distillate to the residue in the cucurbit (the distilling vessel) and redistilling again'. Demachy assumed that even after several *chauffes* they would have to use oil extracts to hide the disagreeable tastes from the 'phlegms' left. He devoted a whole volume to the issue of how to distil the *eaux-de-vie* resulting from the first *chauffe* into *esprit de vin*, which the French merchants sold to their local customers at 67°.

Strength was one thing; quality was another. Demachy distinguished clearly between regions like Cognac which provided 'agreeable *eaux-de-vie* . . . others, like those from Orléans, give a drier *eau-de-vie*. Finally the *eaux-de-vie* from our southern provinces are acrid and disagreeable.' Not surprisingly, most of the nineteenth century scientists who transformed the art of distillation came from the south, where science was needed to make up for the inadequacies of nature.

Using a mere two *chauffes* to produce a spirit which would be agreeable to drink was clearly a delicate matter. Not only did the *eau-de-vie* have to come from Cognac, but it also had to be 'six–eleven' in strength. Demachy was firmly convinced that only the best would do. Some chemists, he said scornfully, believed that if you rectified (distilled again) second-grade brandy, you got as good a result as with a double-distilled, first rate *eau-de-vie*. It might be as dry, he said, but 'connoisseurs do not make the same mistake'. The distillers themselves agreed. They too understood that only the first quality 'combines an exquisite bouquet with all the lightness and dryness it is possible to imagine'.

By Munier's time the conditions for producing the very best cognac had been precisely defined. The distillers used white grapes whenever possible. The favourite variety, which covered the majority of the Cognac vineyard, was the Folle, better known as the Folle Blanche. Writing a century later, Professor Ravaz described how 'an old bottle of wine made from the Folle gives off a bouquet which can be detected from far off and which provides an adequate explanation for the perfume of brandies made from this variety. For it produces the softest brandies and the ones with the strongest and most lasting scent.' The only other widely planted variety was the Colombat (Colombard),[1] which first became famous as the variety used in the

[1] Rémy Martin uses the Colombard to make 'alembic brandy' in California. They have found it matures more quickly than the Ugni Blanc now used in cognac. It is rich and fruity but relatively short on the palate.

Borderies to produce fine sweet white wines. It reminded Ravaz of the Chenin Blanc grape used in Anjou, but Munier found that 'its wine is the most powerful and is indeed needed to provide backbone for those which lack this quality'. These were 'the fattest, that is to say, the most oily' grapes. The grapes may have been 'fat', but as a 1774 almanac put it, the wines should be thin, should have *peu de corps*. The Cognacais had already understood the importance of acidity in the wines they distilled.

Nevertheless, there were still problems associated with defining the right qualities. Half a century earlier Savary had written in his *Dictionnaire universel du commerce* that *eau-de-vie* should be 'white, clear, with a good taste and, as they say, "*d'epreuve*" – that is, when it is poured into a glass, it produces a little white head, which, as it dies down, forms the circle which brandy merchants call the *chapelet* if all the brandy has lost its phlegms, and where there is not too much humidity remaining, in which case the *chapelet* is uninterrupted'. The Abbé Rozier, writing in 1766,[1] was less sure. The strength could be determined easily enough, and it was agreed that 'the force and the concentration of the spirit determines the nature of the brandy.' Nevertheless, tasting was not an adequate way in which to determine its quality because tasting was 'uncertain and relies on whether or not the nerve endings of the palate of those tasting it are more or less affected; for taste is like sight – everyone has his own. Setting fire to it is no more reliable, so people stick to a sort of hydrometer popularly known as a "test-tube". The growers and the merchants have all got their own, and they do not always agree.' They may not have agreed. But they did agree that Cognac's brandies were the best.

[1] *De la fermentation des vins et de la meilleure manière de faire l'eau-de-vie*, Paris–Lyon, 1766.

4 · A Commercial Community

The coniack brandy consumed with such relish in eighteenth-century London was not aged for as long as are today's brandies and was usually the product of one, rather than many, stills. It would be instantly recognizable to a contemporary palate, however. In Cognac itself the 'agro-industrial' community that grew the grapes, made the wine and distilled and sold the brandy was equally identifiable. From numerous contemporary sources we get the picture of an astonishingly modern capitalist society hampered by few of the feudal restrictions usual in pre-Revolutionary France. Many of the feudal rights had been transformed into fixed-money rents, so the peasants could pocket most of the profits from any increased sales. The most burdensome feudal relic was the *ban des vendanges*, the *seigneurs'* right to decide the date of the harvest, a right that used to force the peasants to harvest the nobles' grapes before their own.

Nevertheless, the peasant land-holders shared in the general prosperity. This fact is rather concealed because so much of the evidence left to us is in the form of complaints, directed mostly at the taxmen, which give the impression of grinding poverty. Even Étienne Munier, himself a royal official, was misled. He grossly underestimated the yields and hence the profit available. Other witnesses were equally gloomy. In *A Sad Picture of Rustic Folk*, published in 1786, the author explains that those who could not afford to distil their wines were forced to drink them, 'thus giving their children bad habits from an early age; and as it was natural to serve up worthless wines which would otherwise have been lost, they naturally took advantage of the excess'. Modern sociologists would call the result a cycle of rural deprivation, of which the legacy was a great many widows, deformed children and other signs of misery. It would be fairer to say that there were large pockets of poverty and misery in what was, by eighteenth-century French standards, a prosperous and socially cohesive area. Even in 1789 the peasants directed their complaints against the tax collectors rather than the nobility.

For their part the merchants were not hampered by any of the monopolies that restricted so many other French businessmen, for after Isaac Bernard's abortive attempt to create a monopoly, the trade was remarkably unregulated. According to Savary' *Dictionnaire universel*, the *marchands–épiciers–droguistes–apothicaires* distilled and sold the best spirits in Paris, but the *vinaigriers,* the *limonadiers* and the *distillateurs d'eaux fortes* also had the right to sell spirits.

For centuries everyone in the Cognac area had known that grapes were the most valuable crop, so the clergy and the nobility, as well as humbler tenants, farmed the land themselves and did not follow the usual habit of leasing it to sharecroppers. Jean Gervais remarked: 'Formerly only the rich bourgeois and the better-off cultivated their own vines; nowadays virtually every peasant and simple rustic fellow has planted them for himself, which keeps them busy and means they give up working for others, so that the remaining day labourers, sought by everyone, prefer to work for those who can pay them to excess'[1] – thus putting pressure on small or inefficient

[1] Jean Gervais, 'Mémoire sur l'angoumois', 1725; reproduced in the bulletin of the Société: Archéologique et Historique de la Charente, 1864.

farmers. For the peasants were fully alert to commercial opportunities, even at the expense of farming techniques. As Munier put it: 'In the Angoumois the peasants do not form a class apart, since they apply themselves indiscriminately to every type of cultivation. This over-extensive appetite is perhaps the cause of the bad farming methods in the Angoumois.'

Many of the peasants had their own stills, although there were also precursors of today's *bouilleurs de profession* (professional distillers), some of whom had mobile stills. Claude Masse, writing in 1712 about the previous century, claimed that the 'merest peasant, once he was comfortably off, distilled his own wine and the merchants find a ready sale for the wine in its new form. And it is this which decided everyone to plant vines so that very little land remained uncultivated.'[1]

JARNAC HISTORIQUE

LA VILLE ET CHASTEAU DE JARNAC

JARNAC (Charente) — La Ville et le Château de Jarnac au XV· siècle

Emile Rousseau, édit., - Jarnac

7 — COGNAC - Un coin du Champ de Foire

[1] Quoted in Delamain, op. cit.

The *fureur de planter*, the mania for planting vines, spread throughout south-west France after many of the crops had been devastated by the great frost of 1709. The subsequent famine merely increased the authorities' concern about possible starvation, and they repeatedly tried to stop new plantations and to induce land-owners to pull up their vines. But no one took much notice. Father Arcère even argued that since Nature had clearly intended the inhabitants to plant vines, it would be flying in the face of Nature to pull them up. The growers had more immediate worries – such as the plagues of noxious worms, insects and other pests which periodically afflicted them and the growing shortage of the wood required as fuel for the stills. Father Arcère recommended the use of coal, which provided a more uniform and reliable source of heat and could be imported from England (in peacetime anyway). One merchant even imported coal as ballast when ships were returning from England, but the Charentais were conservative and remained faithful to the cheaper, local wood for another hundred years or more.

The major local obsession was the burden of taxes. The problem was not a new one. As early as 1640 a special royal tax was imposed on brandies, and twenty years later *eau-de-vie* was taxed as an ordinary drink. This was a considerable, if unwelcome, tribute to advances in distillation techniques, since even in Demachy's time many second-rate spirits could not be used even for chemical purposes, let alone drinking, but were suitable only for use in varnishes because of their disagreeable smell. By the eighteenth century the whole Cognac community had to pay taxes. The peasantry were hardest-hit, but the nobility and clergy, who were normally exempt, naturally protested most loudly. In 1713, at the instigation of the archpriest of the small town of Bouteville, the *curés* of the Grande Champagne launched a bitter complaint. In 1744 a group of aristocrats joined in. They complained that their major source of income was in the form of wines suitable only for distillation, so they were hit by an anti-fraud tax dating back to 1687, which supposedly affected only merchants. The 'tax farmers' (notorious entrepreneurs who had bought rights from the monarch) argued that it applied also to the landowners, since brandy was not a natural agricultural product but resulted from art and industry and was therefore liable to the taxes levied on manufactured articles.

By this time the tax system was chaotic. Successive monarchs had been financially stretched for so long that they had pile several different taxes on to any healthy revenue-producing occupation, taxes administered by the tax farmers. The specific 'farm' that hit the locals hardest was that of the *courtiers-jaugeurs*, licensed intermediaries who took a fixed percentage on every transaction within the area. The problem was worse in La Rochelle than in the Angoumois (which included Cognac) where the *courtiers-jaugeurs* had been bought out, and the distillers could transport their precious cargo free of duty.

The woes of generations exploded in the famous 'Doléances' of 1789, the endless pages of complaints that provided such a dense background to the Revolution. Typically, the citizens of la Valette, a small town near Angoulême, had hoped that,

having paid their *Tailles*, their poll taxes, taxes on utensils and equipment, forced labour, subsidies for waifs and strays, personal dues, the first, second and third portions of the 'twentieth', having paid their labourers, the priest and the landlord, and after we have endured bad weather, like hail, frost, rot and drought, we had hoped that what remained of our crops could be gathered into our barns and cellars. But far from it. Our friends the tax collectors are beating at our doors demanding that we pay over three livres for every *barrique* of wine we produce.[1]

[1] 'Doléances de la Sénéchaussée d'Angoulême pour les États Généraux de 1789'.

They had to pay even on the large quantities of wine destined for their own consumption and were victims of their own success – their vines were productive, and taxes on wines were based on the quantity produced.

The tax system as a whole struck especially hard at a largely commercial community like Cognac. A cask of wine or brandy paid up to ten times its value in internal duties on a journey through France to Paris. Royal greed extended even to Cognac's vital – and officially encouraged – export business. The town's brandies had to pay a substantial tax when they passed through the ports to leave the kingdom. These dues trebled during the eighteenth century, and they were increased further in 1782, with the Cognacais paying double the amount levied on the Rochellais, a bias which led to a major protest.

Foreign countries were already exploiting the revenue-producing potential of these luxury imports. Even a free-trade city like Hamburg levied heavy import duties on wines and brandies. In Britain French brandy had been a tempting target since Elizabethan times, and in wartime brandy was always among the first times to be prohibited. An attempt at a commercial treaty in 1713 merely exposed the depth of the opposition – backed by the politically powerful rum lobby.

The penal duties imposed on French brandies affected the whole cognac trade. To the British

Left: The secret side of the Cognacais

taxman 'brandy' became 'spirit' above 66°, and the duty doubled. This was annoying for the Cognacais, who normally distilled their spirit as strong as possible, at between 67° and 70°, to reduce the costs of production. But they then had to reduce this below 60° (*eau-de-vie simple*) for domestic consumption because French taxes doubled above that point (when the spirit became an *eau-de-vie double*) and tripled for *esprit-de-vin* of above 86°. The reduced-strength spirit had then to be strengthened to just below 66° with some *esprit-de-vin* for sale to Britain.

The heavy British duties inevitably led to a lively smuggling traffic throughout the century. In Rudyard Kipling's words, 'Brandy for the Parson' (together with that other highly taxed item 'Baccy for the Clerk') was a staple of the smugglers' cargoes. In the late eighteenth century Adam Smith concluded that smugglers were the biggest importers of French goods into Britain (and vice versa), for by then the traffic had been institutionalized. According to Professor Lipson, the prosperity of Lymington (a town in Hampshire near the Channel) was attributed to the smuggling of French wines,'[1] and even today Matthew Clark, the firm that has been importing Martell cognacs for over a century, finds that the citizens of southern Dorset drink far more of its products than the national average would suggest.

The connection is appropriate. Jean Martell, who founded the firm, was a member of a leading commercial family in Jersey, a major centre for smuggled goods. So it was natural for him to seek his fortune in Cognac, where he arrived in 1715. He started as a broker, buying casks of cognac and wines from the Borderies for buyers mainly in the Channel Islands, but also in Normandy, Picardy and Holland. He made an unpromising start. His arrival coincided with the short-lived boom engendered by the economic policies of a Scottish charlatan, Law. The price of wines and spirits soared and then, inevitably, slumped. Martell was caught in the boom-and-bust and was forced to liquidate his first parnership. But he repaid his debts and enjoyed considerable success when he started up again, greatly helped by successive marriages to the daughters of two major Cognac merchants. He married first Jeanne Brunet and then, after her death, Jacques Roux's great-great-granddaughter, Jeanne-Rachel Lallemand. After his death his widow brought in her brother Gabriel as a partner and changed the name of the firm to Veuve Martell-Lallemand.

She and her handful of fellow merchants faced a good deal of competition. In 1751 the merchants from La Rochelle tried unsuccessfully to reduce the strength of the *eaux-de-vie* coming from up-country to the level of their own (inferior) products. Thirty years later the Cognac merchants complained that they had lost their markets in the Baltic to rivals from Spain and other parts of France who sold imitations – the opening of the Canal du Midi made it much easier for unscrupulous merchants to substitute cheaper and inferior products from the south. The tax system did not help. According to Demachy, merchants would try to smuggle *esprit de vin* into Paris disguised as *esprits odorants* from Montpellier, which paid a lower rate of duty. They would add a drop or two of essential oil, or even rub the cork with it, and try to convince the officials in that way. Some fraudsters did not bother to distil a second time but disguised the basic liquor with lavender oil and water.

The legitimate merchants described themselves as those from Cognac, Jarnac and Pons, for Cognac, in Munier's words, was emerging as 'the major township and trading centre of these provinces' (Saintonge and the Angoumois). By his time *preuve de Cognac* had replaced *preuve d'Hollande* as a measure of a spirit's strength, just as the name of cognac had become the standard by which all other brandies were judged. It was still a small town, with only about 2,000

[1] E. Lipson, *Economic History of England*, vol. 3, London, A. & C. Black, 1931.

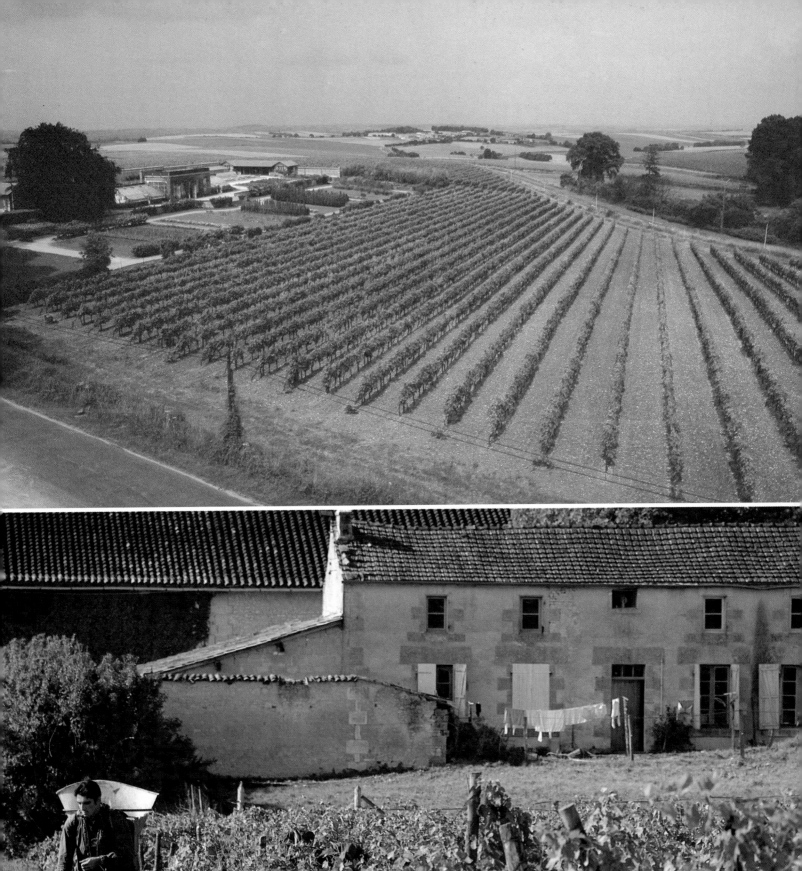

inhabitants, but was increasingly recognized as important. It even enjoyed a superb postal service: there were four services a week to Paris, and letters took a mere four days to get there. Those to England only took ten days, even in wartime. The cognac business itself had become increasingly institutionalized. Only a handful of merchants were actually based in Cognac, but a lot of business was done. Savary described in his *Dictionnaire universel* how 'on Saturday each week a brandy market was held in Cognac. All the merchants and distillers meet to buy and sell.'

Jarnac, Cognac's only local rival, had slipped in importance. It had always been a major centre of Protestant activity, and in 1685 the revocation of the Edict of Nantes put an end to a century of legal toleration; the community was forced to scatter. Many Protestants went abroad to join the 'Huguenot Mafia', which provided local merchants with a network of contacts. These included Europe's leading bankers, who were always prepared to lend money to their co-religionists. Those who remained were forced to convert. Even the Martells had to go through symbolic Catholic marriage ceremonies to ensure that their children would be recognized as legitimate. Nevertheless, throughout two generations of active persecution the Protestants defiantly held secret services in lonely country barns. The Cognacais remained sympathetic, and the soldiers sent in pursuit of the preachers at the behest of the clergy often found it impossible to arrest them,

Where the Gauthiers lived and worked

though their whereabouts were known to hundreds of the local peasantry. For the Church, like the aristocracy, had a far weaker hold on the region than on most of rural France. In the second half of the eighteenth century the Protestants began to benefit from an implicit toleration. The only memorials to their previous sufferings were the solitary cypress trees on the families' estates, each marking the tomb of one of the faithful.

Yet their ambiguous position could still be exploited. As late as 1767 the dowager Countess of Jarnac, who had the monopoly of baking in the town, wrote a ferocious letter from her Paris home to M. Delamain, Jarnac's leading merchant, who had dared to encourage the locals to build their own bread oven. They were related by marriage, but the breach of her rights so infuriated the countess that she exploded: 'Remember your religion is that of neither the State nor of the King. Your profession is a noble one, since it is free . . . your father-in-law was born a vassal of our forefathers, not even a vassal, for only the nobility is entitled to this title.'

Despite the persecutions, the majority of merchant families remained intact during the terrible years. They dealt mainly in cognac and in wine from the Borderies but, to earn a living, often traded in other agricultural products. In 1750 Guy Gauthier sold almost as much tanned hides, walnuts and clover seeds as he did brandy, and Jean Martell also bought leather and goat- and sheepskins. But they were still acting for principals based elsewhere. The three-cornered relationship born of the earlier Dutch dominance persisted, with the ultimate buyers located in London, Dublin, Hamburg or, most often, Ostend and Dunkirk, the Channel ports which acted as *entrepôts* for the English market. As the century wore on, the merchants drifted from La Rochelle to Bordeaux, then France's greatest sea port, although La Rochelle remained the commercial centre for the Charentes, with its heavy concentration of bankers, brokers, notaries and the legal and administrative infrastructure required for the cognac trade. The 'merchants' in Cognac itself were still simply brokers acting on a commission of about 2 per cent, although they travelled all over northern Europe to remain in contact with their clients. The families were truly international: Guy Gauthier – who, although a Protestant, acted as a spokesman for the people of Cognac in Paris – settled his son in the City of London after an apprenticeship in Holland; his brother worked in Barcelona and two other members of the family at Port-au-Prince in Haiti, in the West Indies. The trade was not exclusively export-oriented: Delamain in particular enjoyed a healthy trade in Paris, and the French army and navy were both considerable buyers. Rochefort was growing in importance as a naval base and arsenal, and the ships provisioned there required large quantities of cognac to sustain the sailors and prevent scurvy.

Even in the late eighteenth century the three-cornered pattern remained the norm, as the story of Richard Hennessy clearly demonstrates. He was a member of one of the Irish Catholic families that had emigrated to France to escape religious persecution and had become leading fighters on behalf of their new country against the English oppressors. Hennessy himself had fought in the Irish Brigade before setting up in business, working originally from Ostend (the base for his partner, Connelly), but in 1765 he moved from Bordeaux to Cognac, stating bluntly 'It was the only town in the province with a market dealing in brandy.'

The market was a big one. Every year Cognac produced 200,000 *'barriques de vins propres à brûler'*, from which emerged 13,400 *pipes* (each of 3 *barriques* or about 600 litres), adding up to 8 million litres of *eau-de-vie*. In bad years the yield was somewhat less, since then it took 6, rather than 5, *barriques* of wine to make one of *eau-de-vie*. Surprisingly, the frequent wars between Britain and France in the course of the eighteenth century seem merely to encouraged trade: the outbreak of war in 1756 provided Jean Martell with enough of a boost to enable him to give up dealing in beef and tallow, and the 1782 complaint stated that merchants' trade was virtually confined to England – then, of course, at war with France. This was not strictly true: the Paris market was a great help. Transport was the only problem. In wartime brandies destined for England would generally have to be transhipped through a neutral port like Rotterdam, sometimes getting there overland via Paris. Prices rose after the outbreak of war in the 1740s, the 1750s and 1770s. Jean Martell recorded that consumption of brandy in London and Dublin had tripled during the Seven Years' War. But an even more important factor was the availability of alternative spirits. In Ireland, then a crucial market, bad harvests (and thus reduced supplies of grain for distillation into whiskey) during the late 1750s were enough to send the price of cognac soaring, and any shortage of rum also provided an opportunity for the Cognacais.

By the latter half of the century they were stocking their brandies and not neccessarily selling at the first opportunity. But whereas in Bordeaux it was the merchants who held the stocks, in Cognac the landowners made the running – in the 1770s Richard Hennessy had only a few dozen casks in his warehouses. As Munier noted in 1779: 'When the brandy has been distilled, the rich landowners often store it until they can get a high price for it. I have seen some who have converted into brandy and hoarded in their cellars the several years' vintages which they have sold in one fell swoop at the right moment, making 12,000 to 15,000 *livres* on the transaction.' These were still relatively young brandies. In the 1780s Richard Hennessy noted that shrewd operators with enough capital had bought up most of one year's production and were not prepared to sell until they saw if the next vintage would be good or not. They made money also by storing the brandies, although they did not have to keep them for long. Brandy was called 'old' once it had spent a year in cask, and the oldest Hennessy brandies shipped were generally no more than four years old (although he occasionally sold brandies ten or even eighteen years old). Prices were set by geographical origin as well as by age. During the century brandy from the 'Champagne' region grew in value by comparison with less blessed vineyards nearer the coast.

The growers had been speculating for most of the century. Old brandies had been worth more than new since the 1720s, and speculation became even more profitable when the market soared in the 1780s. The 1782 tax increases were rescinded two years later, and the Treaty of Free Trade with England, which came into operation in 1786, provided a new impetus for the cognac trade. Exports (and prices) rose rapidly; even more important, the Treaty launched the Cognacais on to a new pattern of trade. Even in the 1720s the Dutch were still buying twice as much cognac as the British, but during the century the Cognacais reduced their dependence on Holland and on Ireland, both highly price-conscious markets.

In London, and only in London, a selective market had developed. Buyers were prepared to pay for their fancies and to distinguish between brandies old and new, pale brandies, fortified brandies, strong brandies and double spirit. The existence of so selective a market provided the Cognacais with a unique weapon in their fight against the merchants of Bordeaux, who also included the local representatives of cognac houses such as Martell. Nevertheless, their primary loyalties were now to Cognac. In 1791 the merchants of the district, Augier, Veuve Martell, Allemand, Arbouin & Zimmerman, Hennessy & Turner, Ranson & Delamain and Guerinet & Robin, swore to use only brandies from the Saintonge and the Angoumois and not to imitate their competitors by mixing the local produce with brandies from the south of France or from Spain. They knew that their loyalty to real cognac would prove profitable in the long run.

5 · A Revolution, not a Disaster

In 1789 the Cognacais had worse things to worry about than a mere revolution. The previous winter had been memorably harsh, the worst since 1709. The wine had frozen in the cellars; stocks of grain were almost exhausted by early summer; and famine was averted only by a timely loan from Messrs Augier and Martell. The Martells, like most of the merchants, were largely untouched by the Revolution itself. It was easiest for the Hennessys. As an Irish refugee from the British yoke, Richard was naturally celebrated as 'Citizen Hennessy'; it was equally natural for him to be charged by the local revolutionary committee with the sale of brandy. He was luckier than M. Augier, elected a deputy in 1789 but, like so many others, left stranded by the increasing extremism of the revolutionary tide. By 1794 revolutionary ardours had diminished, and the overwhelming worry remained peasant distrust of the *assignats* and other dubious notes issued by the revolutionary governments. To buy their precious cognacs the merchants had to come up with gold or foreign currency.

Even though many of them were of foreign, enemy, origin, it was during the revolutionary years that they became part of the local establishment, and Martell and Hennessy, at least, were transformed from mere brokers into merchants who sold their wares directly to their customers in London, where they both established members of their family. Cognac could thus escape from the bad reputation it had acquired through the mixtures sold by intermediaries in Bordeaux, Ostend or Dunkirk. Because Jacques Delamain was ageing, he could not adapt and thus his house lost much of its importance to a newcomer, Otard-Dupuy, a partnership of two growers who had accumulated comfortable stocks before the Revolution. Jean-Baptiste-Otard was descended from an old Scottish family which, like the Hennessys, had settled in France for religious reasons. Unlike Richard Hennessy, however, Otard was sentenced to death by the revolutionaries and escaped only through the timely intervention of his loyal friends. Jean Dupuy was a local, who brought a new market to the partnership they established in 1794: his uncle, Léon Dupuy, had pioneered sales to the newly independent United States. They were not alone: the first recorded sale to New York was made in 1794 by Richard Hennessy to one Jacob Schieffelin (an ancestor of the family which remained Hennessy's agents for nearly two hundred years). The American connection became valuable, not only because of the direct sales but also because the Americans were neutral, so their ships could be used to ship brandy to an equally neutral port for trans-shipment to England in wartime.

Otard-Dupuy managed to buy up the finest corner site in all Cognac, the Château des Valois on the river guarding the bridge across the Charente, a fortress which had naturally become vacant with the fall of the French monarchy. Ever since then it has provided an ideal warehouse – and a magnificent shop window for the firm's products. Physically MM. Otard and Dupuy established themselves alongside Hennessy and Martell, and commercially they were quickly catapulted into third place in the cognac hierarchy. But during the revolutionary period Martell and Hennessy established a primacy which they have never lost: indeed, the commercial history of Cognac since then has been of successive challenges to their duopoly, challenges which have often seemed invincible in the short term but have rarely lasted more than one generation, for as Jacques Chardonne points out, even the most important merchants owed very little to inheritance: 'wealth does not last long in this business'. The duopoly was founded not on their cognac business but on the trade as general merchants that they carried on through the war and that enabled them to build up the capital required to concentrate on brandy after 1815. Not that they had a duopoly at the time: shipping documents show that in the mid-1790s the long-extinct firm of Laberge was as big as either and that the two halves of the Delamain business (father and son had quarrelled and gone their separate ways) were together almost as big. By contrast Otard-Dupuy was one-third the size, and Augier, the daddy of them all, a mere one-sixth.

Otard-Dupuy was not the only new firm established at the time. The other important newcomer was Thomas Hine, the descendant of a Dorset family who had originally gone to France to complete his education – a link arranged through the 'Hugenot Mafia'. He settled in Jarnac, went to work for Ranson & Delamain and soon followed Jean Martell's example by marrying the daughter of his employer, James Delamain, whose son had set up on his own. Jacques Delamain's father had started by marrying the daughter of his boss, Isaac Ranson, as had Phillipe Augier, whose father-in-law was a banker and paper merchant in Angoulême. Paul Roullet set himself up by marrying another Delamain. '*Il se fait gendre*' ('he has turned himself into a son-in-law') is an old saying among the peasantry of the Charente,[1] but in-breeding was inevitable in a small community conscious of its foreign origins and very separate from the native aristocracy and gentry. In Cognac itself the two biggest houses were becoming increasingly connected. In 1795 Jacques Hennessy married Marthe Martell, and later Jean-Gabriel Martell married Lucie Hennessy. One Augier married a Martell, another Marie Broussard, from the firm which held the valuable monopoly to supply spirits to the Napoleonic navy. The firm of Renault–Castillon was foreshadowed when Alexandre Castillon du Perron married Sophie Marett and Antonin Renault married Marie Delafargue.

But the Revolution had other important effects. It relieved the peasant landowners of their burden of feudal dues and institutionalized the tolerance unofficially granted to the region's Protestants over the preceding quarter of a century. More crucially, it removed the restrictions and taxes which had impeded the circulation of wines and spirits, and thus, for the first time, enabled the Cognacais to blend brandies from different distilleries. The ability to blend meant that individual merchants could establish their own style of spirit, although this development was slow to emerge.

For the Napoleonic years were not lost. Sales to Britain had been boosted by the Free Trade treaty of 1786 from below 50,000 hectolitres to over 60,000. When war broke out in 1793 sales slumped, but only to between 30,000 and 40,000 hectolitres. Exports – and prices – recovered somewhat, for even the new-style Revolutionary War did not mean the end of all trade with the enemy. Some elements of the former pattern of trade remained. An old-style shortage of grain in 1795–6 had its usual effect of increasing demand, and the Peace of Amiens in 1802 brought the usual result, a slump, which led to the bankcruptcy of Casimir Martini, one of Cognac's leading merchants.

Even the period of blockade and counter-blockade which followed the outbreak of 'total' war in 1804 included elements of sheer farce. Sales dropped, but because of excessive British tariffs,

[1] 'The son-in-law also rises', as they used to say in Hollywood.

not on account of war. The blockade which followed the 'Orders in Council' of 1807 should have put a stop to the traffic. Far from it: imports soared, partly because prices in France had dropped sufficiently to provide bargains for the British, who declined to deprive themselves of their habitual luxuries. In 1808 Sir John Nicholl, a British Minister, recognized that 'we need a little wine and French brandy to rejoice and comfort ourselves'. A system of import licences ensured that the British kept some control over the situation while still slaking their thirsts. As Jean Martell put it: 'We only want freedom to get out, and the blockade will not stop us, above all if we have good letters of credit' (although he also needed political protection at a high level in Paris to obtain the necessary export licences). The ban on purchases of French wines and spirits for the British armed forces in 1807, and later the total ban on French imports, was inspired not by patriotic fervour but by pressure from the 'West Indian interest', the traditional lobby of merchants whose sales of rum had been badly hurt by the success of French brandies. Imports soared in 1809 in anticipation of the ban, which caused a temporary slump but lasted less than two years until counter-pressure from the rest of the commercial community forced a relaxation. In 1812 things began to return to normal, a process that took nearly a decade.

Nevertheless the period had left its scars. As one of Martell's colleagues put it: 'What is becoming appalling for our region is the relentlessness with which our hapless brandies are being pursued; it is much to be feared that people will lose the taste for them, and it is very difficult for a trade which has been thus disturbed to get back on to its former tracks.' Not surpisingly, as Frédéric Martell put it, 'It was with feelings of the greatest relief that the citizens of Cognac greeted the news of Napoleon's deposition.'

Peace brought a short-lived boom in prices and a steady increase in sales – from an average of 30,000 hectolitres during the war to over 80,000 in the late 1820s and over 100,000 in the following decade. Nevertheless, British customs duties continued to rise, and at their post-war worst amounted to six times the value of the cognac itself, far higher than those payable by rival spirits like rum. (So-called 'British brandy' enjoyed a considerable vogue, largely because it carried one-third of the duties imposed on the French equivalent.)

The Cognacais, like their colleagues in Bordeaux, were almost totally dependent on sales to the British market, which took over four-fifths of their exports, so both communities were early campaigners for Free Trade. As one 1838 petition put it:

If the French government does not get a reduction of the exorbitant duties which disrupt our brandy trade, they will cease to be drunk at all ... which will force the wine growers to pull up their vines. This does not mean to say that they can plant other crops ... the soil is too dry ... the government should not forget that it is a question of 200 million francs and the ruin of 4,000 families ... what distinguishes the Cognac trade from that of other spirits is that no merchant here bothers with distillation: the owners of the vineyards, in both the departments of the Charente, are at the same time farmers and distillers.

The pattern established before the Revolution continued, with hundred of small farmers, few large holdings (except those being accumulated by the merchants themselves) and even fewer labourers – a situation that produced the usual crop of complaints about the lack of labour. One authority estimated that there were 1,500 growers with holdings large enough to produce a dozen *barriques* of wine. Most of them distilled their production themselves in small stills which held only 1 *barrique* of wine and cost a mere 500 francs.

The petitioners emphasized that although their traditional methods of distillation were both slow and extravagant, they were essential to retain the natural qualities of the grape and justify the price of Cognac: 'These methods are the only ones that can be employed without damaging these qualities.' Distillers making lesser spirits from grain could use larger, quicker, more modern stills, but in Cognac these gave provably inferior results, although some of the Cognacais did experiment with a new-style apparatus, using a second still by the side of the first, so that the distillation process could be more or less continuous – the second still was emptied only once a week to rid it of the accumulated lees.

Throughout most of the century the growers continued to hold the bulk of the region's stocks of older brandies, and the richer among them could choose whether to sell their brandy new, speculate by holding it for a few months in case the next harvest was bad or age it themselves. In the early post-war years prices were still set in the traditional way.

Every Saturday [wrote J.-P. Quénot in *Statistique du Département de la Charente*, 1818] the day of the brandy market in the town of Cognac, the growers who wish to sell, the middle men who are buying to sell on, and the merchants from the whole region . . . repair to a small square in Cognac called Le Canton where most of the buying is done on the simple presentation of a flask in which the seller has put a small sample of the spirit which he agrees to deliver. The price at which most transactions have been concluded becomes the official market price, which the merchants use when calculating their selling price.

This mechanism gave the merchants a chance to increase their profits. The official price was for brandies from 'la Champagne', defined as the whole of the *arrondissement* of Cognac lying on the south bank of the Charente (as well as some from the neighbouring department). Those from the north bank were worth less, and those from the outlying regions to the west formed a third division. The less scrupulous merchants, said Quénot, 'blend the different brandies and make

119 – COGNAC - Le Pont du Parc

Cognac. – Asile des Vieillards

their foreign buyers pay in relation to the full market price. To this considerable advantage they added the price of the cask, which they also make their suppliers pay, without allowing the amount when dealing with the growers.'

Nevertheless, the relationships between the growers and merchant (or his representative) were usually reasonably harmonious. In Dickens's magazine *Household Words* his friend Henry Vizetelly gave a lyrical description of the relationship as he witnessed it during a visit in 1855:[1]

When a peasant proprietor out in the country has burnt his wine into *eau-de-vie*, if the markets put on an inviting aspect, he loads the chariot before his door with precious tubs, he then washes his face and hands, puts on a clean shirt and blouse, and takes his Sunday broad-brimmed hat out of the closet. He proceeds slowly on his way with stately step, and enters the narrow crooked passages which Cognac dignifies with the name of streets, announcing his arrival by a long succession of what you might take for pistol-shots, but which are no more than harmless cracks of the whip. He stops at the gate of the establishment, say of Messrs R. & Co.,[2] his cargo is set down, taken in, rolled up an inclined plane, and measured at once by transfusion into a cylindrical vessel which has outside it a glass tube, to which a graduated scale is attached, communicating with the interior, and therefore showing exactly how full the measure is. That settled he walks off with the empty casks, goes on his way rejoicing, leaving the rustic *eau-de-vie* to be converted into gentlemanly cognac brandy.

Some proprietors preferred to play the market more actively. Alfred de Vigny had retained the vineyard near Blanzac that he had inherited from an aunt because he loved the place and its setting. Although it did not matter to him financially and had nothing to do with his poetic vocation, he nevertheless kept a beady eye on the cognac market. Like many other growers, he normally sold to one particular firm (in his case it was Hennessy), but this did not stop him from speculating. 'The price of brandy seems to me to be pretty satisfactory' he wrote to his estate manager in April 1854, 'but as the season is inclement and M. Auguste Hennecy [sic] has informed me that prices will neither rise nor fall before the harvest, I will wait until you tell me about the late frosts people are afraid of before deciding.' Four months later he had still not sold: 'I haven't settled anything with M. Hennecy, and you will not deal with anyone over my brandies, because the outlook for the harvest this year is unpromising.'

But there was one group that did not accept the existing order of things. In 1838 Pierre Antoine de Salignac rallied some hundreds of the region's wine growers into the United Vineyard Proprietors Company, the Société de Propriétaires Vinicoles de Cognac. He lauched the new firm as a direct challenge to the 'Big Three' houses – Martell, Hennessy and Otard-Dupuy – which, he claimed, monopolized the purchase of the growers' brandies (according to Quénot, six or eight houses controlled the trade.) Salignac claimed, reasonably enough, that cognac owed its worldwide fame to its quality, and that this was provided not by the trademarks burned into the casks by the three firms but by the growers and distillers themselves. Their fight against the 'Big Three' was soon successful: within a few years the United Vintners' brandy, with Salignac's own name prominent on the label, joined the 'Big Three'. The idea was copied by other groups, and the growers from Barbezieux, for instance, were soon selling their brandies direct to the British market. Salignac, too, had his imitators. Jules Duret and the founder of the

---

[1] According to Charles Tovey, Dickens himself was the author. But Dickens never went near Cognac, and the style is unmistakably Vizetelly's.
[2] Tovey says the firm was Salignac.

firm of Barriasson used their position as managers of growers' co-operatives to launch themselves as merchants. Salignac himself had the strikingly modern idea that cognacs, like the wines of Bordeaux, ought to be graded by their age and quality, arguing that cognac's principal clientèle, the better-off classes in Britain, could afford higher prices. He was the only merchant who actually welcomed visitors. More traditional houses, in the words of Charles Tovey, 'would like the English consumer especially to retain the delusion that a special name branded upon the exterior of a cask has everything to do with the quality of its contents. They would not wish the world to know that any merchant in Cognac who has cash to go to market with can purchase from the farmers as good Brandy as another.' In an understandable effort to retain their aura of mystery they did not even reply to Tovey's letters.

Salignac did not confine his ideas to the market place; they had an additional, political, dimension. This was not especially radical – Salignac was joined by two of the leading landowners of the region, the Marquis d'Asnières and Jules de Bremond d'Ars, and the three of them headed a rather reactionary, Catholic political grouping. In his election propaganda he accused the 'Big Three' of exploiting the growers and making monstrous profits at their expense. He mocked the idea that they had opened new markets: they still depended, he said, almost entirely on British buyers and even used British ships, to the great detriment of the French merchant navy. He finished with a splendid flourish: 'Stop giving yourself an importance which you lack. Your only claim to fame is to have profiteered at the expense of the growers . . . and the region has never forgotten the fact!!!!'

The Martells and the Hennessys were tempting targets, politically as well as commercially. Both families provided Cognac with mayors and deputies, while one Martell ventured, successfully, as far afield as Libourne, the consituency in the Gironde that includes St Émilion. Salignac alleged that they ganged up on outsiders, supporting each other's candidatures against the growers even if they did not share the same political labels or beliefs. These varied but both families tended to be what Continental Europeans term 'liberals': like their constituents, they were secular, luke-warm or hostile to the Church's political pretensions; they naturally favoured Free Trade; and, in French terms, they sometimes strayed into a paternalist sort of radicalism. In any case personalities, not policies, mattered most to what was still a highly restricted electorate. James Hennessy senior was extremely popular because he had been an early opponent of the reactionary King Charles X, whom he had helped to dethrone in 1830, so he was invariably elected. But when his son stood in his place he was defeated.

The political battle gradually became less stormy after Salignac's death in 1843, but his commercial ideas remained valid and the firm continued to prosper, first under Salignac's son and grandson, and then under the management and name of the Monnet family, for the growers still felt the need for a manager of distinction who would lend his name to their product. Nevertheless the firm remained rather different: Jean Monnet remembered that some of the firm's more important 'shareholders' came to dinner every Saturday: 'well-off men, full of wisdom, close to the soil . . . the links between them and my father were closer than mere interest; there was also friendship and mutual trust'.

For all the complaints, the rows and the excessive duties, the second quarter of the century saw a steady improvement in the region's fortunes. Judging by some 1846 tax returns, the Martells, the Hennessy's the Otards and the Dupuys were the richest, but the Commandons, the Planats, the Augiers, the Gauthiers and, in Jarnac, the Hines and the Bisquits all had substantial fortunes.

Their growing financial needs led to the foundation of the town's first bank in 1838.

During the eighteen years of the 'July Monarchy', so abruptly terminated by the 1848 Revolution, many merchants moved away from their cramped quarters in the Old Town. Some of them, like Auguste Martell, bought country houses and estates: by the end of the century some members of the leading families had become landed gentry rather more interested in their estates than they were in their commercial affairs. But others remained within Cognac itself, for it was during the first half of the century that the town had expanded beyond the cramped alleys of the Old town (in 1800 it still covered the same area, 226 hectares, as it had in medieval times). 'Twenty years ago,' Vizetelly pointed out, 'Cognac was only a village; the same dull, steady-going place that it had been ever since the dawn of time. Now, not to speak of the merchants, the peasantry of the *arrondissement* of Cognac are the richest in France.' He contrasted the 'narrow side streets which look as if they were hewn out of the rock itself', covered with vines which 'seem to climb for the sake of reaching the summit of a natural cliff', with the many 'great houses in the town – surrounded by that symptom of wealth, luxurious gardens'. Some of these are now Cognac's municipal pride – the Museum, for example, is housed in a mansion built by Jules Dupuy in front of the Town Hall, itself originally the town house of his partner, Léon Otard. All this activity gave employment to an increasing number of local builders and architects, and, more directly, to 300 coopers, *tonnelliers,* in Cognac and Jarnac. The town, like its principal product, was on its way.

Le petit vicomte.

Turd-boyaux.

6 · An Imperial Glow

The 1850s and 1860s, the reign of Emperor Napoleon III, signalled a golden age for the Charentais, for they, together with the Bordelais, were the biggest beneficiaries of the emperor's policy of Free Trade, unprecedented in French history. Naturally they remained loyal to their benefactor for a generation after his downfall, though they paid for their loyalty: much of the bill for the gigantic reparations imposed by the victorious Germans after the Franco-Prussian War of 1870 was met through a substantial increase in the taxes paid on spirits.

At the beginning of Napoleon's reign British customs duties were still very severe. A first reduction in 1849 had only a limited effect because sales were hampered by the spread of oidium, a small fungoid growth that devastated all the vineyards of the south-west in the early 1850s. It was soon found that dusting the vines with sulphur provided a complete cure, and by the end of the decade the vineyards were back to normal. But in the meantime the merchants had not had any stock to tide them over. Vizetelly's visit had coincided with the worst of the crisis and he noted: 'There has been no wine lately to make into brandy; and everything vinous and spirituous is so dear that every accustomed purchaser is afraid to buy.' Inevitably, 'great complaints' were being made 'of want of employment amongst the working classes. The merchants are obliged to discharge most of their men.' But the crisis was clearly a temporary one: 'Arthur Young's test of a town's prosperity is manifestly visible; public and private buildings are being erected and restored on a liberal scale.'

There were no such obstacles to expansion when the Free Trade Treaty was signed between Britain and France in 1860. The outbreak of the American Civil War that year had sabotaged the growth of a promising market, but the dramatic reduction in British customs duties more than compensated for the lost opportunity. Before the Treaty cognac had cost eight times the 116 francs it fetched on the local market: afterwards it cost a quarter of the previous figure, putting the French product on equal terms with its British competitors. Before the onslaught of the oidium sales had risen to nearly 200,000 hectolitres. They dropped to a mere 110,000 in the 1850s and by 1860 had recovered only to 150,000 hectolitres. Within ten years they had soared to 450,000. Not surprisingly, Cognac is the only town in France to boast a rue Richard Cobden, named after one of the men who had preached the gospel of Free Trade so effectively.

To Vizetelly, as to the Victorian middle classes as a whole, cognac was more than a drink: 'We are therefore ... obliged to a district which supplies stores for our medicine chest as well as for our cellar,' he wrote. In the days before antibiotics brandy was widely prescribed: 'There are countless aged persons and invalids, whose stomachs cannot bear either wine or beer, to whom pure brandy, or brandy-and-water, is an indispensable sustenance.' The notion of 'medicinal brandy', the half-bottle kept in the corner cabinet of even the humblest British home, was firmly implanted in mid-Victorian times and was the foundation of Martell's long and profitable dominance of the British market.

The prosperity was general, but although a number of new firms were formed, the trade remained highly concentrated. Between 1852 and 1870 the top dozen firms were responsible for over 70 per cent of the exports; sales in France were relatively unimportant. Hennessy alone accounted for nearly one quarter of the total, and Martell just over one fifth. The growers assembled under the Salignac banner supplied 9 per cent and Otard-Dupuy 5.6 per cent. No other business came anywhere near these four, but even they were not large businesses; their stocks were not enormous. In the 1870s the venerable house of Augier reckoned that it had the second biggest stock of cognacs, although this amounted to the equivalent of only about 1 million bottles of normal-strength brandy. Much of the region's production was exported immediately to be aged in wood in Britain; the growers still held most of the older brandies – and thus remained in a strong position to bargain with their customers. In the late 1840s two-thirds of Hennessy's stocks were less than two years old, and only one-ninth more than five years old, a proportion that did not change dramatically in the following quarter of a century. The evidence is obvious to every visitor: the older *chais de stockage* are not large.

For in some ways the trade remained set in its traditional ways. The railway line from Angoulême through Cognac to the coast was completed in 1867, but brandies continued to be shipped by barge to Tonnay-Charente. Nevertheless, one relationship was totally transformed in the third quarter of the century: that between the Cognac firms and their British customers. The Cognacais started selling their product in bottles under their own name and not, as previously, in anonymous casks whose contents were to be bottled and labelled with the name of the London merchants. These all-powerful middlemen also controlled other markets in the British colonies (especially India, an increasingly important outlet). So selling direct was a bold and novel step: when the major cognac houses registered themselves under the Trade Marks Act of 1875 they also recorded the length of time for which they had been using their names. Martell claimed that it had been using its name since the turn of the century, Hine that its emergence from anonymity dated back to 1817, the year of the firm's foundation, but all the others (including Hennessy) had started selling under their own name only in the 1850s and 1860s.

The revolution was a dramatic one. Until the late 1850s the merchants had been relatively helpless. Unscrupulous foreigners could – and did – import inferior brandies and have them stamped as of French origin because they had passed through a French port. All this was stopped by the French Law of 23 June 1857, by which trademarks could be registered and thus protected against interlopers. The Tribunal of the Chambre de Commerce in Cognac, which started registering marks in 1858, is a rich repository of brand names. There are 16,000 in all, although only 3,000 are still legally valid because they have to be re-registered every ten years. The locals were anxious to establish trademarks because they could then personalize their products even further by putting them into bottles. Martell owns what is probably the earliest bottle of cognac – it dates from 1848 – but two relatively new firms, Jules Robin and Jeanne-Antoine Renault, also seized the chance early to make their name by bottling their cognacs. By 1855 the practice was widespread: Vizetelly saw a man making thirty or forty cases (or, as he playfully called them, 'volumes') a day in 'MR's establishment'. The Act of 1857 provided a further boost. Between 1860 and 1875 the Martells were sending one-quarter of their sales in cases of a dozen bottles. In the 1870s the trade as a whole matched this proportion – but by that time the Hennessys were selling half in bottle.

Within a few years of the Act of 1857 every house in Cognac had registered several marks. Bisquit Dubouché was early on the scene, registering the firm's mark (a shield, a horseman and the *fleur-de-lys*), and in 1864 the Hennessys got round to registering their famous *bras armé*. By the later 1860s there was evidently some pressure on firms to adopt a trademark. In 1867 the younger Thomas Hine adopted the famous stag mark – possibly a pun on the word 'hind' (a female deer) – only because he felt that his firm's brandies had to have some distinguishing stamp.

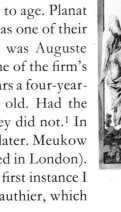

The next step was to identify the contents of the new-fangled bottles according to age. Planat and 'Bellot et Fils Frères et Foucauld', for example, both registered 'Old Brandy' as one of their marks. But this was merely a vague indication. According to family legend, it was Auguste Hennessy who systematized the idea. Noticing a star engraved on a window in one of the firm's offices, he devised a system by which one star meant a two-year-old brandy, two stars a four-year-old, and three stars a six-year-old. The term 'old' meant more than six years old. Had the Hennessys registered the star system, they could have protected the idea, but they did not.[1] In 1868 De Laage registered the three-star system; Martell followed suit sixteen years later. Meukow boasted that its 'Carte Argent' was 'Cognac fine champagne 20 Ans' (also registered in London). This in turn was topped in 1873 by de Laage's Cognac Fine Champagne 1825', the first instance I can trace of a cognac of a specific vintage. The last word was spoken by Messrs Gauthier, which once marketed a brand bearing the label 'Antédiluvien'.

The legislation opened the floodgates to the impressive ingenuity of the town's merchants. In 1870 Messrs J. L. Martel registered a splendid spoof label, virtually the same as that of the double-l Martell's, boasting, truthfully enough, that their *maison* was 'fondée en 1870', a dig at the

[1] The Hennessys were always rather careless in registering their ideas. They also thought up the idea of using the letters XO to indicate an Extra Old cognac, but many other houses now use the mark as well.

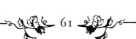

real Martells, so proud that their venerable firm had been founded in 1715. Many labels boasted of their suppliers' successes at exhibitions – Jules Duret, for instance, had been awarded a Médaille Première Classe at the Exhibition Universelle held in Paris in 1855.[1] Martell could afford to be decidedly sniffy; it had 'never submitted its products to any of the exhibitions, large or small, which have multiplied everywhere and which give rise to a veritable avalanche of awards sought by houses of the second rank'.

But the dominance of Martell and Hennessy forced lesser houses to find some distinctive mark to help in specific markets. Bisquit registered 'La Presidenta 1848' to commemorate some long-forgotten event in the history of Guatemala, and Bonniot registered a 'Fine Vieux Cognac' under the pseudonym of 'Paul Dupont' (the French equivalent of 'John Smith') that was 'expressly bottled for India'. Many other firms employed more than one name: P. A. Maurain had used

[1] The exhibition which set in tablets of stone the classification of the wines of the Gironde. In theory, therefore, Jules Duret could claim to be a 'Cognac 1er Cru'. But Cognac has enough problems of its own without opening that particular can of worms.

'John Bellot', with a label, clearly aimed at Far Western thirsts, of a cowboy (or could it be a gaucho, for the Latin American market was growing rapidly) lassoing a buffalo. But my personal favourite was registered by Charles Rousseau: 'Imperial Brandy Proprietors', it showed a dishevelled young lady, clearly the worse for wear, hanging on to some wreaths, in which she was entwined, as though they were life jackets.

During the golden years Hennessy was clearly in front in the century-old two-horse race. The Martells were in the middle of a transition between the Martells themselves and the Firinos, who had married into the family, for the tradition of sons-in-law taking over continued as strongly as ever: Alexander Bisquit's son-in-law, Adrien Dubouché, himself had a son-in-law, Maurice Laporte, who duly added his grandfather's name to his.

Commercial pressure also led to the first attempts to define the different parts of the Cognac vineyard. The inferiority of the cognacs from the Saintonge and Aunis, near the sea, had been known and acknowledged by the price obtainable for them for at least a century. But in the boom years it became increasingly necessary to define more precisely what had hitherto been a rather rough-and-ready series of categories. The initiative was taken by the Salignacs, who felt that their members were being cheated because the big houses used brandies from outside the choicest slopes. So, as Tovey put it in his *British and Foreign Spirits*: 'Salignac bound them to ship only the Brandy grown in a defined district (of which a map is prepared) well known to produce all the finest qualities.' The first map of the Cognac district had been prepared in 1854 by the Coopérative at Saintes and naturally took the town as the beating heart of Cognac.[1] Salignac's response was to commission a well-known geologist, M. Coquand, to carry out the first proper survey of the area in order to pinpoint the superiority of the Champagne districts. By the late 1860s there was a *Dictionnaire de crus* and a series of maps, drawn up by an engineer called Lacroix, defining and redefining the boundaries between the different *crus*. Unfortunately, he set a precedent by being too tidy-minded to cope with the fragmented geology and geography of the Cognac region.

Originally, brandies had been defined simply as coming from either the Champagne or the Bois. The Borderies remained somewhat apart because of their historic fame as a supplier of sweet white wines. The principal effect of the mania for classification was a proliferation of names for the enormous area covered by the Bois. One small area across the Charente from the Grande Champagne acquired some considerable fame as the Premiers Bois: Tovey refers to a 'fine brandy known as Premiers Bois'; one much-liked cognac was marketed under the name of Château de Chassors, the heart of the area; and in the 1930s Charles Walter Berry, the leading English connoisseur of fine cognac, tasted and approved of a 'fine Fin Bois'. But the Premiers Fins Bois were merely top of a hierarchy, which naturally included Deuxièmes Bois, followed by Fins Bois, Bons Bois, Bois Ordinaires, Bois Communs, Bois à Terroir and so on. Tovey listed 'Champagne fine and common, Champagne de Bois and Eau-de-Vie de Bois, as well as that of Annis (Aunis) produced from the vines on the banks of the river'. Robert Delamain claimed that some London buyers divided the region into no fewer than sixteen different *crus*.

The distinctions made were commercially important, since a Champagne cognac could be worth 40 per cent more than a mere Bois. The gradations, depending as much on age as on the *cru*, can be seem from the valuation of the brandies in the family's *magasin* when the widow of Pierre

---

[1] Some years later the merchants of Angoulême followed suit: their map was so biassed that Segonzac, the historic heart of the Grande Champagne, was placed firmly in the Bois.

Comandon, a leading merchant, died in 1861.[1] An anonymous 'eau-de-vie nouvelle' was valued at a mere 160 francs per hectolitre, A three-year-old 'Fine Champagne' – a mixture of both Petite and Grande – was valued at 225 francs, while ten-year-old cognacs from the Bois were valued at around 200 francs. Some Borderies 'Vieille', clearly more then ten years old, was worth 300 francs and some Old Fine Champagne 400 francs (to confuse matters further one lot was described as being 'Saintonge vieille').

The inventory also gives an insight into the business as a whole. The Comandons owned 1,500 cases of *eau-de-vie,* lodged with Mr Oppenheim in London, and a small quantity at Messrs Blancan Ewen in New York. At home they possessed, as well as the brandy itself, 16 hectolitres of the *sirop blanc et colorant* required to sweeten and darken the cognac for market. The result was in the nine cases 'préparées à destination d'Angleterre', diluted by some of their 50 hectolitres of *petites eaux,* the mix of brandy and water used to reduce the spirit to 40° strength.

Not surprisingly, the distinctions gave rise to all sorts of frauds. The growers naturally blamed the merchants, but everyone was at it. In 1858 a report by the Sous-Préfet of Barbezieux firmly blamed

an enormous number of the smaller distillers [who] buy a little wine and distil it at home. It is these fellows . . . who have given the local brandy trade a bad reputation. For most of them mix the local product with raw alcohols from the Nord and spirits from Languedoc. Unfortunately it is almost impossible to convict them of the frauds of which they are undoubtedly guilty.

He was being a little unfair to the authorities' efforts. Tovey noted that in 1857–8 a number of growers were convicted of fraud and received long sentences which 'had a very salutary effect, and contributed in a great degree to stop all adulteration and sophistication.'

In Tovey's time these fraudsters could plead a lack of local grapes caused by the oidium. But the frauds continued in the 1860s and early 1870s, when the area growing grapes for conversion to cognac started to expand even faster than the market. Indeed, by the mid-1870s it formed the largest single vineyard in France. Thirty per cent of the *arrondissement* of Cognac was already planted with vines, as heavy a concentration as could be found anywhere in France, so the growth was concentrated in the woods to the north and west, in the Deux-Sèvres and more especially in the Charente-Inférieure,[2] where nearly 60,000 additional hectares were planted with vines in the third quarter of the century, all adding to the acreage of 'bois'. In the peak year of 1875 production from the whole vineyard was more than double the 1850 figure.

The area's vineyards may have been the biggest in France but they were emphatically not the best-kept. Vizetelly had remarked how 'the culture of vines for making *eau-de-vie* differs considerably from the management of mere wine-making vines. It is also more careless or slovenly in appearance.' A contemporary *enquête agricole* had commented on how loosely the rows of vines were planted, with enough room between them for an ox team to plough. The inhabitants echoed the slovenliness – and the prosperity – of their vineyards. In the late 1850s Tovey shrewdly remarked:

Anyone who observed these people congregated together at the Cognac or Jarnac market or fair, would at once recognize them from their appearance as a class of men who, having had a difficulty in

[1] Archives de la Charente, *série notaire* 2E 13640.
[2] This is now known as Charente-Maritime. The inhabitants naturally did not want the inferiority of their product emphasized by the name.

getting what wealth they possess, are determined to keep it, and are earnest in their endeavours to increase it. Although in their best apparel, they are ill-dressed and shabby-looking; the clothes they wear might at some time or other have been genteel. Some appear in dress coats, with outrageously large coloured silk handkerchiefs round their necks. The ill-fitted clothes show that the present wearers are not the original proprietors ... one keen and subtle-looking man, whose clothes would not have fetched five shillings, was pointed out to us as a man worth eighty thousand pounds.

His observations were echoed by a later visitor. Charles Albert d'Arnaux was a well-known illustrator who signed himself 'Bertall' at the suggestion of Balzac, whose novels he illustrated. In 1878 he published *La vigne*,[1] an entertaining account of a visit to the Charente – although it was inevitably rather patronizing, he being Parisian and they provincials and therefore, by definition, simpletons. He had arrived from Bordeaux, where the vines were grown in fastidiously tended rows, and the contrast was startling, given the nearness of the two regions. Bordeaux and Cognac, both dependent on the export of a luxury product derived from the vine, remain worlds apart even today. In Cognac, he noted, 'The vines seem to grow haphazardly, like cabbages or beets in a field. Their branches wander at whim, without stakes, laths or ties, and the general impression of a vineyard is of a vast carpet of greenery, which is not dulled, as it is elsewhere, by the powdery grey tints of the stakes or posts intended to support the vine and its fruit.' This neglect extended to the wine making. The growers did not even bother to destalk the bunches of grapes, which were crushed either mechanically or by the peasants' feet. It was all rather casual. But it did not matter much. As he pointed out, the wine was merely an intermediate product. What mattered was the cognac, especially the older stuff, and he was lucky enough to meet an owner of some of the best.

M. Curlier, a partner of M. Courvoisier, introduced Bertall to a grower, M. Saunier, rich and sage like those who dined with the Monnets every Saturday. 'A small, grizzled man, completely tanned, baked and baked again by the sun; his face was wrinkled as a dried grape. His slim face, sharp and fine like a fox's muzzle, like some Norman countenances, is illuminated by small clear grey eyes, shining with intelligence and good-will.' he was modestly dressed, and even his precious *pressoir* and still were 'old, covered with a sheen resulting from long years of use.' M. Saunier was not a superficially worldly man. He suspected Paris: he had only been there once and regarded it merely as the refuge for local ne'er-do-wells (one of whom had been shot as a *communard*; another had been transported for his part in the same revolutionary uprising). This provincial outlook and modest exterior concealed a fortune (estimated by Bertall at 2 million francs) in old cognac, which M. Saunier was in no mood to sell. 'Keep your money, I'm keeping my casks,' he told M. Curlier. He was not alone in his wealth. Twenty years earlier Vizetelly had noted that 'the peasantry of the *arrondissement* of Cognac are the richest in all France. Some few are worth as much as sixty thousand pounds sterling.'

In the late 1870s the contents of casks like M. Saunier's were increasing rapidly in value because of the ravages of the dreaded louse, *Phylloxera vastatrix,* which had first invaded the Charente a few years earlier. In 1871 and 1872 the louse had become firmly established on the dry uplands and in the valley of the Charente. It spread outwards from Cognac itself, speeded by a dry year in 1873,[2] when it first got a grip on the grapes in the Champagnes. By the next year it had

[1] Recently republished by Bruno Sepulchre and quoted in his: *Le Livre du Cognac: trois siècles d'histoire*, Paris, Hubschmidt & Bouret, 1983.
[2] The louse did not like water – indeed, it could be exterminated by flooding the vineyards.

spread to the Charente-Inférieure. Once established, the pace of its spread was frightening. On 7 July 1874 the Sous-Préfet of Jonzac declared that all was well. Ten days later he reported the first outbreak; by September a number of villages had been hit; and by the next year 1,250 hectares had been ravaged. The relatively wet summers of 1876 and 1877 came too late to save most of the area's vines. Ironically, the louse was almost welcomed at first, for the frantic planting of the 1860s had outstripped even the increasing demand of the British buyers.

But when Bertall visited M. Saunier the magnitude of the disaster had become all too clearly apparent. Even in untouched areas he noticed the telltale signs that the 'little louse' had begun its destructive work: 'Here and there, unhappily, a few stains, yellow or earth-coloured, had appeared and darkened the carpet of greenery.' Once the louse had taken hold the damage was appalling: 'We easily pulled up a stump whose roots, frayed, blistered, destroyed, had retained neither their strength nor their life.' These were not isolated outbreaks. On both sides of the road between Cognac and Jarnac they saw 'a stretch 5 miles long and 2 miles wide, where the devastation was so complete that the roots were fit only to burn, and the harvest did not produce a single grape'. Within a decade the stocks of growers like M. Saunier had been exhausted. Thousands of growers like him would never again know the prosperity they had enjoyed in the imperial years of the 1860s.

7 · A Disaster – and a Revolution

There are regions where the collective memory stops short at the war of '14–'18; others, like the Vendée, stop at the Revolutionary wars; phylloxera serves as a full stop in the collective memory of the Charentais. There is before and after; before implies halcyon days, the Golden Age; after implies the hard grind of daily reality. For many years after the crisis, the word 'phylloxera' remained the ultimate threat hurled at naughty children, while many growers preserved a row of old vines 'out of friendship', in the same way that you keep a family souvenir.[1]

François Julien-Labruyère, the author of these words, was barely exaggerating. The growers lost not only their new-found prosperity but their independence as well. Phylloxera completely upset the long-established balance of power between the merchants and the growers, who were forced to sell their precious stocks in order to survive. Many tried to sell their land but, not surprisingly, found that the price had dropped to a mere one-tenth of its former value during the first years after the onset of the plague. Others looked for jobs in other parts of France, for there were precious few available in Cognac. In 1873 2,000 coopers were employed in 200 workshops in the town; ten years later there were 93 workshops employing a mere 321 workers.

The merchants were better off. Nevertheless, the old fear that once customers lost the habit of buying a specific drink they would not easily be recaptured proved true, partly because phylloxera sent the price of cognac soaring and made it, for the first time, purely a luxury beverage. The Cognacais, like the Bordelais, tend to pin all the blame on the pest. Preoccupied with their own troubles, they ignored the world slump which afflicted other luxury industries at the same time. A wave of protectionism, set off by the tariffs imposed by the French in 1892 – which undid all the good work done by the Free Trade Treaty thirty years earlier – helped to prolong the slump effectively until after the Second World War.

Ironically, phylloxera shielded the growers from a different type of crisis, though it is no consolation to the collective memories of thousands of broken-hearted peasants to say that without the plague they would have suffered not from a shortage of stock but from a severe crisis of over-production. One estimate, based on the figures given in Berrault's annual survey of Cognac, is that between 1861 and 1876 the region produced nearly 11 million hectolitres of cognac but exported under 4.5 million. The remaining 6.5 million represented no less than twenty-four times the exports shipped annually at the height of the Napoleonic boom, and without phylloxera would have hung over the market for a generation.

Phylloxera transformed the shape as well as the size of the Cognac vineyard, for it was simply not worth replanting the outer areas. The most dramatic example was in the far north of the vineyard, in the Deux-Sèvres, which had nearly 24,000 hectares under vines as late as 1882. Twenty years later the figure was down to 6,300 and since then has always remained at less than a third of the 1882 figure. These outlying areas, which in any case had never produced very good

---

[1] François Julien-Labruyère, *Paysans charentais*, La Rochelle, Rupella, 1982, vol. 1, p. 306.

cognac, soon found their true vocation as dairy farms. By the end of the century Charentais butter, in particular, had become renowned through the efforts of a number of pioneering agricultural co-operatives. The rest of Cognac had to struggle to return to the only product it knew, but progress was slow. In France as a whole there were more vines in 1900 than there had been before the onset of phylloxera. By contrast, the acreage within the Cognac area, which had risen to nearly 290,000 hectares in the 1870s, dropped to 54,000 by 1890 and had recovered only to an average of 74,000 in the second decade of the present century.

Replanting in the very special conditions of the Charente was a painful and costly process. The growers could live off their stocks for a few years but had no financial reserves left to pay the costs of replanting, so most of them had to sell their precious stills and market the produce of their grapes as wine, not as cognac. The mobile stills they were forced to use could not be guaranteed to make spirits of the delicacy and quality required by the buyers.

Elsewhere in France the growers rapidly took to vines grafted on to American rootstock immune to the louse. But in the Charente a stubborn lobby fought for more than a decade to avoid this solution, pinning its faith to chemical remedies, notably the injection of sulphur-based compounds into the soil. These chemicals were both expensive and unsatisfactory, since they never completely eradicated the pest and the treatments were seemingly endless. In 1877 a group of growers headed by André Verneuil of Segonzac, one of the region's most heroic figures, sent the first of a series of missions to the United States to discover rootstocks suitable for grafting on to the Charente's precious Folle Blanche and Colombard vines. It was ten years later that they finally discovered the solution in Texas, where a pioneer viticulturalist, T. U. Munson,[1] had found suitable wild vines. His nursery at Denison on the Red River became a place of pilgrimage for desperate growers.

At first the grafted stocks were thought to be unsuitable for the soils of the Champagne because they were liable to be choked by the chalk in the soil, a malady described as *chlorose* (chlorosis). Fortunately for the Charente, the old habits of communal solidarity had not died out. The merchant families, who alone had the funds, found that, if properly handled, the American stocks would thrive even in the Champagne. In 1889 they even set up a viticultural research station, the first in France, to help with the reconstruction. It was run by a young man, Louis Ravaz, a pioneer of scientific viticulture and a leading missionary for grafted vines, who was only 26 when he was appointed.

For when the Charentais did come to replant, they did so in an unprecedentedly scientific fashion. Cultivation was rationalized. Where previously the vines had been planted higgledy-piggledy but often very close together (with only 1 metre between the rows), the new vineyards left enough room for a horse or ox-drawn plough. Before phylloxera, planting was simply a matter of bending a branch into the ground and letting it take root. This was clearly impossible with a grafted vine. At first the growers could not graft the plants themselves and had to buy their vines at the special nurseries which sprang up all over the Département, many of which were run by dubious characters who sold inferior, albeit higher-yielding varieties. In the end the Charentais found another variety, the St-Émilion, which came to dominate the area as the Folle Blanche had done before the plague. But the St-Émilion produces cognacs that are less aromatic than those distilled from the Folle Blanche. So the region's products, like its economy, suffered a

[1] Ms. Sarah Jane English kindly told me about Mr. Munson.

transformation unique in France – for elsewhere the same varieties were planted to replace those destroyed by the vine louse.

We can appreciate the pain and expense involved from a description of Malaville, a village in the Grande Champagne, written by the local school-teacher in 1901.[1] He painted a depressing picture. Forty years earlier Malaville had had 800 inhabitants: by 1901 the number was down to 633 – and as elsewhere in the Cognac area, many of these were newcomers from other parts of Poitou, filling the gap left by former inhabitants who had fled to the towns. Whereas vineyards had previously been worth 4,800 francs a hectare, by the turn of the century many were on the market at between 600 and 900 francs. The pay of domestic servants had fallen by half, 'in addition to their keep, grudgingly allowed'. The growers were no better off: 'Innumerable

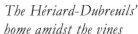

*The Hériard-Dubreuils'
home amidst the vines*

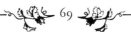
[1] J.-A. Verdon, 'Une commune rurale vue par son instituteur d'alors: Malaville en 1901', *Annales GREH*, 1982.

growers in this corner of the Grande Champagne first tried, alas without any success, to replant the varieties which had brought such prosperity to our region.' Even in 1898 over half the area which had been replanted with grafted stocks belonged to a handful of major proprietors. The smaller growers started up only at the very turn of the century. Only by then had they found how to graft plants for themselves, thus saving the (to them) immense cost of new plants.

The money the merchants invested in their estates, in Malaville as in the rest of the Champagne, was not their biggest cost. They alone had access to the bank credit required to improve their estates and to buy and hold the stocks formerly stored by the growers. Banks flocked to Cognac in the last twenty years of the century, led by the then privately owned Banque de France, which established a branch in the town in 1882. The credit was vital. Before the plague Hennessy had held in stock only enough cognac to supply its customers for six months. After 1880 they held enough for up to six years' sales. These had dropped, but by only 20 per cent – from an average of 290,000 hectolitres in the 1870s to about 250,000 in the following decade, a drop far less severe than the slump in production.

ENVIRONS DE COGNAC — Distillerie d'un domaine

They then, quite literally, built round their stocks, erecting the first major industrial buildings the Cognacais had ever seen. By 1892 the *Revue Périodique Mensuelle* found it natural to include a survey of the Martell establishment in its series on major industrial undertakings. It informed its readers that Martell's stillroom was 50 metres long and that each of its four stills held 6 hectolitres – six time the previous average. Martell, said the article, had been forced to become distillers in their own right. They had to defend themselves against 'frauds on the part of unscrupulous growers; and that is why their purchasing service is so sophisticated and why Martell possesses a laboratory so well equipped with apparatus and instruments' (a far cry from the informality of Vizetelly's day less than forty years earlier). The business had suddenly become modern and capital-intensive. The three-storey *chai au coupage* (blending hall) was dominated by fifty immense cylindrical tuns, each holding 175 hectolitres. On the top floor the line of thirty-six tuns could hold 6,300 hectolitres and was connected by 300 metres of piping. This 'gigantic hall' was unique in Cognac.

The Martells and their competitors did not abuse their power – although Martell and Hennessy found that they were able to fix the annual price for each year's vintage and expect it to become the norm, a duopoly broken in 1954. They could have gone much further and bought up the whole vineyard, but they did not. They extended their estates, to be sure, but they never aimed to be more than substantial country gentry. The principal reason, according to Maurice Hennessy,[1] was that Cognac's leading families were still politicians, aware of their civic responsibilities to the electors on whom they depended. (The Martells, for instance, were ardent defenders of the rights of the *bouilleurs de cru*, the growers who distilled their own cognac.) They obviously felt they had a leading role to play in the region, but they did not want to own it. Until his death in 1907 the electors of Cognac remained faithful to Gustave Cuneo d'Ornano, an absurd, moustachioed, theatrical but effective Bonapartist loyalist. He was succeeded by Maurice Hennessy's father, James.

As the description of its 'factory' shows, Martell was staging something of a come-back. It had bought stock so aggressively that sales were not reduced by phylloxera. Its new installations were also required to increase the proportion of its sales which were despatched in bottles. According to some rather dubious 1894 export figures Hennessy was still outselling its great rival three to one abroad, but Martell was already selling 90 per cent of its output in bottle, as against a mere half for Hennessy, and was also stealing a march at home. 'James Hennessy thought it was really rather vulgar to bother with the French market,' says Alan de Pracomtal, his great-nephew and chairman of Hennessy. As a result the Hennessys were virtually unrepresented in their native country apart from in the smarter bars and restaurants. By contrast, Martell painstakingly built up its distribution network throughout France and has always been the leading brand in what is now a major market.

The Hennessys had acquired some rather grand metropolitan habits during the golden years. Even before he succeeded d'Ornano James spent much of his time in Paris. When his wife died in 1900 he turned his back on the house and the town associated with her and spent only a few days each month in Cognac. By contrast, the Firino-Martells were prepared to get down to the grinding hard work of selling: 'I remember going around Liverpool with Michel Firino-Martell,'

---

[1] This charming veteran, born in 1896, is apt to apologize (both in French and in impeccable English) that he is growing senile and forgetful. In reality he is a shrewd and courteous mine of information about the history of Cognac.

says Jacques de Varenne of Augier. 'He was quite prepared to knock on doors, and every evening we would go round the pubs to see if they sold his cognac.' In lean times the Martell's reputation for being rather dour and plodding, for acting as *l'epicier du coin* (the corner grocer's), served them well.

The merchants' attempts to impose themselves on the outside world were greatly helped by a revolution in the art of bottle making. Until nearly the end of the century bottles were hand-blown by men whose lungs and throats routinely suffered permanent damage from physically blowing thousands of bottles from molten glass. 'Beside every glass works they build,' wrote Max de Nansouty in 1901, 'they had to lay out a cemetery which was never idle.' The hero of the revolution was one Claude Boucher, a Cognacais of humble origins, who invented a machine for blowing glass – previously the only machine-made glass bottles seem to have been inferior, moulded varieties.

Boucher is a local hero, although not all the firms bought from his newly established works (in the 1890s the Martells brought their uniquely shaped bottles all the way from Montluçon, 200 miles away), and contemporary enthusiasm did not extend to his social position. As Jean Monnet remarked: 'Although he had literally revolutionized the glass industry, and thus the marketing of Cognac, in local society he always remained within the ranks of the suppliers.'[1] Monnet knew what he was talking about. His grand-father had been a small grower (Maurice Hennessy remembers how well he played the fiddle at village weddings) and it had been his father who had climbed into the ranks of the merchant class. And climb it was: 'Cognac society was divided into two very distinct classes: on one side there was the merchant class, and on the other everyone else, which in practice meant mostly suppliers.'

Boucher's invention provided a colossal boost to the merchants' efforts to impose their brand names on the world. This was symbolized by the confrontation in Britain between Martell and the Gilbeys, then far and away the dominant force in the market with 2,000 licensed agents throughout the country. At the end of the 1860s the Gilbeys tried to force Martell to supply cognac for their own 'Castle' brand. Martell refused, and for several years the Gilbeys contemplated his plight with some smugness. But by the 1880s they were forced to stock his cognac, not under their name (and thus on their terms) but under his – even though in the meantime Sir Walter Gilbey's favourite daughter had married into the Hine family. Martell, Hennessy and the other Cognacais were benefitting from a worldwide trend which, in the 1880s, established the major brands of Scotch whisky and champagne as well as of cognac. But there was another, parallel trade in bulk brandies: at least one firm boasted that it had installed special equipment for creating and designing brands in buyers' own names – a practice which foreshadowed the 'buyers' own brands' now sold by retail chains the world over. These were sold largely on price, whereas before the introduction of bottles 'own brands' were those sold by the smarter wine merchants, who were emphatically not competing on price.

Business remained poor, and the Cognacais had to search for markets all over the world – Berrault's annual provided exchange rates for dozens of currencies from Turkey to Uruguay. Jean Monnet found it perfectly natural to be sent to London at the age of 16 for a two-year apprenticeship before embarking on a prolonged tour of Canada when barely out of his teens. He had already learned to think of the world as a string of clients to be visited: 'If that took us to Singapore or New York that was scarcely felt as a privilege attached to our profession because it

[1] Op. cit.

was our primary responsibility.' It was a good education for a statesman – and not just because of the training in languages and modern politics absorbed at the family table:

I went to Egypt where I learned other forms of persuasion. I would accompany our Greek agent from village to village. We visited the wholesalers, who bade us sit down, we drank coffee while they busied themselves with their own business. We learned that you had to wait for the appropriate moment. At a certain point Chamah, the Greek, decided that we must bring the matter to a head. At that point he would write in his notebook the quantity which he considered it reasonable for our customer to take, a figure which was never discussed. He had simply respected local customs. Later, in the East, I rediscovered the importance of time, which made me wonder sometimes whether Cognac was not in fact closer to Shanghai than to New York. In China, you had to learn to wait. In the United States you had to learn to persist. Two forms of patience to which Cognac, itself the result of a certain length of time, predisposes you so well.[1]

As markets grew more difficult, so the merchants' search for novelty grew ever more frantic. By the turn of the century there were half a dozen more or less standard qualities: one-, two- and three-star, VO, VSO, VSOP and WSOP. The 1907 catalogue of the Army and Navy Stores in London lists eight cognacs from Martell alone: X, XX, XXX, VO, VSO, VSOP, ESOP ('guaranteed over forty years in cask') and Extra ('guaranteed over fifty years in cask'). But this was not enough. In the museum in Cognac there are bottles of every shape designed to take the buyer's fancy, many of them on maritime themes (in the shape of ships or sailors). The merchants registered dozens of trade marks involving various combinations of 'Grande' 'Fine' and 'Champagne' brandies, as well as a rash of dire-sounding mixtures, like 'Le Coup de Jarnac', described as 'Liquer hygénique à base de fine champagne' and 'Brandy Bark', a 'tonic elixir containing as chief ingredients genuine champaign brandy and royal yellow bark.'[2]

Other companies looked for specific markets: labels were registered for a cognac to be sold in railway buffets, a *Cognac des dames* and 'pocket bottles' (each containing 'Five glasses of excellent Cognac'). Other brands were topical. In 1876 Bellot's 'National French Brandy Company' had commemorated the hundredth anniversary of the Independence of the United States. Ten years later Gabriel Marchand rushed out a new label designed to appeal to supporters of the popular insurgent General Boulanger; and in 1889 the anniversary of the French Revolution and the construction of the Eiffel Tower were duly acknowledged (a more recent tribute from the house of Hine took the form of a bottle shaped like the famous tower).

More ominous were the labels stressing that the contents were 'real' or 'pure' Cognac and the boast of one firm that all its cognacs had been produced in its own distilleries. While there was not enough real cognac, fraudsters, native as well as foreign, had rushed in to fill the gap. As early as 1882 the Pall Mall Gazette was writing that: 'Cognac in large quantities now enters England which comes out of potatoes and not out of grapes. Pure cognac can now be secured . . . only through English holders of old stocks.' However, the machination of the fraudsters set off a train of consequences that, in the long run, provided the Cognacais for the first time with effective legal protection for their precious name.

---

[1] Ibid.
[2] Presumably that new wonder drug, quinine. So 'Brandy Bark' resembled a kit for making brandy and tonic.

8 · The Good Name of Cognac

For a quarter of a century the Cognacais were preoccupied with fighting phylloxera. When they finally emerged from their ordeal it was only to find that their markets had been largely usurped by a wave of 'industrial', mass-produced grain alcohols, some of them even daring to take the name of cognac. 'Fraud stalks the land, powerful and unashamed,' wrote a local author at the time; 'it sows confusion in the mind of the consumer and the inferior quality of its products depreciates the market value of genuine cognac.'[1] These spirits were so dangerous that, for the first time, a strong temperance movement sprang up in France. Unfortunately, its supporters did not distinguish between 'healthy' drinks like cognac and 'poisonous' ones like absinthe; this lack of discrimination induced the state to increase taxes on spirits of all descriptions.

The French Revolution had done away with many dues and duties on the production and transport of alcoholic drinks, but they were far too tempting a target to escape the tax man's attention for long. The first post-revolutionary retail tax on spirits was introduced in 1824; it was sharply increased in 1860 from 60 to 90 francs per litre of pure alcohol and boosted again, to 156 francs, in 1871 – the tax increase which helped so greatly to pay reparations to the Germans. But the biggest blow came in 1900, when the tax was increased by a further 50 per cent. As a result, the total tax burden borne by a bottle of spirits, including the local taxes payable in major cities, amounted to six times its original value. In a report to the Chambre de Deputés in 1902 M. Clementel, one of Cognac's stoutest defenders, remarked: 'The regions worst affected by the increase of taxes on spirits must surely be the Charente and Armagnac. The quality of the spirits they produce and their cost of production obliges the distillers from these regions to demand unnecessarily high prices, which effectively puts an end to their sale in France.' Not surprisingly, throughout the present century the Cognacais have been convinced that they are being unfairly discriminated against. In the bitter words of Jean Lys, in his thesis on the cognac business: 'Spirits are products that have to pay dearly for their right to be consumed.'[2]

Of course the Cognacais fought back. In 1909 the Minister of Finance, one M. Cochery, proposed that every bottle of cognac should carry a guarantee bearing the name of the merchant who had supplied it. In theory the measure was designed as a weapon against frauds, but everyone in Cognac took it merely as a tax in disguise, since the state would have taken 10 centimes merely for stamping each bottle as authentic. The proposed 'guarantee' triggered off a splendidly dignified mass protest led by Edouard Martell, James Hennessy, the Mayor of Cognac Georges Briand, and M. Roullet, the President of the 'Syndicat de défence du commerce des eaux-de-vie de Cognac.'

For a short time the tensions produced the sort of conflict between growers and merchants which affected most French wine-growing regions (including Champagne) in the years before World War I. As in the rest of France the growers in Cognac were wholeheartedly in favour of the

[1] Henri Boraud, *De l'Usage commercial du nom du Cognac*, Bordeaux, 1904.
[2] Jean Lys, *Le Commerce de Cognac*, Université de Bordeaux, 1929.

government's attempts to stamp out frauds. In Cognac the growers even demanded an export tax and a state monopoly for the sale of spirits in France itself. The merchants were naturally wary of a tax on exports and the effective nationalization of their domestic trade, an attitude the suspicious growers took as further proof that they benefited from the sale of fraudulent spirits. The merchants then brought up reinforcements: they recruited the thousands of workers involved in ancillary trades, from glass to cooperage, who depended on the cognac trade and organized their own mass demonstrations against the proposals (in 1907 James Hennessy had already demonstrated the political power of the merchants when he beat a radical opponent in the election that followed the death of D'Ornano, the veteran Bonapartist deputy).

The growers in Cognac, however, bore only a superficial resemblance to those involved in radical demonstrations elsewhere in France. They were not only farmers, they were also distillers, *bouilleurs de cru*. So, of course, were millions of other French farmers, who in other regions constituted the wine-growers' worst enemy. For these other *bouilleurs* were using lesser raw materials, like pears, apples, grain, potatoes or beetroots, to produce rough raw hooch to be consumed at home or supplied illicitly to cafés throughout the French countryside. By contrast even the humblest peasant in Cognac was distilling a noble (and expensive) spirit designed for a discerning, generally foreign, buyer. So, in the long run, the Cognac growers were bound to break ranks with their fellow growers and support the merchants. They were also naturally opposed to the over-generous rights granted to the *bouilleurs* in non-wine-growing regions who in 1902 accounted for over three-quarters of the spirits produced on a domestic scale in France. These 'back-yard distillers' formed a political lobby that was sufficiently powerful to block the controls introduced by successive governments until the 1950s.

Cognac's competition came not so much from other *bouilleurs* but from large-scale, systematic commercial fraud. As Professor Alglave wrote in a legal thesis at the time, 'fraud is not proportionate to the amount of the tax, but to the profits that can be made from each fraudulent act'.[1] The imitators, including a fair number of locals, had moved in as soon as the phylloxera had struck. In the short term the fraudsters were of some benefit to Cognac – although no one in the town was ever going to admit the fact. Yet the wave of fraudulent cognacs which swept the world in the 1880s at least ensured that the customer base for brandies alleged to have come from the town was not lost. These imitations filled the gap in the years when there was not enough of the real stuff. But by the end of the century production was returning to normal: the frauds had outlived their usefulness and were damaging the market, not only because of their poor quality but also by their sheer size. In 1900 the world was probably buying fifteen times as much 'cognac' as the 5,500,000 cases actually being produced in the Cognac region itself.

The Cognacais fought back in the law courts at home and abroad and in the field of international diplomacy; they even fought against the lexicographers. Not unreasonably, the town council protested against the definition of cognac in the great dictionary of M. Littré: 'A brandy from Cognac, and thus by derivation, an excellent brandy.' Although the Cognacais blamed foreigners for most of their troubles, unscrupulous merchants from all over France as well would set up post-boxes in Cognac with their names on them, arrange for someone to re-direct the letters addressed to them and thus establish legal residence. By 1889 it was reckoned that 179 firms were operating that one type of fraud alone.

The council and the merchants, either individually or through the Chambre du Commerce,

[1] Quoted in Maurice Néon, *De la Crise viticole en Charente*, Paris, 1907.

hoped that the French courts would prove an adequate defence, basing their case on a miscellany of laws. Article 1382 of the Civil Code stated firmly: 'Anything done by anyone which causes an injury to anyone obliges the guilty party to make amends'; and the Cognacais hoped to follow the Champenois, who had turned a law of 1824 to their advantage by extending the protection it provided to the name of their region to its best-known product. But the judges let Cognac down. In 1886 a court in Bordeaux ruled that one M. Perpezat, a Bordeaux-based merchant, could label his offerings 'Old Brandy Perpezat et Cie Cognac'. The Cognac region, it said, extended to Bordeaux because merchants based in that city sold it. After that it was relatively useless for a court in Douai to rule that cognac was a 'special spirit, whose qualities derived from the soil which produces it', condemning a local man on the grounds that the 'special soils' did not extend all the way to the Pas de Calais.

Martell's 'compound' in the middle of Cognac

The worst offenders, however, were foreign, and therefore even harder to prosecute. A local court condemned one German who set up under the name of 'Albert Bucholz, Cognac'. And Martell, together with Moët & Chandon, Benedictine and Grande Chartreuse managed to pursue one delinquent, whose premises in Barcelona were found to contain copies of their labels, 'bold and widespread forgeries, carried out with rare skill'. The fraudster, M. Rapau, fled to Bordeaux and was duly sent down for a year. But in most countries the Cognacais were helpless. In Italy, for instance, the French found that they could sell little or no cognac. By contrast, the Italians themselves exported fifty times as much so-called cognac as they imported. In the words of an official French diplomatic report: 'The Italians lowered the reputation of our product by the low, inferior quality of what they sold and by the price war against which we could have struggled only by selling diluted industrial alcohol under the name of cognac.'

But the Germans were the worst offenders. As early as 1892 the Cognacais were complaining about brandies 'chemically fabricated in Germany, employing essences of every description including those most harmful to public health'. The German government actively encouraged imports of wine rather than brandy, which paid twenty-seven times the amount of duty levied on wine (fortified wines paid even less, half the duty on ordinary wines). So German merchants would send fortified wines (*vins vinés*) to Germany strengthened with industrial alcohol or even grape brandy. Once it was over the frontier, the Germans promptly renamed the product 'cognac', for the customs documents which accompanied it were clearly marked with the name of the area it was produced. In another widespread fraud, shiploads of industrial alcohol were sent from Hamburg, touched at a French port and returned duly baptized.

All French producers, not only the Cognacais, quickly realized that domestic legislation could never provide adequate protection. At the Universal Exhibition of 1878 the French raised the subject of international protection for trademarks. A first congress on the subject in Paris in 1883 proved ineffectual, but seven years later the Convention of Madrid was signed by a number of major powers. Article IV, in particular, provided legal protection to 'regional trademarks for products derived from grapes': it also covered products manufactured from grapes – like cognac and champagne. The Treaty, including the precious Article IV, was speedily ratified by the French and applied when prizes were awarded at the 1900 Paris Exhibition. The precedent was followed by the St Louis Exhibition of 1904,[1] where the judges ruled that cognacs were a class apart, not to be compared with lesser spirits.

Unfortunately for the French, not many authorities were as understanding as those in St Louis. The two major empires of Germany and Austria-Hungary ignored it, and even the British played them false for a while. A judge ruled that the Convention did not apply in Britain because the Treaty had not yet been ratified by Parliament. The French naturally assumed that the ruling was biased and that His Majesty's judges could be relied upon to bend the law to protect local interests – those of the producers of British brandy, that old enemy of the Cognacais. But in the long run Article IV served its purpose. Eventually even the Germans had to give in. One of the few effective clauses in the Treaty of Versailles stipulated that the Germans should conform to the Convention of Madrid.

But even Article IV could never have worked without proper protection at home. This was more difficult for the Cognacais than for the producers of other threatened products because their brand name was the same as that of the town itself. In the end it was that old enemy of the

[1] Immortalized as the fair in the famous Judy Garland film *Meet Me in St Louis*.

growers, the 'Aides', which came to their rescue. The Aides was a system devised in the seventeenth century to extract as much revenue as possible from the movement of goods of all kinds through France. 'If it moves, tax it' was the motto, and as a result every ship- or cart-load carried with it a movement order, an *acquit* certifying that the proper dues had been paid. The Aides multiplied the cost of brandy as it was carried through France in the eighteenth century, yet 150 years later served as the basis for providing Cognac with proper legal protection. Ironically, the legal mechanisms now welcomed by the growers were precisely the same as those against which they had revolted in 1789. They had complained bitterly about the obligation to declare the quality and strength of the spirits they were going to distil; now they accepted the requirement as a guarantee against imitations.

Mere revolutions have little effect on the French bureaucracy, and the *acquit* emerged in a new form in 1872 as a *titre de transport* ('permission to move'). Unfortunately for the Cognacais, this form did not specify the geographical origin of the goods. Since then the growers and French legislators have worked long and hard to refine the definitions of the *acquits* and the mechanism protecting the producers from fraudulent imitations. More detailed versions of these *acquits* – and their foreign imitations – now pinpoint the place and conditions of production of all the proudest products of the French countryside – not just wines and spirits but also foods like Roquefort cheese as well. All these regulations are designed to protect the producers; the idea that they originated in an attempt to protect the consumers is a useful myth which the producers are clearly not going to deny.

It took nearly half a century to surround Cognac with a complete protective system. The first effective legislation, in 1905, was designed to suppress frauds committed when describing any agricultural product. Adulteration was defined as adding alien substances or omitting essential ones. But the legislation was so general that it took thirty-five more years to complete the legal framework. The first loophole found by the region's less scrupulous merchants was that authorized warehouses or cellars could house brandies made from lesser grapes grown in nearby regions like the Vendée or the Gironde. This gap was plugged by a new law which came into force in 1909. It was this piece of legislation which, over 200 years after the superiority of 'coniack brandy' had first become apparent, belatedly gave legal recognition to 'Eau-de-vie de Cognac'. This was enshrined in the famous *appellation d'origine*, the guarantee not of quality but of geographical provenance.

Cognac's boundaries, as defined by the law of 1909, were pretty generous. The locals defend the size of their *appellation* by referring to the words of Professor Ravaz, who had asserted that from Angoulême to the sea the vineyard was a compact whole, interrupted only by the river valleys.

All the cultivable soil is covered with vines, plains as well as slopes. Only valley floors which are too wet or 'patches' of over-rich earth are used for other crops or left uncultivated. And everywhere the products are of good quality and possess, to a greater or lesser degree, the special 'aroma' which has earned them this 'indisputable reputation'.

In 1919 these *appellations d'origine* were provided with further protection by a law making it a criminal fraud to pretend that any imitation which did not meet the standards historically associated with the product – *les usages locaux loyaux et constants* ('local, honest and habitual usage') – could be prosecuted. These were further refined a couple of years later when it was ruled that only caramel, oak shavings and 3.5 per cent of sugar could be added to the spirit. And in 1929 cognac's special status was recognized when it was allocated its very own *acquit jaune d'or*, or its 'golden identity card', to distinguish it from lesser wines and spirits; this accompanies even the smallest quantity of cognac when it moves on to the public highway. Fraud at the vineyard itself was supposedly prevented by regulations forcing growers to declare the size of their holdings and, before every harvest, the quantity they were going to ferment and distil. A law passed in 1900 ensured that every still was registered and duly hallmarked.

It took another ten years to refine the legal description of cognac. This was no mere legal technicality. Throughout the 1920s Hennessy – and, to a lesser extent, Martell and Bisquit – were battling against Chinese imitations. They paid informers and even thought of hiring private detectives to increase the number of prosecutions they brought in the law courts. Some agents preferred to take on lesser-known brands because they were less likely to be imitated. Appropriately enough, it was the question of ageing that took the longest to regulate. In 1924 the Australians had protested against the only evidence the merchants could provide of the age of their brandies – a certificate signed by the mayor of Cognac. After the end of Prohibition the Americans queried the authenticity of brandies being sold as five, ten, twenty or even 100 years old, and in the 1930s a system was devised to ensure that the age of every lot of cognac was registered.

But these rules apply only to young brandies, since not even the tentacles of French administration can guarantee the authenticity of brandies more than six years old. It is this inability to certify old cognacs as the product of specific years that has led to the prohibition of 'single vintage' brandies. Outsiders can argue that reputable merchants would not put their name to frauds connected with old and expensive brandies, but the authorities have to legislate for everyone in the business. The case which led to the present situation makes their point. In 1933 a group of merchants suffering from the effects of the slump passed off brandies from the 1930 and 1931 vintages as 'Grande Champagne 1811'. The locals took immediate action, but only on 4 July 1940[1] did the civil court at St Jean d'Angely confirm that age was an essential element in the legal description of cognac and that cheating would be subject to the same penalties as other frauds. After the war the labelling was further refined. Brandies calling themselves VO, VSOP or 'Reserve' had to be at least four years old (technically Compte 4 – see page 176) and those labelled 'Extra', 'Napoléon' or 'Vieille Réserve' six years old (Compte 6).

Another major gap in the market was even more basic: double distillation. It was only in 1935 that a decree was issued confirming that 'real cognac' had to be distilled twice. (This was designed to counteract a legal ruling which had greatly upset the Cognacais. In 1930 the Fédération des Viticulteurs Charentais, worried by the increase of continuous stills, brought a case to prove that double distillation was required to produce true cognac. But the local court decided that brandies could be called cognac even if distilled only once, provided that the wine came from the correct region.)

The decree went on to say that cognac must be distilled only to 72° Gay Lussac, to prevent distillers from producing high-strength brandies which would lack the flavours extracted at lower strengths. This measure put an end to the irregular forms of distillation used even by reputable firms since the continuous still had been developed in the early nineteenth century. (At

[1] Just after the Armistice, when the roads of France were choked with refugees and, supposedly, the whole administration had ground to a halt.

the back of the Gauthiers' house in the rue Saulnier is the brick tower which used to house a steam continuous distillation apparatus. According to Guy Gauthier-Auriol, it provided a much smoother product than any other type.) There was one curious exception to the rule. It applied only to brandies distilled on the French mainland. Distillers on the Iles de Ré and d'Oleron were allowed to distil once only; but they were permitted to call their result 'cognac' and nothing more. They could not use any of the sub-*appellations*, not even Bons Bois, and recently, they too have been forced to distil all their cognac twice.

Double distillation was one instance where the law was merely providing backing for the historic norm. The same applied to the 1936 definition of the varieties of grapes which could go into a bottle of cognac. In 1927 high-yielding hybrid varieties had been banned, and nine years later the varieties were divided into those which could form the bulk of the production and 'supporting' varieities. To no one's surprise, only three principal varieties were allowed – Folle Blanche, St-Émilion[1] and Colombard – and five others – Sémillon, Sauvignon, Blanc Ramé, Jurançon Blanc and Montils – which could only form 10 per cent of the total.

During the 1930s too the Cognacais defined their boundaries more precisely. A commission of inquiry was appointed which included such well-respected local figures as Robert Delamain and Gaston Briand. In contrast to other parts of France, where the process was accompanied by the most frightful squabbling, they soon agreed on boundaries between the sub-*appellations,* Grande and Petite Champagne,[2] Borderies, Fins Bois and Bons Bois. The lack of argument was not just a tribute to the members of the Commission but also a recognition of their generosity. Like Lacroix eighty years earlier, they followed the administrative boundaries rather than the more refined definitions established by Coquand or Ravaz. So they naturally left room for argument – particularly over the *petites Champagnes d'Archiac*. These are the wrong side of the river Né to be called Grande Champagne but can produce undeniably finer cognacs than the alluvial plain of the Charente which was included in the Grande Champagne because it was in the canton of Cognac.

Although the rules were refined after the Second World War, by 1940 all the conditions for making cognac had been established, first by trial and error, human effort and happy accident over several hundred years, then belatedly enshrined in French legislation. This provides a convenient point at which to examine in detail the making of this extraordinary product.

---

[1] In 1971 this was allowed in under its other name, Ugni Blanc.
[2] 'Fine Champagne' was also defined, as a cognac containing at least 50 per cent spirit from Grande Champagne. The Cognacais scrupulously obey the ruling. But neither they nor the legislators have ever succeeded in changing the habits of French drinkers, who still refer to brandy and water as *fine à l'eau.*

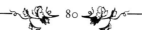

THE MAKING
OF COGNAC

9 · The Land, the Vine and the Wine

Over the past few years the French have been battling to defend the idea of *terroir*, the physical conditions governing the making of wine, against attacks (mostly launched from California) claiming that climate, and above all the skills of the wine maker, are more important than the factors which combine in the notion of 'terroir'. The French are naturally touchy, for the idea of *terroir* forms the basis for their system of *appellations contrôlées*. They could do worse than call the Cognacais to testify on their behalf. For geological and climatic factors are the only variables in the cognac equation. All the brandies entitled to the *appellation* are made from the same grapes, harvested in the same way at the same time, fermented in the self-same vats, distilled in the same stills and matured in the same oak. Nevertheless, his colleagues in other firms would agree with Maurice Fillioux of Hennessy that 'after cognac has been in cask for ten years, out of all the hundreds we taste, 95 per cent of the best come form the Grande Champagne.'

Cognac's *crus* form a series of concentric circles, with the Grande Champagne as a rough semi-circle at its heart, surrounded by a series of rings of steadily decreasing quality. This is rather misleading, for in geographical fact there are three separate areas (four including the Borderies), not the seven indicated on the map. To the west there is the coastal plain, with its vast, ever-changing skies, its marshes, sandy beaches, oyster beds – and thin, poor cognacs. The heterogenous mass of the Bois is mostly anonymous, rolling countryside which could lie anywhere between the Loire and the Gironde, the vines mingling with the arable and pasture. But the heart is the Champagnes, Grande and Petite, a landscape unlike the Bois, resembling rather the Sussex Downs, albeit covered in vines and not pasture, but with the same mixture of gentle rolling hills and snug wooded valleys.

The comparison with the Sussex chalk is no accident: 'Cognac is a brandy from chalky soil' is the repeated theme of the standard work on distillation.[1] For the finest cognac there is no substitute for pure chalk, found only on the south bank of the river. In an irregular quadrilateral, bounded on the north by the Charente, to the west and south by the river Né and petering out towards Châteauneuf to the east, are found the famous 'cretaceous' soils which make up the Grande Champagne: twenty-seven parishes and 35,700 hectares (38 square miles) in the canton of Cognac, devoted almost exclusively to the vine for over 200 years. The various formations were first defined by H. Coquand, the mid-nineteenth-century geologist who did the first scientific study ever undertaken of any wine-growing area (before his time all of them had been lumped together more generally as *Maestrichtien*). The heart of the Grande Champagne is composed of a special sort of chalk, the Campanian, a name which echoes the Latin origin of the word *champagnes*. But the Campanian emerges only on the crests of the gentle slopes of the Grande Champagne, for it is one of three layers of variously chalky soils which come to the surface in the area. The other two are also rather special: the Santonian – named after the old name for the

[1] René Lafon, Jean Lafon and Pierre Coquillaud, *Le Cognac, sa distillation*, Paris, J. B. Baillière et Fils, 1964.

province, the Saintonge – covers much of the Petite Champagne, the belt round the Grande Champagne; while the town of Cognac itself is built on the appropriately named Coniacian chalk.

The Grande Champagne, like all other chalky soils, is basically the accumulation of small fossils, including one particular species found nowhere else, *Ostrea vesicularis*. In the words of the French Geological Survey, it is 'a monotonous alternation of greyish-white chalk, more or less marly and siliceous, soft and incorporating, especially in the middle of the the area, faults made up of black pockets of silica and lumps of debased marcasite'. Marcasite is composed of crystalized iron pyrites, and this iron (also found across the Gironde in Pauillac) is important, but it is the sheer intensity of the chalkiness in the soil which is crucial – that and its physical qualities, its crumbliness, its friability.

The second best soil, the Santonian, is described as 'more solid, less chalky, but incorporating some of the crumbliness of the Campanian slopes, into which it merges by imperceptible degrees'. (One good test is the density of the presence of the fossil of *Ostrea vesicularis*.) The heart of the Grande Champagne, its backbone, is formed by the ridge between Ambleville and Lignière, Cognac's equivalent of the Montagne de Reims which produces so much of the best champagne. But the colouring of the modern geological map is specifically designed to underline how blurred is the boundary between the Santonian and Campanian. As the modern geologists put it: 'The boundaries established by H. Coquand and H. Arnaud have been adhered to, although they are vague round Cognac itself where the visible features are much the same.'

The only *crus* whose boundaries are completely clear-cut are those of the Borderies, with their very special *groies*, dating geologically from the Jurassic era. Ever since the Tertiary period some 10 million years ago, when the Charente was carving out its river bed, the soil has become steadily more decalcified, but the process is still incomplete and the result is a mixture of chalk which is breaking down and intermingling with the clay. The mixture produces a unique, and often underrated, cognac.

The Borderies are by far the smallest of all the *crus,* a mere 13,440 hectares (52 square miles). The Fins Bois are nearly thirty times the size, 354,200 hectares (1,367 square miles); the Bon Bois are even bigger, 386,600 hectares (about 1,500 square miles); and the Bois Ordinaires are smaller, 274,176 hectares (1,058 square miles). The figures are, of course, misleading. Half of the cultivable area of the Grande Champagne is covered with vines, 30 per cent of the Petite Champagne and 46 per cent of the Borderies. By contrast, under 2 per cent of the Bois Ordinaires have vines on them, and they account for a mere 3 per cent of Cognac's vines. The Bois as a whole include 90 per cent of land entitled to the name but only 63 per cent of the vines, and two-thirds of those are in the Fins Bois.

Inevitably, in an area the size of the Bois the geology is much less well defined than it is in the Champagnes or the Borderies. Even Professor Ravaz was rather vague, saying that the brandies of the Bois were 'produced on slopes formed by compacted chalk or by arable soils covered with sands and tertiary clays' – the first being better because of the chalk.[1] Indeed, there is one curious little pocket of virtually pure chalk on the east bank of the Gironde extending inland to Mirambeau, whose growers have long wanted re-classification. By the river at St-Thomas-de-Conac (yet another spelling) the land is very chalky and so, in theory, the area ought to be in the Grande Champagne. Nevertheless, says M. Gay-Bellile of the Station Viticole, 'the grapes are heavily affected by the river mists and by the iodine carried in the breezes from the sea' – yet

[1] Op. cit.

another unexpected element in the cognac equation. The result is that the intensity of viticulture varies considerably even within individual *appellations*. Within the Fins Bois vines are clustered thickly in a semi-circle around the north-east and south-east frontiers of the Champagnes, while elsewhere, especially to the west, successive generations of growers have become discouraged with the profits to be made and have reverted to other crops.

Not surprisingly, Professor Ravaz turned his back on a purely geological explanation of cognac's qualities. As he said: 'The clayey, siliceous soils of the Borderies produce brandies of a higher quality than those of the dry *groies* or even some of the chalkier districts in the south-west of the Charente-Inférieure. For the geological make-up of the earth is not as important as Coquand makes out.' Ravaz emphasized the combination of the chemical and physical constituents of the soil, with the physical predominant: 'the highest qualities are produced from chalky soil, where the chalk is soft and highly porous and where the subsoil is composed of thick banks of similar chalk' (the topsoil is invariably merely a few centimetres thick). In these soils, said Ravaz, 'the subsoil hoards rainwater, thanks to its sponginess and its considerable depth, and releases it slowly to the surface soil and to the vegetation. It is thus to a certain extent a regulator of the soil's moisture content, and so, in chalky soils, the vine is neither parched nor flooded.' This description explains why the Borderies, relatively poor in chalk, produce such good brandies: the soil is friable and is thus physically, if not geologically, perfect.

The same factors apply on the other bank of the Gironde, where the thicker the gravel banks, the better the drainage and the steadier and more reliable the growth as the water seeps through to the roots in a sort of drip irrigation from below. The parallel with the conditions further south extends to the importance of the lie of the land. A well-drained slope is obviously preferable to a

Cypresses, probably planted to commemorate a Protestant

flat stretch of river valley, liable to clogging. North-facing slopes are less highly prized. The sunlight is less strong, and in grey years, when the best southern slopes produce wines of a mere 7°, the northern slopes cannot even manage that.

The politicians and the administrators responsible for defining Cognac's *crus* could not afford Ravaz's fine distinctions and naturally followed Coquand's more definite lines. Broadly speaking, the classification accords with that established by market forces before the geologists moved in, a pattern found in other regions, like Bordeaux, which had depended on sophisticated – usually Anglo-Saxon – customers for two centuries or more. Inevitably, those responsible for guarding cognac's reputation adhere to it, for no one can face the problems which any attempt at re-classification would present.

There is no dispute about the validity of the distinction between the various categories; only the boundaries are in question. The first, and most obvious, is that the river Charente marks the frontier,[1] so the Grande Champagne includes the alluvia of the river bed and the strip of Santonian chalk that separates the alluvium from the Campanian, which starts several miles south of the river at Segonzac. This sleepy little town is the heart of the Grande Champagne (not surprisingly, the only merchant located in the town is that most old fashioned and traditional firm Frapin). At the other boundary the further bank of the River Né towards Archiac, officially in the Petite Champagne, produces cognac arguably superior to some from the Grande Champagne.

[1] With one exception, the pocket around Bourg-sur-Charente, the only land north of the Charente entitled to call itself even Petite Champagne. This anomaly is composed largely of an estate owned at the time of the classification by the Martell family. Its brandies are subjected to particularly severe scrutiny when they reach the family business for blending.

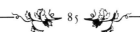

But most of the blenders agree with Maurice Fillioux that the Grande Champagne should never produce bad brandy and that its boundaries are broadly correct. Francis Gay-Bellile does not sound ridiculous when he affirms that they are 95 per cent accurate.

No one disputes the borders of the Borderies, nor the quality of the brandies they produce, two-thirds of which are bought by Martell and Hennessy. Inevitably, the position is much less clear-cut when you reach the Bois. Nevertheless, there is a consensus among the more serious firms, who have established solid links with hundreds of growers over the years, that they should concentrate their purchases in two well-defined sections of the Fins Bois: in what were formerly called the Premiers Fins Bois (and are now often referred to as the Fins Bois de Jarnac) just north of the town, and in the area around Blanzac to the south-east. Neither Hennessy nor Martell buys any Bons Bois at all regularly, and those serious houses that do buy here concentrate their purchases in a narrow strip to the south around Chevanceaux and Brossac. None of them buys even Fins Bois from the west, brandies they find too 'foxy', with too much *goût de terroir,* an unappetizing earthiness (the only exception is the chalky pocket near the Gironde). Indeed there is a general, albeit tacit, agreement to ignore brandies made west of a line running from St-Jean-d'Angély through Saintes to Pons. These, like the even thinner products made on the islands off the coast, are sold mainly to the tourists who flock to the beaches of the Charente or to passing travellers. Indeed, one enterprising producer has arranged for the coaches carrying pilgrims to Lourdes to stop at this hospitable estate.

If the *cru* matters enormously, the making of the wine emphatically does not. The wine is merely a raw material, akin more to the barley used for malt whisky than to wine made for drinking, and accounts for between 10 and 15 per cent of the quality of a cognac. It merely has to

be 'correct', with a proper balance of sugar and acid, free from defects and of a uniform quality. As Lafon puts it, 'The still does not purify the wine but simply extracts the alcohol and the aroma, whose virtues and vices it accentuates.'[1] The ninefold concentration of the inherent qualities of the wine in the distillation process reinforces the Cognacais' obsession with its purity and reliability.

By definition, then, nothing about the wine can be other than pedestrian. To start with, the varieties of grapes cannot have too pronounced a character. They merely have to provide a suitable blance for a *moût neutre* (a 'neutral must'). When Cognac first made its name the district was given over largely to the Balzac grape, which had several characteristics found in today's favourites: it was highly productive; it was a Mediterranean variety and thus did not fully ripen as far north as the Charente; and it was relatively late and thus not susceptible to the region's late spring frosts. Its major rival at the time was the Colombard, which had produced the Borderies' delicious sweet white wine. The Colombard lingered on, although in the nineteenth century the Balzac was almost entirely replaced by the Folle or Folle Blanche, which had already been planted before the Revolution and was also a great favourite of the Armagnacais. In Ravaz's words, its wine was 'so acid, so green, that it is something of a struggle to drink it'. It was the ideal grape for producing fine, aromatic, fragrant cognacs, and it is still remembered with much affection. But its fate was sealed by the phylloxera. When it was grafted on to American root stock it flourished so vigorously, its bunches were so tightly packed, that the grapes in the middle were liable to the dreaded grey rot (they are still beyond the reach of modern anti-rot sprays). A good many over-productive hybrids were planted after the phylloxera, but the brandies they produced smelled foul, so since 1900 the St Émilion has been triumphant, and although other vines are permitted, they now account for only a tiny percentage of Cognac's production.

Elsewhere in France the St Émilion is known as the Ugni Blanc, but it originated as the Trebbiano Toscano from the hills of the Emilia Romagna around Piacenza. In the words of Philip Dallas, it produces 'a wine that has invaded all Central Italy, a wine, like bread and potatoes, that one can consume every day without complaint'.[2] Its other major characteristic is also welcome to the Cognacais: 'it has no exaggerated characteristics, yet it is strong and firm-bodied', always neutral and therefore a variety much in demand as a base when blended with more aromatic varieties. It forms a part of the blend used in Moët & Chandon's new Pierlant sparkling wine and by itself produces some refreshing white wine both in Bordeaux and in the Charente.

The Italians too make brandy with the St Émilion grape, but even in Italy it matures late, and in Cognac, at the very northern limit of its cultivation, it remains relatively green and acid and produces a different type of juice than when grown in Italy. Its other major advantage is that it starts budding late and is, therefore, like the Balzac, less susceptible to the area's late spring frosts. Cognac's long, light but not hot summers ensure that there is a certain intensity in the juice. Since the grapes are not fully ripe when they are picked, it lacks even the little aroma and bouquet it develops when fully mature.

As with the variety, so with its cultivation, which was higgeldy-piggledy until phylloxera. Replanting was carried out either in rows or in blocks. Ravaz, writing at the turn of the century, said that one could plant in the shape of either a square or a diamond – he preferred the square form because it was easier to work. In the last twenty years the vineyard has been adapted to the

[1] Op. cit.
[2] *Italian Wines*, London, Faber & Faber, 1983.

machine. The vines have been trained far higher than previously. It is easy to see the result with the older, thicker trunks pruned right back, the newer trained up to 1.2–1.5 metres (4 or 5 feet) high on trellises. (The Cognacais replace their vines roughly every thirty-five years.) For the same reasons the space between the rows has been doubled to just over 2.8 metres (9 feet), and although the vines are planted more closely, there are still only 3,000 to each hectare, 1,000 fewer than under the old system. Yet with modern clones the yield has steadily increased. The major disadvantage of the change is that the grapes ripen a week later because they are further away from the ground and therefore benefit less from the sun's rays reflected from the chalky-white soil.

Nevertheless, the viticultural assembly lines of the Charente share one important characteristic with their nobler brethren elsewhere in France. Growth must not be encouraged, either by pruning too lightly to leave room for more bunches of grapes, or by lavishing too much manure on them: otherwise the balance will be disturbed, and the acid level will inevitably be reduced.

The St Émilion matures late, and even relatively unripe grapes are ready for picking only in October, after those in the Médoc. But the only limit to the date of the harvest is the frosts generally expected in late October, which, in a bad year like 1980, can ruin the quality of the wine. Harvesting machines would seem a natural choice for the region because the Cognacais are not particularly interested in quality, but they have been relatively hesitant. Bisquit Dubouché, for instance, now takes the precaution of pre-distilling samples of wines made from machine-harvested grapes because of a bitter experience. With early models of the machines the wines were rather 'green' for the very obvious reason that the machine sucked in everything, twigs and leaves as well as grapes. Their hydraulic machinery was badly insulated and tended to leak tiny quantities of oil on to the grapes – oiliness was inevitably exaggerated by distillation. These problems have now been solved, but they have left a legacy of mistrust.

The 'vintage', like the wine itself, is not of crucial importance. Of course, every year will be slightly different, and single vintages are an obvious way in which to elevate the status of a spirit (as the Armagnacais have demonstrated over the past few years), but in Cognac the differences in most years are perceptible only to the most expert palates. The exceptions are years remembered as particularly difficult. The classic recent problem year was 1980. The season was late, and the grapes were picked very cold, so their juice had almost been neutralized, rectified by the cold. This in turn made it difficult to get fermentation started. As a result the wines were thin and flat, and their faults were duly multiplied in the distillation process. In 1962 the problem had been exactly the opposite. The grapes were picked in very hot weather, up to $35\,^{\circ}$C ($95\,^{\circ}$F), and because the wine makers could not control the temperature the precious yeasts were killed before they had time to complete their work. Better cooling techniques prevented a repetition of these worries in the unprecedentedly hot summer of 1982. In 1976, another hot year, the grapes could not be picked until they contained a full $12\,^{\circ}$ of alcohol and thus produced cognacs that were flat and uninteresting. It is tempting to compare cognac vintages with those of Bordeaux, a mere 80 kilometres (50 miles) to the south, but the rhythms are completely different: in a cold, wet year like 1977 the grapes simply did not ripen in Bordeaux, but in the Charente this did not matter and the quality was perfectly adequate. In 1929, greatest of years for the Gironde, the wines (and hence the brandies made in the Charente) were so rich that they were unbalanced for distillation.

The wines used for distillation are, of course, undrinkably acid. They are also very weak, between $7\,^{\circ}$ and $10\,^{\circ}$, for one very basic reason: the weaker the wine, the greater the degree of concentration involved in producing a freshly distilled cognac of around 70°. When the St Émilion is fully ripe its wine will reach 10–11°. But even a wine of 10° would be concentrated only seven times; one of 7° (the lower limit of practical distillation) will be concentrated ten times, so it will be infinitely more aromatic. The ideal strength is between 8° and 9°. In theory wine as weak as 3° or 4° could be turned into acceptable brandy; the major problem is that the lower the strength, the less likely the grapes are to be wholly sound or even half-ripe.

The wine making itself is naturally pretty basic. As Gay-Bellile of the Station Viticole says, it relies on nature: 'We adapt our wine-making techniques to the needs of the still.' For all they are doing, as he says, is to 'preserve the interesting elements in the juice'. Even so, the obsession with reliability is all-pervasive. One of the many regulations issued in the 1930s banned the continuous presses, in use since the late eighteenth century, which pressed and squeezed the grapes at the same time. The additional pressure crushed the pips and released a stream of undesirable tannic and oily substances into the must. Even now the lightest of modern presses use enough pressure to leave solids from the skins in suspension in the wine.

The must is fermented in vats holding 100–200 hectolitres (2,000–4,000 gallons). Until recently these were made from concrete, but modern wine makers now prefer vats made from soft iron lined with epoxy resins or resins reinforced with glass fibre. In the past few years the fermentation of the first few vats has been triggered off by the use of cultured yeasts, but otherwise there has been total reliance on nature as the juice ferments for an average of five days at a temperature of 20–25°C (68–77°F).

For modern scientific knowledge has led to remarkably few changes in the tried and tested historical methods, the major difference being a fuller understanding of the wine making process and its problems. For a long time, for instance, it was thought that the taint of bitterness, of greenness, found in some cognacs could be traced back to tannin from the skins of the grapes. But there is virtually no tannin in a wine made, as in cognac, by lightly pressing the St Émilion, and any residual tannins are eliminated by the distillation process. The disagreeable bitterness did indeed come from tannins – not from the skins but from volatile substances like hexanol and haxanal contained in the pips, leaves and twigs swept up in the harvesting process.

The need for purity creates one major problem. White wines being prepared for drinking are invariably dosed with a little sulphur to prevent oxidation and to deter bacteria. It is simply impossible to use sulphur dioxide (SO_2) when making wine for distillation.[1] Nevertheless, wine as acid as that made by the Charentais has several advantages: it is so acid – the level of residual sugar is a mere 1 gram per litre, far lower that that if any wine made for drinking (technically it has a pH of between 3 and 3.4) – that it keeps well, does not suffer from bacterial problems and lacks the pectins which can make wine rather cloudy.

Before the wine can be distilled it should undergo malolactic fermentation, known in France simply as *le malo*, when the malic acid in the wine is transformed into lactic acid.[2] In many wines this sort of viticultural puberty does not take place until the spring following the fermentation, too late for the Cognacais, who have to finish distillation before warm weather stimulates fresh

[1] Even without SO_2 the yeasts produce a certain quantity of aldehydes. Encouraged by SO_2, they produce up to twenty times as much. The compound formed by the SO_2 and the aldehydes decomposes when heated in the still, and the resulting mixture of aldehyde and alcohol produces acetal, giving off a smell reminiscent of hospital corridors.

[2] You can distil pre-*malo* wines, but you must not distil them in mid-maling, as the resulting brandies give off a rather fetid smell.

fermentation. Fortunately, their wines are precocious: when wines have a high proportion of malic (as of other) acids, are free from sulphur and have not been racked, the lactic acids develop very quickly. By early December, a mere six weeks after the vintage has been gathered, the wines are ready for distillation.

Wine-making – in cement vats – is pretty basic

10 · Distillation: the Heart of the Matter

Wine is the raw material of cognac, its only influence a potentially negative one if it should not be correct, healthy and free from any impurities that would be multiplied in the distillation process. The newly distilled brandy is no more than an intermediate product, yet the still has transformed it not only into ordinary spirit but into cognac. 'It is one thing to manufacture alcohol,' wrote Professor Méjane; 'it is quite another to create a high-grade brandy ... with the same raw materials, brandies produced in batches are greatly superior to those produced in continuous stills. This gain in quality justifies all the inconveniences of re-distillation: increased energy consumption, the need for the distiller's skills, its limited flow.'[1]

Even the distillation process itself is unlike that used elsewhere. Ordinary distillation involves the separation of the volatile elements in the original liquid according to their boiling points, whereas in distillation *à la charentaise* the alcoholic vapours simply sweep through the distillation apparatus. A local author writing at the end of the last century, in an attempt to ban more efficient but less satisfactory stills, compared 'the cooking of brandy to that of *pot-au-feu*. Who does not prefer a nourishing home-made broth to that made in a restaurant, even though it has been made by steam?'[2] Michel Caumeil of Hennessy puts it even more simply: 'The production of cognac is simply controlled evaporation.'[3] The process is not completely scientific but is an art, a balancing act between the desire to preserve the character provided by the grapes with the need to eliminate undesirable elements by rectification. It is at this point that the crucial element of personal judgment, the 'distiller's skills' referred to by Professor Méjane, enters into the equation.

Fortunately for the Charentais, the Dutch found the type of distillation apparatus needed to 'evaporate' their thin white wines in the late sixteenth century, at the same time as distillation was increasing its share of the market for them. The still had to heat the wines, trap the alcoholic vapours and then cool them. In theory this is simple enough. But, as with the wine making, everything has to be perfect: the heat must be applied uniformly to all the liquid in the container; only the desirable vapours must be extracted; they must flow smoothly; and the cooling process, like the heating, must be gradual and regular. It is a tribute to the Dutch engineers of the early seventeenth century that the formula they brought to Cognac has worked so well ever since.

So the first detailed picture we have of an *alembic charentaise*, dating from 1710, would be instantly recognizable to a distiller today, as would Munier's, written half a century later. The still itself, the *alembic* or *chaudière à eau-de-vie* (literally a 'spirit boiler'), is surmounted by a smaller *chapiteau*[4] to trap the vapours, which are then led down a *bec* ('beak') to a cooling coil. The *alembic* is still housed in a massive brick square containing an open fire. Only the dimensions of the

[1] In *Annales de technologie agricole*, 1975.
[2] Quoted in: A. Baudoin, *Les eaux-de-vie et la fabrication du Cognac*, 1983.
[3] In *Pour la science*, December 1983 (an invaluable article).
[4] Literally, a circus tent, the 'big top'.

The Comte de Ruffignac at the Chateau de Chesnel

alembic – and the fuel used – have altered. Then, as now, the whole apparatus was constructed of 'several pieces of red beaten copper, fitted together with copper nails and without solder'. Copper is a catalyst but does not change the taste of the spirit: it is easy to work, impervious to most acids and a good conductor of heat. Experiments using alternative materials, like steel and glass, were conducted around the turn of the century. They merely confirmed how ideal copper was for the purpose. The copper used today is special, very pure (electrolyzed) and polished to smooth out the pores in the metal. But copper also has a chemical role to play. It fixes the fatty acids in the wine, as well as any of the sulphurous products in the vapours that would harm the quality of the cognac.

The shape of the apparatus has not changed either. The *cucurbite*, the vat in which the wine is heated, has always been onion-shaped, *un cône tronqué* (a truncated cone). This provides an expansion chamber in which the fumes released by heating can swirl like a tornado. They sweep upwards into the *chapiteau*. This is also rounded, the combination resembling an old-fashioned cottage loaf sculpted in gleaming copper. In Munier's day it varied in shape, although it always broadened above the neck, which captured the alcoholic vapour rising from the *cucurbite*. Munier's own text was illustrated with a *chapiteau* which strongly resembled an old-fashioned stove-pipe hat, but he also provided a sketch of a much more modern, more rounded shape he had devised himself. The *chapiteau* prevents the froth from spilling over to the condenser, allows the less volatile elements in the vapour to fall back into the *chaudière*, and thus guarantees the quality of the spirit. The *chapiteau* should be about one-tenth the size of the *cucurbite*. If it is any bigger, the vapour gets too rectified.

The vapours then trickle down the *bec* or, as it was called locally in Munier's time, the *queue* ('tail'), which is effectively an extension of the *chapiteau*. Then as now the individual components were not merely nailed together but 'strongly soldered with a compound of tin and zinc' , which 'helped to ensure that [the *bec*] was not blown off by the expansion of the vapours during distillation'. This insistence on the construction of the apparatus was not accidental, for every element had to be gas-tight. Munier was a 'physiocrat', one of the small band of inquiring spirits who believed that it was their mission to improve anything they came across. In his case the obvious problem was the *col* ('neck'): 'I have heard a number of progressive distillers say,' he wrote, 'that the neck of the still was usually too flat; that there was not enough distance between the surface of the liquor and the roof of the *chapiteau*, so that the vapours do not travel far enough to rid themselves of "phlegms", and the liquid spills over too easily.'[1] Until his time the *bec* had been a straight pipe leading from the *chapiteau* to the *serpentin*, which condensed the vapour into liquid. The combination resembled, it was thought, a Moor's head *(tête de Maure)*; to modern eyes it resembles, rather, a cartoon animal, bullet-headed with a long sharp nose. Earlier in the century Claude Masse had suggested bending the pipe, and Munier went further towards the modern idea, the elegantly shaped *col de cygne* ('swan's neck') which provides an infinitely smoother flow path than the earlier, more angular designs.

It is not surprising that the distillers of Munier's time found the flow problem *délicat*, as some unwanted *mousse* ('froth') seeped into the *serpentin*. With the older shape, as Bruno Sepulchre notes: 'You got very personalized brandies. The evolution of the present olive or onion shape of the *chapiteau* also reflects the evolution towards brandies that taste more neutral and standardized because they are rectified by the increased height of the *col de cygne*.'[2] To correct this, *chapiteaux*

[1] Munier, op. cit.   [2] *Le livre du Cognac.*

Eternal vigilance at the Château de St Sorlin de Conac

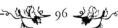

were not made any larger than about one tenth the size of the still itself, and care was taken that the 'swan's neck' did not arch upwards too much (although the *chapiteaux* used in the peripheral regions still capitalize on this point: they are larger in order to block off some of their undesirable *goûts de terroir*). Cognac is a conservative place: it was not until well into the present century that the *col de cygne* triumphed over the *tête de Maure*. The distillation apparatus was completed by the cooling coil, described by Munier as 'the *serpentin*, which forms five circles in a slope of $3\frac{1}{2}$ feet ... submerged into a barrel called the *pipe* ... the spirit flows from the *serpentin* into a circular double-bottomed (*foncé de deux bouts*) tub; it is called a *bassiot*.'

In terms of size the apparatus used in Munier's day was a mere pilot plant for the much bigger stills employed today. Then – and indeed, right through the eighteenth and nineteenth centuries, when most cognac was distilled by thousands of growers – the *cucurbite* was relatively tiny, with an internal diameter of a mere 53 centimetres (21 inches) and only 75 centimetres (2 feet 6 inches) high. The size varied, but overall it held only between 30 and 40 *veltes* (216–288 litres). Everything else was in proportion: the furnace was 0·9 metres (3 feet) in diameter; the *bec* was only 0·5 metres (a couple of feet) long; the *serpentin* a mere 1 metre (3 feet 3 inches) high; and, according to Munier, the whole apparatus could be contained in a 'small one-storey building, consisting of single room about $3\frac{1}{2}$ by $4\frac{1}{2}$ metres (12 by 15 feet)'.

Modern technology has changed all that. Some of the stills used for the *première chauffe* hold up to 130 hectolitres, but those used for the second *chauffe* are legally limited to a maximum of 30 hectolitres and can be filled only with 25 hectolitres of liquid. If they are any bigger, the brandy they produce cannot be called by any of the *sous-appellations* (just plain cognac). For the balance has to be preserved: the bigger the still, the more neutral the spirit. So in any case there is an absolute limit to size: above a certain point too little of the wine or *brouillis* is in actual contact with the *alembic*.

The stove heating the wine has always been crucial. Now, as in Munier's day, it is made of thick masonry, with a large door occupying a third of the front, strong enough to resist the heat of the furnace. Behind it the chimney was in brick, as was the lining of the furnace. Considerable skill was required to ensure that the heat was absolutely steady. In Munier's words: 'Too high a flame upsets everything; with the strong spirit water it carries off acids and oils, which do not have time to mix and which alter the taste of the brandy; too low a fire provides a light, pleasant brandy but one that is too strong, with too burning a taste; it removes neither enough water nor all the bitterness.' Even today if the flame is too high, it over-heats the copper, and the resulting brandy is *rimé* ('burned').

For a *bouilleur de cru* distilling his own wine the fuel was by far the biggest cash cost he incurred – two thirds of a cubic metre (over twenty cubic feet) of wood or 100 kilograms (2 hundredweight) of coal were required to produce a hectolitre of cognac. Until the nineteenth century wood from the Bois or from the forests to the east was the normal fuel. But wood burns quickly, so the furnace had to be refilled every two or three hours during a distillation season that lasted, day and night, for up to three months. This imposed a colossal strain: James Long recounts how when the distiller wanted a nap he would 'hang a tin on the swan's neck suspended on the end of a piece of string stuck there with wax; so that when the wax melted the tin would fall and wake him up!'[1] Munier insisted that the *brûlerie* 'had to be separate from any other building to reduce the danger of fire', for he had seen 'distillers grown sleepy and careless who had, through

[1] *The Century Companion to Cognac and Other Brandies*, London, Century, 1983.

Overleaf: Hennessy's cognac factory at Le Peu

sheer clumsiness, lit with their candles the spirit that came out of the serpent'; the fire spread up the 'stream of spirit' and could be stopped only by blocking the outlet at the bottom of the *serpentin* with a wet rag. Vizetelly was only half-joking when he wrote: 'Various little precautions have to be observed; among others, not to set the premises on fire.'

During the nineteenth century wood was gradually replaced by coal, which required less frequent attention, although this meant rebuilding the furnaces to provide more draught. Fuel oil was tried but proved difficult to insulate from the still itself. Fortunately, the natural gas discovered at Lacq in the south-west of France in the early 1950s has proved an ideal fuel – reliable, regular and requiring no attention. Even so, it took over twenty years for the infrastructure of pipes – and tanks of propane or butane – to reach the region's thousands of scattered stills. The gas is adjusted to heat the liquid at the same speed as wood. An even more modern heating method, electricity, is strictly fobidden. The alembic has, legally, to be heated by a naked flame.

Distillation needs less heat, and thus less fuel, if some of the heat dissipated in the cooling process is transferred to the cold wine through a heat exchanger. So during the nineteenth century the idea of heating the wine by using a *chauffe-vin* gradually caught on. The pipe containing the wine was simply diverted through the barrel-shaped cooling chamber. But conservatives like Martell still do not employ a *chauffe-vin*; they are afraid that the more complicated refrigeration chamber could not be properly cleaned, that the pipes would be blocked and the incoming wines over-heated. Supporters of the *chauffe-vin* say that it is simply a mechanical process, designed to save heat, but even they admit that it can be dangerous if the wine is heated above 40–45°. The *chauffe-vin* can then cause oxidation, so it is often used only for a few hours during a *chauffe* (usually the last few).

The wine can, of course, be distilled with or without its lees. Scientists are now gradually separating the two different types of lees – those from the grapes, their skins and twigs; and the relics of the yeasts. 'The 600° heat of the fire cooks the lees and infuses the cognac with their aroma,' says Robert Leauté of Rémy Martin, which distils all its brandies on their lees. The yeast lees contain a number of esters, including three fatty acids, which turn out to be absolutely critical in giving the cognac its much prized *rancio* quality when it is in cask (see page 109).

Distillers start work in early December, as soon as the wine has completed its fermentation, but have only three months to complete their work before an early warm spell might awaken the dormant wines. They work day and night, for distillation is a long process, with each *chauffe* taking about eight hours (some distillers take up to twelve hours in order to extract the maximum grapiness from the wines). The first produces a *brouillis* of between 26 and 32 per cent alcohol, about three times the strength of the wine. The first vapours to emerge are much stronger, about 55°, and are removed because they are bound to contain impurities already in the system. At the other end of the cycle the flow is cut off when the alcohol meter below the *serpentin* shows that the spirit contains less than 5 per cent alcohol. Because the *première chauffe* does not result in any permanent product (and in any case the *brouillis* is difficult even for the distiller himself to taste), outsiders assume that it is less important than the second. Precisely the opposite is true: virtually all the chemical reactions that provide the cognac with its final quality take place during the first, not the second, *chauffe*. 'It does 60 per cent of the work,' the professionals all agree.

The stills used for the *première chauffe* are sometimes bigger, but there is inevitably a short time during which enough *brouillis* are being produced to load up a still for the second, *la bonne chauffe*

(it helps if the wine has a strength of 8 per cent). Too long a gap can have unfortunate effects. Between 1973 and 1975 there were three enormous crops and not enough vats to hold all the wine, so a great deal was reduced through an early *première chauffe*, and there was some oxidation during storage.

The second, *la bonne chauffe*, is the glamorous one. Nevertheless, 'It simply selects and separates; it is not creative,' says Jacques Rouvière of Bisquit Dubouché. As with the first *chauffe*, a small percentage, a *tête*, is drawn off the top before the brandy is allowed to flow into the *bassiot*. The point at which the *tête* is cut is not crucial. As Gay-Bellile points out: 'The first 0.5 per cent is used merely to clean out the *serpentin*, which is full of diluted wash. After that it doesn't matter too much. There is some difference depending on whether you start allowing the spirit from *la bonne chauffe* through after 1 or 2 degrees, but since the *tête* goes back into the next load of *brouillis*, the effect is minimal.'

By contrast, the point at which the flow is diverted and the *secondes* are put on one side is a matter of considerable skill. *La bonne chauffe* starts flowing at about 78 per cent alcohol, and the legal maximum for the final spirit is 72 per cent alcohol, but below that point the break is a matter of subjective judgment. Distillers used to apply the rule of the *trois perles*: the break was made when three bubbles formed on the surface of the brandy when it was shaken in a sample glass – a habit that persisted long after the development of reliable alcohol meters made it unnecessary.

The basic point is simple enough: the higher the degree of the final spirit, the more neutral and rectified it will be; the lower the strength of the last drops allowed through, the more essential aromas they will contain but the greater the danger of noxious elements. Leaving more *tête*, and thus allowing more neutral spirit, can be a useful precaution in a bad year when the solids may turn out to be particularly nasty. In a good year you can afford to let through more of the nutrients. Even in a good year Martell deliberately cuts both *têtes* and *secondes* early as a matter of style, aiming to produce a dry, clear-cut, relatively neutral brandy that will absorb character from the wood in which it will be housed for so long. At the other extreme is Jacques Rouvière of Bisquit, who tries to extract as many of the secondary elements as possible. The decision is a delicate one: 'Even half a degree makes a difference,' says Rouvière, and he even distinguishes between the Champagne brandies and those from the Bois. Since the Champagne brandies are going to be kept for longer, they can be stronger, more neutral, so they are kept to 70.5 per cent, half a degree more than those from the Bois.

But there is more than one decision to make before the brandies are ready. If the *secondes* are mixed with the wine, this strengthens the raw material used in the *première chauffe* from 9 to 11 per cent, so the *brouillis* comes out at around 30 per cent. This is useful if, like Martell, you are looking for a relatively neutral result, for some of the wine will be distilled four times. (It is also useful if you are using grapes that are even more unripe than usual and therefore low in alcohol.) If the *secondes* are mixed with the *brouillis,* then you get a greater depth of aroma, with the brandies extracting the maximum benefit from the original grapes.

For two hundred years the end result has been much the same. In Demachy's words: 'The liquor flows into the receptacle forming a thread, which thickens imperceptibly; and when this thread is roughly the width of a medium-thick pen, the distillation process is well established.'[1] The cognac is now ready for its long years in wood.

---

[1] Jean Demachy, *L'Art du distillateur des eaux-fortes*, Paris, 1773.

11 · Brandy + Age + Cellars + Oak = Cognac

The thin trickle emerging from the *alembic charentais* is not yet cognac. Over the years the Cognacais have come to understand that a spell in oak casks is necessary to produce true cognac.[1] The oak and the spirit react, both physically and chemically. With greater understanding of the complexity of the ageing of cognac has come an enhanced capacity for blenders in different firms to define their house styles more accurately. Nevertheless, an element of mystery remains. Michel Caumeil of Hennessy, arguably the town's greatest expert on the chemistry of cognac, says simply: 'We know how a man is made, but not cognac.'

Style starts with the wood. From the outset *Quercus pedunculata*, the common oak, was chosen for casks, originally for its physical properties. In the words of Francis Gay-Bellile, these included:

its strength; elevated density of texture, which increases its strength; its hardness, which protects it from shocks and mechanical tension; its suppleness, which allows the curved lines of the cask to be formed by bending; its water-tightness, which prevents the liquid from leaking; its lack of permeability, which prevents the spirit from being diluted by the humidity in the atmosphere; and its light colouring.

The French are lucky: theirs is still a very wooded country, and oak occupies one-third of all their woodland. Even today *tonnelleries* use less than 10 per cent of all the oak sawn in France (even though there is an increasing demand for the wood from the wine maker's abroad, especially in California). Only two types of oak, both French – the Troncais and the Limousin (the name derives from the same root as Limoges) – have ever proved suitable for ageing cognac, although in the past many distillers, anxious to minimize their expense, have experimented with lesser woods, like chestnut or oak from the Baltic (Danzig) or the Atlantic (Trieste). But none of the alternatives has provided the unique combination of physical and chemical qualities required to turn raw-brandy-from-the-Cognac-region into cognac. In Tommy Layton's words: 'American oak gives the spirit a fraction too much bitterness, while those from Austria and Germany are so hard that they do not release a sufficiency of tannin.'[2]

The difference between the Troncais and the Limousin go back to their very different origins. The Limousin forests, centred in the hills to the east of Angoulême, conform to the British idea of oak woods: they are small, and the trees widely scattered, thick and sturdy. The wood is appropriately tough. In his detailed work on the making of cognac's casks, Jean Taransaud explains:

The oak from the Limousin is a rough heavy, hard and sinewy wood, with big fat grain up to 1 inch in size. It is difficult to work and more porous than oak from the Troncais, but it is renowned for its

[1] Oak is also used for the massive *tonneaux* required for blending and short-term storage, which have to be chemically neutral. Their only properties are physical.
[2] *Cognac and Other Brandies*, London, Harper Trade Journals, 1968.

tannic qualities, and if its best recommendation to the merchant is its rate of evaporation, none the less it provides a much appreciated tannin for taming the harshness of cognac.[1]

Limousin wood, floated down the Charente, was the only oak available when Cognac was just beginning its rise to fame. Troncais, its only rival, comes from a man-made forest first planted in the middle of the seventeenth century. The great French statesmen, Colbert, reckoned that the only way to combat the over-mighty warships of Holland and England with their 'Hearts of Oak' was for France to grow its own. The Troncais forest was the result. It is in the 'Bourbonnais', the very heart of France between Montluçon and Moulins, extending north towards Nevers and east towards Burgundy (Ravaz calls it 'wood from Burgundy'). The forest itself is a major tourist attraction, awarded two stars by the editors of the *Guide Michelin*. The trees are more crowded, and therefore taller and slimmer, than those grown in the Limousin – and thus unfamiliar to British eyes accustomed to naturally grown oaks. The forest's wood is darker than that of its rival, copper-coloured where that from the Limousin is a lighter yellow. In the words of Jean Taransaud, 'Mature clumps of trees provide an oak which grows thin and straight. The wood from it has a delicate and soft grain which is easy to work. It is particularly impervious to alcohol, very unporous. It has an excellent tannin, soft and slightly sweet, which permeates the cognac only slowly.' The Troncais has less tannin and more lignin than wood from its rival and so imparts a less woody flavour to the cognacs. So Limousin is not entirely suitable for the cheaper cognacs, which are going to spend only a few years in wood; they are liable to absorb too much tannin and to become too *boisé* ('woody'). In the long run Limousin is more suitable for the same reason: it has so much tannin to impart that the cognac still has reserves to draw on after a decade or more in the wood.

But the tannins form under 5 per cent of the chemical make-up of the wood. Seventy per cent is cellulose, some of which is chemically inert. It is important mainly for the 'backbone', the mechanical strength, it gives the wood, although the spirit does absorb some of the sugars in the hemicellulose as the molecules shrink during the ageing process. But more important than either is the lignin, which forms about 23 per cent of the oak and hence has a much more important influence on the maturation process than the better-known tannins. Luckily for the Charentais, oak contains only about 0·5 per cent of resinous matter, which pollutes the grapiness of the brandy with the turpentine taste so marked in brandies matured in casks of pine, which contain 8 per cent of resinous matter.

Cognac's casks are special in every respect. The oaks have to be at least fifty years old (most of them are at least centenarians). The only part that can be used is the *fût* (the trunk), and then only from just above the roots to the lowest branches, to ensure that the planks and their grain are straight and free from knots and faults. But not all of even this limited selection is suitable: the heart itself is too knotty; the sappy wood under the bark is too rich in soluble organic essences, which would pollute the brandy. The drying, too, is special. The ready-sliced trunks are piled up in the open air in stacks, which allow the air and the rain free access, for they play a crucial part in the chemistry of cognac. The trunks dry naturally and slowly – at the rate of a year for every centimetre of thickness. Most of the planks are 5–6 centimetres (2–2½ inches) thick, so most firms dry their oak for considerably longer than the statutory minimum of three years – most of them use planks dried for five or six years.

The wood needs to mature, but the drying also has a chemical role to play: lengthy exposure to

[1] *Le Livre de la tonnellerie*, Paris, La Roue à Livres Diffusion, 1976.

the air and the rain washes away some of the more bitter tannins in the wood; others are broken down into more palatable tannins; and a mould develops that works on the lignins in the wood. The enzymes split the big (and tasteless) lignin molecule into four smaller ones, all of which taste of vanillin. The acid and the alcohol in the cognac dissolves the vanillin lignins. These emerge with the vanilla aroma that is so essential in the finished cognac.

The fuss about air-dried oak sounds absurd. It is not. With the help of the co-operative that markets the Prince de Polignac brand, the Station Viticole compared brandy stored in oven-dried oak with the same spirit stored in the air-dried equivalent. After a year in the oven-dried oak the spirit was bitter and astringent, fuller of acids and tannin than if the air had been allowed to do its work unaided.

The cognac cask itself has always been special. Its shape was not unusual – the bulge in the middle, making it easier to roll, was a feature of other regions as well – but it was instantly recognizable by the hoops made of thin strips of lath laid around most of the sides of the cask, only the wood in the middle remaining visible. The staves of today's cask are circled only enough to enable them to be rolled more easily. The size of the cask is crucial, since it determines the extent to which the brandy will be exposed to the wood: the smaller the cask, the woodier the cognac. As with the size of the *alembic*, balance has to be achieved. In the past the *barrique de cognac* held over 205 litres, although the brandy was housed in *tierçons* which held over 500 litres. But now the more reputable distillers have standardized on smaller casks. By trial and error they have found that casks holding around 350 litres provide the correct balance.

Not surprisingly, *la tonnellerie* (the craft of the cooper) has always been important – Taransaud proudly styles himself *maître tonnellier de Cognac* – and one little affected by modern production techniques. Because they are such substantial users of casks, the major firms now own some of the biggest *tonnelleries* in France (Hennessy took over the Taransaud family business twenty years ago, while Rémy Martin claims to own the largest in France). Their self-reliance is explained by the horror stories they all have to tell of the leaks that developed in casks bought from outside, defects that ruined the quality as well as reducing the quantity of the spirit. The slightest flaw in the cask can mean that the precious contents drain or become infected: 'A split stave will cause a woody taste,' wrote Charles Walter Berry,[1] the wine merchant who was probably the leading expert on cognac in London between the wars. Despite the size of the workshops, the casks are still made in the traditional way; the wood has to be cleaved along the line of the grain, not sawn across, and although some of the staves can be relatively mass-produced, the actual fabrication of the casks remains the task of individual craftsmen, each with his own rhythm of work.

Even though the wood is so dense, the casks so carefully made and the bungs so tight, there is inevitably some evaporation when cognac is stored in wood: the art of the cooper and the distiller is to ensure that the evaporation is controlled, so that the necessary reactions between wood, air and brandy can proceed at the appropriate pace. The spirit evaporates at between 2 and 4 per cent annually, depending on the humidity of the *chai*,[2] a loss described by the locals as *la part des anges* (the 'angels' share').

The ageing process is both physical and chemical. Rémy Martin divides it into five stages: in the first year the cognac loses its 'boiler taste' and takes on its first colouring, a pale yellow tint. In

[1] *In Search of Wine*, London, Constable, 1935.
[2] Strictly speaking, a *chai* ought to be partly underground, as it is in Bordeaux. In Cognac a *chai* is any type of warehouse used for storing spirit.

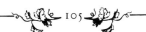

The art of cask-making: at the Tesserons'

... and at Seguin Moreau, owned by Remy-Martin

Part – but only part – of Martell's stocks

the next couple of years the spirit starts to absorb some 'woodiness' and ceases to be merely a raw spirit. In the two subsequent stages – covering the next seven or eight years – the 'woodiness' diminishes, the cognac mellows, a hint of vanilla starts to creep into the taste. From its twelfth birthday the *cognac simple* gets more complex and harmonious.

More prosaically, the spirit also gets progressively weaker, at the rate of about one percentage point a year in the first ten years in cask but much more slowly after that – a brandy with fifty years in cask behind it contains only about 46 per cent alcohol. The balance is a delicate one: if the *chai* is especially humid, then the loss of alcoholic strength will be much greater, whereas an unusually dry warehouse induces unnaturally fast evaporation of an unnaturally strong spirit. Maurice Fillioux of Hennessy reckons that a cognac left for twenty years in an especially dry *chai* will retain the youthfulness of a ten-year-old. The same period of time spent by brandy in an unusually wet *chai* will add five years to its physical age.

The traditional brandies sipped by the British aristocracy were bought young by their wine merchants, shipped immediately to London or Bristol and stored for decades in damp cellars in the docks. This produced the classic taste of 'early-landed' cognacs,[1] pale and delicate, much to the taste of the English but disliked by many of the French blenders, who find them flabby. Maurice Healy described such a cognac as 'of almost unearthly pallor and a correspondingly ethereal bouquet and flavour'. A number of merchants still buy cognacs a year or two old from such traditional suppliers as Hine and Delamain and bring them to London or Bristol to mature for a decade or more. Unfortunately for drinkers in search of the ethereal, in recent years the casks have been stored in much drier warehouses. The merchants were not accustomed to visiting the warehouses and did not realize what was happening. So they are now faced with cognacs far stronger, drier and less aromatic than they, or their customers, are used to – a fate escaped by Berry Bros who store their Cognac at their suppliers' Messrs Frapin.

Modern scientists now perceive this controlled evaporation as a continuation, albeit at a much slower rate, ot the processes begun in the *alembic*. The evaporation is still the most important element in the ageing of cognac, but it is only part of the most important reaction – that of the oxygen in the air outside the cask and the wood of the cask itself. The wood allows the oxygen to seep steadily through to the spirit, and its metallic elements act as catalysts. This slow oxidation ensures that the aromatic elements in the spirits are preserved, although they would be lost in a speedier chemical reaction. The wood itself is profoundly affected by the spirit and gradually drained of the elements which enrich the cognac – inevitably, the more often the cask has been used, the more neutral its wood.

The tannins play an important role, as they do with maturing wines: they bring colour to the spirit, which is colourless when it emerges from the *alembic*, and at first they increase its bitterness. But, after a few years, chemically the molecules are enlarged and the flavour has mellowed. The lignin brings with it an aroma of balsa wood and, when it breaks down, results in the vanilla and cinnamon overtones detectable in some cognacs. These processes are slow; tannic matter really starts to build up only after eight years in cask: and while the aldehydes reach their peak after a mere thirty years (they have absorbed one of them, vanillin, within five), the volatile acids build

---

[1] The usual phrase is 'early-landed, late-bottled'. The two are not the same, since virtually all cognacs are 'late-bottled', in the sense that they are bottled only just before they are sold.

up over the fifty years a truly old cognac spends in cask before it is transferred to glass *bonbonnes* for storage in sterile conditions.

The tannins and the lignins dissolve at different rates, so after five years only 10 per cent of the lignin in the cask has been absorbed but 20 per cent of the tannins; after ten years only 60 per cent of the tannin is left but 80 per cent of the lignin. The conventional wisdom that cognac takes up to fifty years to absorb all the tannin in the wood is challenged by Michel Caumeil, who reckons that after twenty or thirty years virtually all the tannin has been absorbed, so that the only role of the wood is a physical one – it continues to allow air through for oxidation.

But age does not automatically bring quality with it. After fifteen or twenty years some cognacs – not all, by any means – become maderized and acquire the very particular *rancio charentais*. Charles Walter Berry (who did not like it) described *rancio* as 'a special character of fullness and fatness in some Brandies . . . rankness (*rance, rancio*)'. This richness of savour reminds some tasters of Roquefort cheese; indeed there is a sort of mild cheesiness in the nose, a sense of hidden depths, far removed from the foxy *goût de terroir* of young, inferior brandies but

Saintes – imitating Venice in 1982

Overleaf: Cleaning up in 1982

nevertheless a reminder of the earthiness of the spirit's origins.

Chemically, *rancio charentais* derives from the oxidation of the fatty acids in the spirit, producing the ketones that feel so rich and fat on the palate. But this is only one of many such reactions. The scientists are still busy analyzing the chemical reactions and their results on the palate. One team under Dr Heide detected 334 ingredients in cognac: 24 acetals (ethylates of aldehyde and alcohol), 27 acids, 63 alcohols, 34 aldehydes, 25 ketones, 77 esters, 19 ethers, 3 lactones, 8 phenols and 44 'diverse substances'. The scientists have still separated and analyzed only seventy of these, either because they form an important part of the mix or because they strongly influence the taste. The two are not the same: with Michel Caumeil I sniffed certain entirely neutral ingredients present in some quantity, and others – like some ethyl compounds – whose smallest whiff is strongly reminiscent of rotten fruit. But these considerations are for the perfectionists. The vast majority of cognacs are sold before their fifth birthday, before they have time to develop any of the complexities of a great cognac. The decision as to what is worth keeping and what is good merely for immediate sale is largely in the hands of the blenders in a few major firms. In Cognac the market reaches right into the cask.

12 · The Personality of Cognac

Between the distillation and the consumption comes the merchant, who blends the brandies and under whose name most of them are sold. Most of these blends will be unremarkable, and most of the merchants – there are still over two hundred of them – resemble their eighteenth-century predecessors; they are largely brokers between the growers and foreign buyers. Most have stocks, but these are largely 'tactical', held for a few years, like those in Richard Hennessy's cellars in the late 1770s. Like him, they rely on growers' stocks for most of the older brandies they need. Only a handful are big enough or – the classic case is Delamain – enjoy a sufficiently high reputation to be able to afford a 'house style' of thir own and hold a balanced stock extending back through the decades. Like great craftsmen the world over, the blenders in all the better houses have a clear idea in their heads and in bottles in their tasting rooms, rather than on paper, of the essential qualities historically associated with their name.

The obvious comparison is with the merchants of Reims and Épernay. They too have lovingly cultivated house styles; they too usually depend on raw materials bought from hundreds of individual growers. But most of the major champagne houses rely on their own estates for a substantial proportion of their raw materials (one, Louis Roederer, is almost completely self-sufficient), and many of the others depend on them for crucial elements in their house styles. By contrast, in Cognac the ownership of estates seems largely irrelevant. Four of the biggest merchants – Martell, Hennessy, Rémy Martin and Bisquit – own vineyards of their own, but these account for an insignificant percentage of their requirements.[1] The Martells and Hennessys operate an informal separation of their interests: the estates and the vineyards are run by members of the family, more interested, like the English gentlemen they so greatly resemble, in farming than in trade. Rémy Martin has extensive estates in the Grande Champagne, and Bisquit a vast estate at Lignières in the Fins Bois, north-east of Rouillac. But none of them mentions these estates as other than routine suppliers. The only partial exception to the rule is Frapin, historically a grower which marketed its own brandies, which still relies on its extensive estates in the heart of the Grande Champagne to supply all its more expensive brands.

For none of the major firms is truly integrated. None of them buys grapes; all buy wine and new brandy – even Martell buys half its requirements after distillation. They all have to buy in parcels of old cognacs when they are mixing their finest blends, for not even Hennessy & Martell can guarantee an adequate supply of every one of the twenty or more cognacs required. Obviously, all the 'serious' firms keep a tight control over the brandies they buy, mostly through contracts with hundreds of supposedly 'independent', but closely supervised, growers. Some of them, like Hine, Courvoisier and Delamain, do not distil any of their own cognac but rely entirely on growers from whom they buy young cognacs. Neither Hine nor Delamain buys newly distilled cognacs at all.

[1] The co-operative that markets Prince de Polignac sells the output of hundreds of growers but cannot dictate to them, and therefore has less freedom than an ordinary firm to develop a house style of its own.

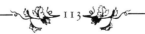

Right: The Fillioux at work: Yan (left) and his uncle Maurice (right)

Opposite: The 'Petite réserve' at Hine

All of them are playing with a number of variables: the type of oak they are using; the age of the casks; the length of time for which they mature their different 'brands'; and, crucially, the area from which they buy their cognac – two of them, Rémy Martin and Delamain, sell only brandies from the Champagnes. For their cheapest blends, the VS (formerly Three-Star) and VSOP, all the other merchants inevitably rely on brandies from the Bois but are usually looking only for a 'correct' brandy that fits their house style.

Inevitably, the brandies from the Bois are less capable of development, but the best can acquire a certain fragrance. The arch-exponent of the potential of the best cognacs from the Bois is M. Voisin of Leopold Gourmel, one of the few merchants who sells a cognac purely from the Fins Bois. His offerings have poetic names: Age des Fleurs, Age des Épices and Quintessence, and he compares the aroma of his best Fins Bois with the scent of new-mown hay. Indeed, his Fins Bois, which come from a small area east of Jarnac, are delicate and delicious, with an aura of pot-pourri, a dried flowery scent. Many drinkers prefer it to a run-of-the-mill, heavily caramelized champagne cognac, but even the Fins Bois of M. Voisin will never have the length, the depth or the subtlety of a great cognac from the Champagnes; and as time goes on it will bear an increasingly distant relationship to its more expensive brethren.

A number of the bigger and more serious houses have a secret weapon: using brandies from the Borderies for their VSOP and other medium-quality cognacs. They find these cognacs very special, 'nutty' and intense even after a mere ten years in cask. When Eric de Rothschild of Château Lafite decided to launch a cognac under the château's name, he chose a pure Borderies,

a tribute to the area's reputation. 'Brandies from the Borderies mature very quickly. They are well-rounded after fifteen years,' says Pierre Frugier of Martell, which uses a great deal of the brandy in its Cordon Bleu. 'We pay the same for cognac from the Borderies as we do from the Petite Champagne,' says Maurice Fillioux. 'I can always distinguish a cognac from the Borderies – there's that little something. To talk about violets, as some people do, is a little poetical; to me the essence is of nut kernels.' This 'nuttiness' so characteristic of the Borderies forms an essential part of the better Three-Stars and VSOPs. Indeed, the brandies from the Borderies are tailor-made for VSOPs made up of brandies of between five and ten years of age. Some purists claim that the whole idea of VSOP is unnatural, that the age range is too old for brandies from the Bois, too young for those from the Champagnes (though Rémy Martin has made its fame and fortune by refuting this particular old wives' tale).

But for all their better brands, the innumerable XOs, Napoléons and the like, the merchants rely on cognacs from the Champagnes. In theory, these are so intense as to be almost undrinkable before they are ten or more years old. But Rémy Martin disagrees. 'They don't mature more slowly. They are simply more complex, and therefore it is more interesting to age them longer,' says Robert Leauté. Impressions of the aroma and taste of Champagne cognacs revert to the vine, to the flowers and twigs as well as the fruit of the grape, resulting in the preservation, in a uniquely concentrated form, of the natural qualities of the raw materials, nature transformed by man.

Not all cognacs, even from the Grande Champagne, have the capacity to age so vigorously and gracefully, for there are obviously some bad brandies made in the Champagnes. Although the growers now all know how to distil good cognac, some of them are still careless. The Station Viticole imposes some form of discipline, since all the cognacs have to be sampled (given the *agrément*) before they can be sold to the public, and this eliminates the truly worst brandies. Yet, broadly speaking, the buyer has very little legal protection. Blends up to six years old have to be marked with the age of the youngest brandy in them, but there is absolutely no control after that point. A buyer of a cognac claiming to be 100 years old can be sure only that all the brandies in it are at least six years old. There are plenty of inferior, well-aged cognacs on sale, for any unscrupulous blender can fabricate a 'venerable' Grande Champagne cognac with some undrinkable, albeit genuinely aged, cognac plus a generous dose of caramel and oak shavings to increase the age of the blend's taste. The reputation of the firm selling the cognac is inevitably a better guarantee of quality than the legal descriptions. Any good blender can produce a Petite Champagne blend that is far superior to all but the very finest products of the Grande Champagne.

House style starts with the cognac itself, but it inevitably also includes the type of oak used and the age of the casks. A high proportion of Rémy Martin's cognacs, which are all from the Champagnes, are destined for VSOP brandies, to be sold within six, or at the most ten, years of distillation. So it is looking for a type of wood which will speed the maturation process and naturally uses Limousin oak. Martell uses Troncais because it is looking for precisely the opposite qualities: the wood has less tannin and is denser and therefore less porous, so ageing is slower and less wood is imparted to the cognac. Indeed, the secret of the dry Martell style, originally destined for the British market, was that the cognac itself and the oak in which it was aged were both directed towards a target which is ascetic in theory, but in practice, fills the mouth with a balanced fullness.

The same considerations apply to the age of the casks. In theory, most firms keep their cognacs in new wood for a year to provide an initial 'attack' of tannin before transferring it to older casks to prevent them from becoming too *boisé*. At the Tesserons, where the average is three months in new wood, the length of the stay depends also on the quality of the casks. The only exception is Delamain: none of their cognacs has ever seen any new wood. At the other extreme the equally reputable house of Frapin keeps its best cognacs in new oak for up to two and a half years, depending on the amount of colour (and hence, by inference, the tannin) the spirit has absorbed. Both are exceptions: Delamain is seeking a light, almost ethereal style, and the cognacs that the Frapins use for their Château de Fontpinot brand all come from a particularly favoured corner of the Grande Champagne, so they can respond to the strength of the new wood.

All the houses are aiming at a standard product from grapes that inevitably vary from year to year. If the year has been especially wet, the cognacs could be flabby, so Rémy Martin, for instance, stiffen their backbone by a longer stay in new wood. In very dry years the opposite applies. Bisquit uses old oak for Champagne cognacs and new wood for a third of those from the Bois. There is a regular routine as the brandies are gradually transferred to older and older casks. But the pace varies for as Alain Braastad of Delamain says, 'Every cask has its own personality because of the very different qualities of the wood in which it is lodged.' All the blenders agree with him that while the brandy is above 40 per cent, the wood still contributes something to the final result.

So, of course, do the *chais* in which the brandies are housed. These are a cross between a commercial warehouse and, in the case of the fabled *paradis* housing the oldest cognacs, a living museum. Originally they were located on the banks of the Charente, so that the casks could be loaded on to the *gabares*. This was another lucky accident. Initially the Cognacais probably did not realize the contribution made by the dampness of the riverside atmosphere to the quality of the cognac. So the north bank of the Charente in Cognac, and both banks at Jarnac, are still lined with handsome stone warehouses, inevitably blackened by generations of *Torula compniacensis*.

The old sites had two problems, fire and flood, neither entirely conquered even today. A few years ago the Charente flooded. Casks of brandy bobbed about like life rafts, and the dark stains left by the receding waters can still be seen half-way up the walls of the Royers' *chais* by the river in Jarnac. Fire is an even more serious hazard. Vizetelly remarked that if Cognac 'were once to catch fire at any point, it would explode like a mountain of lucifer matches struck by lightning, and would blaze afterwards like an ever-burning *omelette-au-rhum*, intended to be gazed at but never eaten.' Rather more limited conflagrations are a regular occurence, and both Rémy Martin and Martell have suffered within the past decade.

Despite the disadvantages of a riverside location, both Martell and Hennessy still rely on their old sites. Rémy Martin did not inherit any historic *chais* and now owns a number of rather unromantic sprawls in and around Cognac. In Jarnac Courvoisier dominates one bank of the river, although its stocks have never been as large, in relation to its size, as those of other major firms. Bisquit has deserted its historic site on the other side of the bridge; nevertheless, it has insulated its massive new *chais* out in the country so that they enjoy the same degree of humidity as the ancient ones. Bisquit's new *chais* are designed for modern handling methods, with each cask in a little cell in a kind of prison block a dozen or more cells high, ready to be picked up by a fork-lift truck. In more traditional *chais* the casks are piled three high, each labelled with a (rather childish) code designating its origins and age.

The blenders clearly have an immense palette from which to work. Typically, Hennessy has 700 growers under contract. Rémy Martin buys from 500 individual growers who provide particular qualities to add to the basic cognacs bought from twenty *bouilleurs de profession* (professional distillers) who themselves draw wines from 1,200 growers. All of them have been trained, often over several generations, to distil their brandies in the specific fashion best suited to the house's requirements. At least once every year (twice at Hennessy) the blenders taste the thousands of individual casks they have in stock. Historic contracts with the growers offer the immense advantage of records indicating just how cognacs from a particular holding have developed in the past, making it easier to know which are capable of further improvement.

At a certain point even the most venerable are ready for blending – mixing with distilled water to bring them down to 40 per cent alcohol – and 'adjustment' with a little sugar and caramel. Both are delicate operations. The most prominent feature of every tasting room is the long line of bottles, each containing examples of the house's products and samples of different casks that will be required in the future.

Only the oldest cognacs, those of at least forty years old, are weak enough to be sold without dilution; the younger the blend, the stronger the basic spirit. to bring a three-year-old down from perhaps 60° to 40° is a delicate business. 'The dilution can never be too brutal,' says Michel Caumeil, who compares it with landing an aeroplane. The decision is irreversible: 'once a cognac has been cut,' says Caumeil, 'it can never go into one of our best blends.' But even the meanest spirit cannot be brought down from its cruising altitude (or undiluted strength) in one go. The process occurs in several stages, each of them separated by a period of months. At one major house they start reducing the strength of their Three-Stars to 48° as soon as they have been bought, so that they reach the 40° level at which they are to be sold without further disturbance. 'At Hennessy we prefer to keep the brandy's character,' says Maurice Fillioux, so they mix it a year before the brandy is to be sold. At Martell they taste even the distilled water, while Delamain uses a mixture of distilled water and old cognac, itself left to mature for a few months, to dilute the brandy.

Since the arrival of the *appellation* system the merchants have not been able to tamper with the cognacs. They can add one part of caramel per thousand and 8 grams of sugar per litre, and that is all. Because the sugars from the hemi-cellulose in the wood gradually infiltrate the cognac after twenty years, Hennessy for one finds that it has to put only 2 grams of sugar, a quarter of the permitted level, into each litre. The sugary syrup softens the young cognacs – it 'rounds' them – while the caramel, neutral to the taste, merely standardizes the colour. There is another widespread habit, which is frowned upon: artificially ageing the cognac by tipping oak chippings – *la boisé* – into the casks and thus boosting the tannin. This 'turbo-charging' is disapproved of for reasons that go back to the basic rhythms of ageing. It speeds up the process of ageing too much, it swamps the spirit with a harsh heavy coating of tannin which is in theory natural, but because of the intensity and the suddenness of the oakiness, emerges as an artificial woodiness on the palate. Even less well publicized is the alleged use of artificial flavours imported by a handful of unscrupulous houses from Dutch fragrance manufacturers.

Things were very different in the goodish old days when the merchants enjoyed complete freedom as to the additives they could employ. Then they were particularly aware of the need to darken their brandies. The British (like the Chinese) were fond of 'brown brandies', partly because of a fond delusion that a dark brandy was an old brandy. Prune juice, sweet, dark and a trifle nutty, was a great favourite, and if more nuttiness was required, almond could be added to the casks. Vizetelly was shown a special locked storehouse and was offered a sample

from an enormous cask of the burnt-sugar syrup, which 'brownifies' the brandy (English customers admiring a gypsy complexion), and which syrup is not nice at all; and also a glass of softening syrup, made of one-fourth sugar and three-fourths *eau-de-vie*, which sweetens and smooths the cordial for lickerish lips, and which is so delicious that you would not have the heart to reproach your bitterest enemy if you caught him indulging in a drop too much.'

Even the normally puritanical Tovey approved of such additions:

The old Cognac houses are very particular in the quality of their colouring, and prepare it with great care; it is important, too, that it should be old, and it is made up with Old Brandy. Consequently good old colouring imparts a fulness and roundness to Brandy which is not to be met with in the uncoloured spirit, although the latter may merit the preference in character and finesse.

Even today the houses add a little caramel to bring each cask up to the level of the darkest individual blend, and because the Chinese equate darkness with age, so the blends sent to the east may well be darker than those sold in Europe or the United States.

The physical blending, like the dilution, is conducted on a large scale but with considerable respect for the fragility of the product. The brandies are left to enjoy each other's company for several months before being refrigerated to $15\,°F$ ($-9\,°C$) and filtered (generally centrifugally) to ensure that they do not throw any deposits even if they are left on tropical docksides or in icy Alaskan warehouses for weeks at a time. For a house style has to be capable not only of being applied on an industrial scale but also of surviving the many accidents that can happen between the Charente and the drinker.

To appreciate a spirit which may have travelled a long way from the Charente a drinker must use not only his palate but his nose as well (the eyes are less important, although colour does provide a preliminary clue as to the nature of the cognac). At their best dark cognacs can be fruity, but they are also liable to be woody, or heavily caramelized, or both, while, in general, paler ones will be less woody (and possibly purer). Tasters obviously have to rely exclusively on their sense of smell – even the strongest stomach could not survive the small sips ingested when sampling fifty or more cognacs in a row, especially freshly-distilled or immature ones.

They, like the rest of us, are judging on three criteria: age, *cru*, and the general style which results from the combination of the age, the *cru* and the oak. They will instantly reject the harsh oiliness imparted to both nose and palate by the raw spirit used in even the best grape brandies. The *cru* is more difficult to distinguish. Most cheap cognacs are relatively anonymous: the better will, however, have a certain character. Courvoisier is round and rather caramelly. Bisquit has more fruitiness than any other, while both Martell and Hennessy are both rather more round and mature than their competitors. None, of course, has the freshness or the fragrance of the pure Fins Bois sold under the Gourmel name.

With less routine cognacs it is immensely enjoyable to look for the nuttiness provided by cognacs from the Borderies, and to try and detect the age of the cognac employed in different 'Champagne' cognacs. Some merchants disguise the characterlessness with relatively heavy doses of caramel, but with most you can tell the age not only from the rawness of the alcohol, but from its depth and complexity. The easiest individual element to detect is, of course, the *rancio*, but for me a good or great cognac is more than the sum of its parts.

Like the locals I drink very little of it. For me, like them, the nose is almost more important than the palate, so I spend far more time 'nosing' it, absorbing the complex sensations provided by its bouquet, than feeling its warmth on my palate. In the end I am looking for the greatest possible impact from the fruit from which the cognac was made. This can be richer or leaner. It is no more ridiculous to talk of the 'backbone' of a good Martell, the 'elegance' of a Delamain, the 'fruitiness' of a Hennessy cognac than it is to attribute the same qualities to clarets from Pauillac or Saint Émilion.

Whatever the sensations, the drinker can generally be guided by the style of the house which blended the cognac. These house styles are a strange mixture of the taste for which customers developed a fondness in ages past, of the personal favourites of the blenders, sometimes of a deliberate, almost perverse complexity: 'The more you simplify cognac, the easier it is to imitate,'

Bottling is still an art, even at Martell

says Robert Leauté of Rémy Martin. For once you rise above the VSOP level, the choice is almost infinite: 'The old cognacs vary so much that you have an enormously wide choice of style from XO upwards,' says Jacques Rouvière of Bisquit. As might be expected, Martell and Hennessy have very different house styles: Martell, as we have seen, is almost obsessionally dry and clear on the palate; Hennessy does for a much richer, almost voluptuous, taste in its blends. The theme of 'richness', of a desire to extract as much of the grapiness as possible from the fruit, is also common to Rémy Martin and Bisquit, although they use different methods: Rémy distils all its cognacs on their lees; Bisquit relies on keeping more of the *secondes* by not cutting the 'tails' until late in the distillation process. Recently the firms have had to adapt to new markets: the Japanese were unhappy at the dry intensity of Martell's cognacs; Hennessy recently changed its VSOP, making it lighter, less woody (they simply kept it in older casks): before launching its new XO, Bisquit

The industrial side of cognac

tested a number of blends on a panel of a thousand Chinese in Hong Kong. At the other extreme, Alain Braastad of Delamain says simply: 'I blend what I like.' But then his house is very special. It employs only eighteen people, and the bottling (and even the twisting of the wires over the necks of the bottles) is done by hand. Historically, Hine, like Delamain, was aiming at the top of the English market, which was looking for a pale but intense cognac, relying on a combination of good raw materials from the Champagnes and ageing in old oak.

The house styles of Martell and Hennessy are also greatly affected by two families, the Chapeaus at Martell and the Fillioux at Hennessy, who have blended their cognacs for the past two hundred years (the mother of Pierre Frugier, Martell's present head blender, was a Mademoiselle Chapeau). At times they were more like chief executives than chief blenders – Maurice Fillioux's father, Yves, worked with, rather than for, Gilles Hennessy. One Fillioux

Delamain: where cognac is still a cottage industry

ventured abroad to help Jean Monnet, but both Frugier and Fillioux seem genuinely puzzled by the idea that they could exploit their historic importance. The Fillioux have resisted numerous tempting offers from the United States and were furious when a distant relative started a firm trading on the family's fame. The reason is simple: as Pierre Frugier puts it, 'We are part of the furniture.'

These stylistic rules apply less to the ordinary blends and to the truly old cognacs, those that have absorbed all they can from the wood, which are a class apart. As we have noted, they 'expand inside the mouth'. Once they are fifty years old, the best of them have acquired an inimitable, golden-bronze colour and feel: a harmony achievable only with age. Age can also bring with it a kind of anonymity, blurring the original distinctions between different styles, so some of the real golden oldies, like Rémy Martin's Louis XIII and Hennessy's Paradis, resemble each other more than they do their makers' more ordinary blends. Style applies more to younger, mid-range blends. The contrast between two widely respected cognacs, Frapin's Château de Fontpinot and Delamain's Pale and Dry, is striking. The Frapin is infinitely more woody; the oak, though dissolved and matured, is still emphatically present. In pre-feminist language, it is a 'masculine' cognac, where the infinitely more delicate Delamain is 'feminine', all lightness and elegance. To my palate, the best balance is achieved by a single-vineyard cognac, that of Madame Raymond Ragnaud, which somehow combines the strength and delicacy of the two extremes. But a cognac like this is rare enough to prove the rule that the only way to establish a reliable house style is to blend the products of many stills. There is only a handful of single-vineyard cognacs worthy of the name – notably from the two branches of the Ragnaud family and from Guy Lhéraud; for most of the other 500 or so direct sellers are relying either on price or inverse snobbery – the French desire to get away from 'commercial' drinks in favour of the *vente directe* by a 'little man' known only to them.

The other great rule, which argues against single-vintage cognacs, is equally sound. The Cognacais do not allow themselves to put dates on the bottles they sell, for two reasons: cognac vintages do not vary greatly; and some of the merchants could not be trusted if they did. Charles Tovey put it bluntly: 'We place but little reliance upon the cognac shippers' declarations with regard to vintages; and the only security the merchant has is to get his vintage brandy over to England into his own bonded stores as soon after the vintage as is convenient.' Maurice Healy described how some merchants operated a sort of 'solera' system: 'Bisquit Dubouché offered to supply apparently unlimited quantities of their 1865, their 1834 and even their 1811. . . . If a cask of 1811 brandy had got down to its last tenth, and was then refilled with brandy of a younger but sympathetic vintage, say 1834, the cask became within a few days a full cask of 1811, the older vintage having endowed the younger with its quality, while receiving the strength and virility of the other.' The merchants in Armagnac, who can legally offer single-vintage spirits, seem to have an inexhaustible supply of such esoteric vintages as 1940, making Healy's point for him. If you follow Tovey's advice and buy a single-vintage cognac from one of the handful of merchants who still import cognacs young and age them in Britain,[1] you will be getting an undeniably superior drink – but only because the cognac has been lovingly chosen and aged; it will not necessarily be superior to the non-vintage, early-landed cognacs that have been through the same scrupulous commercial chain.

Demand for pale, early-landed cognacs was always limited. The Cognacais needed a sales tool

[1] The prohibition on the sale of single-vintage cognacs applies only to the cognac houses themselves.

with broader appeal. Evelyn Waugh hinted at their new weapon in a famous scene in *Brideshead Revisited*. The hero, the insufferably superior Charles Ryder, is dining with the upstart Rex Mottram at a restaurant clearly identifiable as the Tour d'Argent. The cognac offered to them is 'clear and pale and it came to us in a bottle free from grime and Napoleonic cyphers. It was only a year or two older than Rex and lately bottled. They gave it to us in very thin tulip-shaped glasses of modest size'.[1] Predictably, Rex does not like it: he 'pronounced it the sort of stuff he put soda in at home'. So 'shamefacedly, they wheeled out of its hiding place the vast and mouldy bottle they kept for people of Rex's sort . . . a treacly concoction', which left 'dark rings round the side of his glass . . . a *ballon* the size of his head' (still often seen in pretentious surroundings the world over, but *never* in Cognac itself).

Waugh was being deliberately, outrageously snobbish. But he had clearly separated the two markets which developed amid the cigar smoke and lush living of Edwardian England: the older, 'purer' tradition, of aristocratic sips of light, intense, delicate cognacs shipped early and bottled late, and the newer and more vulgar novelties symbolized by 'vast grimy bottles' and 'Napoleonic cyphers'. The Cognacais could not afford to be so choosy. The 'Napoleonic cypher' was a brilliant marketing idea that helped them recover at least some of the markets they had lost in the years of the phylloxera.

[1] Like those used by the Cognacais, anxious to combine small quantities of spirits with the maximum capacity to entrap and concentrate the bouquet.

MODERN TIMES

13 · Struggle

The name of Napoleon proved a powerful weapon in the hands of the Cognacais in their fight back after the disasters of phylloxera. The imperial name was seized on as a guarantee of legitimacy, a pledge that the brandy was indeed from Cognac, for the frauds of the phylloxera era had cast a long shadow. The name started to spread in the first decade of the century, when the trade was still convalescent, when the Army & Navy Stores still felt itself obliged to say that its brandies were 'guaranteed grape spirit from Cognac district'.

The success of the identification of the drink with the emperor is rather puzzling: for a century Napoleon remained an arch-villain in Britain, and he had never been a particular hero for the Cognacais, whose affections had been exclusively lavished on his nephew, Napoleon III. Since the onset of phylloxera came soon after the latter's deposition, it would have been natural to use his name, and not that of his uncle, to indicate a pre-phylloxera spirit. Yet the connection was made with the first emperor, and it served its purpose: it did help in the restoration of Cognac, and even today the name provides a splendid sales weapon, especially in countries outside Europe, where the name of Napoleon is better known than that of Cognac itself and is especially associated with the image of virility and strength for which the drink has become profitably renowned in the East.

The weapon was used at three levels. The name was freely attached to any dusty old bottle of brandy, like those demanded by Rex Mottram. Even today the London salerooms still offer for sale bottles of so-called 'Napoleon' brandy. These are usually labelled 1811, the 'Year of the Comet' which remain embedded in the subconscious of the world of cognac (and of claret). Not only the name of the emperor himself was exploited: the Napoleonic magic was sufficiently powerful to cover bottles labelled with the names of his first wife ('Impératrice Joséphine'), his house (Maison de l'Empereur') and even his tragic offspring ('Le Roi de Rome').[1] Some merchants went for a belt-and-braces approach, aware that the mere name of Napoleon might not be sufficient to impress the buyers. A bottle of 1928 'Bonaparte' cognac from Croizet was 'guaranteed to be the distillation of the fermented juice of fresh grapes produced in the Cognac area' – but I should not scoff: it is a smooth and delicious cognac.

These 'Napoleonic' bottles were almost certainly phony. At the very best they were the products of the 'solera' system referred to on page 123, but most were simply sham. One clue is provided by the alleged date of bottling: this is often given as the first decade of the present century, ninety years after the date the brandy was allegedly distilled. During the years 1900–10 the merchants bottled up any brandies they still had in stock and slapped 'Napoleonic' labels on them, for at the time any old cognac was called 'Napoleonic' after Napoleon III, in whose reign it had been distilled. The automatic association of the name with his uncle was natural enough.

[1] Not only the emperor and his family were recalled. One rather tactless label celebrates 'La Grande Armée', the army which was led to its frozen fate in the Russian winter, although the contents of the bottles might well have come in handy on the army's retreat from Moscow.

La crue de la Charente
(18 Février 1904)

Cognac — La Place de la Levade et le Minage

6 COGNAC (France) — Les Quais
Embarquement de " COGNAC ROY "
pour l'Exportation

VUE GÉNÉRALE
DES
ÉTABLISSEMENTS
DU
COGNAC "MONNET"

Succeeding eight pages:

The distinctive shape and decorative style of the old alembics

Sex and symbolism: selling the product in the time-honoured way

Measuring the strength of the new cognac

Bottling the past, in a blender's library of the old

Cask storage modern-style, chez Bisquit at Lignières

Even in serried ranks, all alembics must conform to a regulation size

Another life on the Charente

At a much humbler level the name Napoleon was, and is, attached to particular quality (oddly enough not the best), the one above VSOP. Only a handful of firms can afford not to offer some form of 'Napoleon' – so, in theory, discriminating buyers should avoid any house so insecure that it feels obliged to use the magic name rather than relying on its own reputation. But this would be unfair to Courvoisier, which for the past seventy-five years has used the name, and the picture of the emperor, in a brilliant and sustained piece of image-building. This was due not to native Cognacais but to the Simons, Anglo-French wine merchants who bought up Courvoisier in 1909 and promptly introduced the Napoleonic image. The name was probably already being used in London and Paris, but it was perfectly reasonable to attach it to Courvoisier. The firm's founder, Emmanuel Courvoisier, was a native of the Jura, near the Swiss frontier. He had based himself in Paris, cultivating the business available at Napoleon's imperial court, even supplying the emperor himself. His partner, Louis Gallois, was the builder of the first of the wines and spirits warehouses which have turned Bercy, a dreary suburb on the outskirts of Paris, into the centre of the French trade in basic wines (*la grosse cavalerie*: figuratively 'plonk', literally 'the heavy mob'). Their sons transferred the brandy business to Jarnac, and in the 1840s Courvoisier's son bought out his friend and partner. He retained the Napoleonic connection by supplying spirits to the court of Napoleon III. The business passed to his nephews, the Curlier Brothers (it was a M. Curlier who showed the Parisian artist Bertall around in 1877).

So Courvoisier had never been a traditional firm, and remains something of a maverick to this day. The Simons inherited none of the legacies usually associated with more orthodox concerns – no stocks, no hereditary contracts with hundreds of growers. The only asset was the Napoleonic connection. This they exploited to the full: Courvoisier became, and remained, 'the brandy of Napoleon', and the shadow of the great man became Cognac's most familiar trademark.

The Simons were the exception, the only outsiders in a narrow, introverted world which had

EAU·DE·VIE·FINE
J & L
COGNAC

J & L. ALEXANDRE & C.ie
COGNAC

JULES MUMON
Propriétaire & Négociant

TRADE   MARK

COGNAC

OLD BRANDY

TRADE   MARK

PROUTEAUX & CHAUBIN   DÉPOSE

M. BOITARD

COGNAC

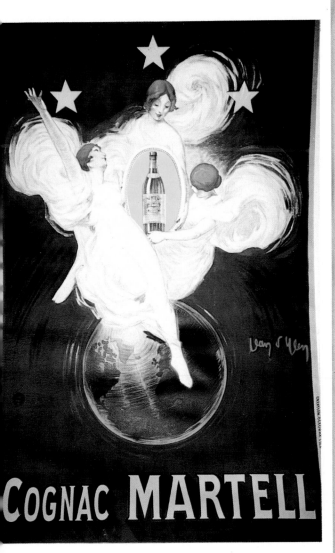

many parallels with the Chartronnais of Bordeaux, another largely Protestant merchant oligarchy living surrounded by Catholic peasants in a major centre of Anglo-French trade. The world of the Cognacais was recently recalled by Jean-Frédéric Gauthier-Auriol, sitting in his study in the family house in the rue Saulnier a few hundred yards from the river. He was talking of the 1920s but could just as well have been referring pre-1914 Cognac:

There were four employees in the office and one very important gentleman, the *maître du chai*. I remember well how the *gabares* were loaded: the workers from the warehouse loaded the cases on big wheelbarrows we called 'twins'. They also loaded cases on to horse-drawn carts: they were branded wooden cases (cardboard packaging was a revolution).

Domestic life was equally traditional:

My grandmother had a ladies' maid who stayed with her for forty years and a manservant she kept for forty-three years. Our governess ('*la* miss') came from England. At lunch we spoke English. If you spoke a word of French, they whisked the dessert past your nose ... as I loathed caramel flan, when I saw it in the kitchen before lunch, I automatically spoke English! For me English was another native language ... there wasn't a single merchant who hadn't spent a year's apprenticeship in England.

The Gauthiers' world was one large family (Gauthier's grandmother was Mademoiselle Delamain) firmly, exclusively Protestant:

the Protestants were like a plate of macaroni cheese: if you pulled one strand you brought with it the whole plate ... we adhered to certain principles in our house: we went to the chapel every Sunday ... my uncle Guy remained a bachelor. He had a mistress whom we called 'the admiral' because she was the daughter of a Breton admiral; my grandmother never allowed him to marry her. For she was Catholic and, what is more, she did not come from the same class as us.[1]

[1] M. Gauthier-Auriol's memories have been recorded by Catherine Petit in *Les Charentes: pays du Cognac*, Paris, ACE, 1984.

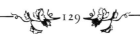

Poor uncle Guy (but perhaps he never wanted to marry *l'amirale* in the first place) was the very model of the all-round merchant-athlete. In later life he was described by a British trade magazine as 'A sturdy, vigorous, full-statured man, with a toothbrush type of moustache, slightly beetling brows' with 'all the alertness, all the sprightliness of the trained athlete' – which he was: holder of the French record for the 100 metres, and a rugby international. The Cognacais were the most northerly French supporters of rugby football: even today the major firms are quite prepared to take on to their staff any foreign rugby star imported to beef up the local XV in its efforts to rejoin the first division of the French rugby championship.

SPORT ATHLÉTIQUE COGNAÇAIS

Life for a well-established merchant family could be temptingly easy. According to Gerald de Ramefort, whose family bought the business in 1930, the Otards were 'more interested in public and social life than business, living like lords in the beautiful *châteaux* they bought around Cognac or in their Paris apartments, and of course, they used to spend a lot of money'. The biggest spenders were probably the family of Jules Robin, a firm that was almost as big as Martell and Hennessy in the late nineteenth century. Older Cognacais can still remember their gorgeous equipages and the state they kept.

Nevertheless, the Otards and the Robins were the exceptions. Most of the Cognacais spent much of the year tramping round the world diversifying their sales, and their efforts did bear some fruit. Before the First World War a number of countries – Belgium, Holland, Sweden, Denmark, Canada, India, Argentina and, to a lesser extent, the United States, Russia, Norway and Egypt – had all become substantial customers. But the bulk of the exports went to two contrasting outlets, France's numerous colonies, which took nearly 15 per cent of the total, and

Britain, which took 40 per cent. The colonials bought cheaply in cask, while the British imported virtually all their brandy expensively in bottle – and the major exception, the early-landed brandies destined for long years in the docks, was among the most valuable. Not surprisingly, 55 per cent of Cognac's total export receipts came from Britain. Half-bottles of Martell Three-Star could be found in millions of humble British medicine chests, while the cognacs of Hennessy, like those of Hine and Delamain, were largely confined to the aristocracy, who otherwise drank the cognacs sold by their traditional wine merchants.

The First World War inevitably resulted in the mass of personal tragedies familiar to anyone who has ever read the endless lists of names of the *Morts pour la Patrie* in the tiniest of French hamlets. But apart from the absence of able-bodied men, it did not change the pattern of Cognac's life – although Meukow, one of Cognac's most reputable concerns, was seized because it had been owned by Germans, the Klaebisch family.

By contrast, peace brought an avalanche of problems. The flood of legislation designed to protect the good name of the town did not help financially between 1918 and 1939. In France itself sales were badly affected by a tax on luxuries first imposed in 1917. This started at 10 per cent but was raised to 30 per cent in 1924. The locals naturally complained: their drink was taxed, they said, at a higher rate than imported luxuries like furs and diamonds, which paid only 10 per cent. Not surprisingly, the French turned increasingly to the mass of newly fashionable, and infinitely cheaper, wine-based aperitifs. Between the wars these largely replaced the famous *fine à l'eau* as a staple drink at the corner café. Women were increasingly drinking in public, and they too turned to lighter, sweeter drinks.

Abroad the situation was even worse. The only consolation was the article in the Treaty of Versailles that obliged the Germans to recognize the name of cognac. But even this relief was temporary. By the mid-1920s the Germans' financial problems were so severe that they would keep their purchases down for a generation. Elsewhere the prospects were almost unrelievedly gloomy. The Russian Revolution dealt a severe blow to the firms – especially Camus – which had specialized in sales there. A number of countries, Greece, Spain, Italy and Portugal among them, protected their local wine and spirits makers with heavy import duties. These were a crucial factor: exceptionally, the Egyptian market remained healthy because duties were low. But the habit of heavy import duties spread to Argentina, whose economy had, in any case, declined dramatically after the war. Indeed the market in much of Latin America suffered from a similar combination of economic misfortune and increased duties – a pattern which was to recur half a century later. In a few markets – such as Holland – a reduction in sales volume did not involve too great a loss in cash terms because imports were increasingly in bottles.

Duties were a perennial problem. Prohibition was a new terror. It wiped out the American market (although vast quantities were smuggled in through the tiny French-owned islands of St Pierre and Miquelon, south of Newfoundland). The custom spread to Canada and the Scandinavian countries. If sales were not totally forbidden, then they were channelled through state-run liquor boards with little interest in increasing sales. Their baleful influence can be felt to this day, although a small group of merchants – such as Tiffon and Larsen – have specialized successfully in supplying such markets. But the worst problem was in Britain. The merchants were still effectively on a 'sterling standard', since most of their costs, like transport and insurance, were payable in that currency. After the war the franc was weak, which vastly increased their costs. And in 1920 the British Government suddenly imposed an extra 33 per cent levy on imported spirits. The effect was so severe (revenue from customs' duties dropped by half despite the increased rate of duty) that the increase was soon withdrawn. But the damage was done: by 1923 even the Germans were buying more cognac than the British. In the years after the war their purchases were a mere sixth of the quantity they had taken in the golden days of Napoleon III, and under half of the less glorious days of Edward VII. Excise duties on all spirits had risen fivefold since 1914 and dashed any hope of a rebound after the duty increases were rescinded.

The mood in Cognac was naturally defensive. The most dramatic result was the agreement in 1922 between Martell and Hennessy effectively to divide up the world between them. They were already used to working together: since the mid-nineteenth century they had set an agreed price for the cognacs they bought from the growers, a lead that was followed by the rest of the trade. The families had, of course, been connected by marriage and friendship ever since the 1870s, but fears that one side or another would be dominant had prevented any formal business links. As we have seen (page 74), Maurice Hennessy's father spent most of his time in Paris, leaving his son alone in Cognac. The Martells became a second family to him: 'I spent weekends with them in their house near Royan,' he says. 'I had a room in their house. I remember leaving my gambling winnings in a drawer and finding them there untouched the following weekend. It was like home to me.' The dramatic drop in the British market altered all that. Maurice himself was in Bogotá at the time. He returned post-haste and talked his idea over with his friend, Paul Firino-Martell, who convinced his father and uncle of its soundness.

The agreement was formal, intended to last twenty-five years. Each side took substantial shareholdings in the other; they worked so closely that the post was opened in the same room. They then divided up the world between them. The Martells were allocated the crucial English market, which gave them an immense short-term advantage. The Hennessys retained their traditional Irish connection and in the longer term benefited greatly from the running start they enjoyed after the war in the Far East and the United States. (The partners did not actually prohibit sales in each other's territories. The Hennessys retained an agent in Britain, and in China, traditionally a Hennessy fief, the local agents got together in the 1920s to agree on a common price structure.) Between the wars both families had relinquished active management of their businesses. Maurice Fillioux's father, Raymond (who had worked for Jean Monnet for a time), was responsible for a great deal of the Hennessy business, while at Martell distant relations – MM. Castaing and Castillon – enjoyed a great deal of power.

The arrangement at least ensured the continuing supremacy of the two houses. In the 1920s, according to one authority, there were only 'two cognac firms of the first rank'.[1] Most of the others had suffered from one or other of the region's many problems. The Otards, for instance, had relied too heavily on the Latin American market. They had also got left behind. The last Otard, Marie-Thérèse, had married the Comte de Castellane, and they refused to change. Gerald de Ramefort put it bluntly: 'When their competitors began to sell their brandies in bottles under their own names, they did not follow the trend. "We are not grocers," they said loftily.'

Less aristocratic houses also suffered. In the mid-1920s Jean Monnet was called back to Cognac from Geneva, where he was the inspiration behind the fledgling League of Nations. As he wrote in his memoirs, 'At Cognac I found a situation which was financially bad and psychologically worse. No sooner had I arrived than I met a friend at the Café du Chalet. "I must

[1] Lys, *Le Commerce du Cognac.*

talk to you," he whispered, "not here, but round the corner." I had forgotten that side of life in the provinces. "It seems that you are going into liquidation," he whispered.' Monnet established himself in a delightful little house a few miles outside the town and analyzed the problem. It was simple enough: because Monnet's father believed in quality and loved good cognac, he had accumulated enormous stocks of old cognacs, which he could not sell at a time when the fashion was for young spirits. So sales and working capital were precariously low: 'You could go bankrupt in Cognac,' he wrote, 'despite having a good product and a well-respected brand name; it was enough to believe in what had always been, but was no longer true – the value of rarity and the danger of change. Many other firms were killed by their founders' obstinacy in preserving the practices that had earned them the esteem of a clientèle which was both small and sophisticated.' Monnet, anxious above all to prevent his father from suffering the same fate, arranged to

Rue Saulnier

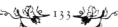

exchange some of his oldest cognacs for younger, more saleable spirits, which would not, however, damage the firm's reputation for quality.

As he admits, Monnet was lucky. His stay coincided with a temporary resurgence in the business, and he left a sound enough enterprise in the hands of his relations before returning to the wider world. But he, like everyone else, was on the defensive. They all retreated into their shells. The ablest of them all, the Delamains, had already made names for themselves as scholars, scientists and amateur archaeologists investigating the region's numerous remains. In the 1930s one brother, Maurice, became a well-known publisher; Jacques made his name as an orchidologist (many small French orchids bear the family's name); and Robert wrote the classic history of Cognac – a brilliant essay that largely ignores the commercial history in which his family played such a crucial role.

The only region where sales were showing signs of life was the Far East, particularly China and Japan. In his analysis of exports Jean Lys attributed the increase in sales to the fact that the local intelligentsia had returned from their education in France with a taste for the drink. Hennessy was the market leader (although much troubled by local imitations) and enjoyed considerable success with European expatriates as well as the locals. In 1921 Sincore & Co., the Harrods of Shanghai, was selling 500 cases of cognac a month, and M. Randon, their agent, was adjusting his prices to ensure that Chinese restaurateurs could afford to put two bottles of cognac on a table seating six or eight diners (he also gave regular gifts to the better-known night-club singers). But it was an outsider, Otto Quien, the local agent for Rémy Martin, who had the greatest effect. Rémy Martin had been founded early in the eighteenth century by two growers who built up a modest business, largely in anonymous cognacs sold in bulk. In 1910 a much more substantial grower, André Renaud, went into partnership with Paul Émile Rémy Martin II, and in 1924, exactly 200 years after the firm's foundation, bought up the firm completely. Quien, by contrast, was a truly international figure, half-Dutch, half-German, born in Shanghai and educated in Switzerland. As a young man he spent six months of every year in Indonesia (then the Dutch East Indies), working for an uncle who owned a major wines and spirits business with substantial sales throughout the Far East. Rémy Martin supplied the Quiens with cognacs, which they shipped mostly in cask, and in 1929 Otto Quien went to work for them, originally on a temporary basis. He persuaded Renaud not to sell, as previously, only Three-Star cognacs ('Special Quality' or 'St Rémy'), for he was probably the first person to realize that the Chinese were natural buyers of better-class cognacs. This perception led to Rémy's concentration on VSOP cognac from the Champagnes, a decision that was to have far-reaching consequences after the war.

With the end of prohibition and of the slump, there was some improvement in the 1930s, but the recovery was naturally aborted by the defeat of France in 1940. Nevertheless, Cognac suffered from the occupation less than almost any other area of France. At first the German forces – especially the Navy – confiscated any stocks they could lay their hands on, but order was restored with the arrival of a local commandant, Otto Klaebisch, a remarkable man who seemingly took neither pleasure nor personal profit from his powers – he did not even re-commandeer the property that his family had lost at the outbreak of the First World War. He was also an old friend of many of the merchants, for he had been educated in the local *lycée* when his family had been running Meukow. He was no Nazi and, as early as October 1940, foresaw Germany's fate. 'The worst thing that can happen to a man,' he told Maurice Hennessy, 'is to see his country defeated twice within a generation.' The only local firm that was in trouble was Courvoisier, liable to confiscation as enemy property, for it had been an English-registered company since the Simon brothers had taken it over. Two of the managers, George Hubert and Christian Braastad, calling themselves 'Hubert et Cie', bought the stocks and rented the name, using pre-dated documents. Unfortunately, eighteen months later the Germans found out and put in a sequestrator to run the company.

But the key figure of the occupation was Maurice Hennessy. He had only one eye, yet had somehow managed to become a pilot in the French Air Force and could have stayed in Britain after the fall of France. However, he returned home with one simple object: 'to try to safeguard our productive capacity, in the form of our vineyards, and our working tool, our stocks of cognac'. His basic strategy, as he explained it to his fellow merchants in 1941, was equally simple: 'We should think ourselves lucky if after the war we are in a position to start again.' He ensured that they all regarded the increasing volume of cognac they were forced to deliver to the Germans as 'a tribute imposed by the occupying power on a number of named persons of the occupied country. To keep to this definition of "tribute" the merchants were obliged to furnish supplies under a quota system decided in proportion to their previous volume of business, while no such obligations were imposed on the growers.'

The 'tribute' was enormous: 'In 1940,' said one observer, 'the Germans took two years' sales in four months.' The pace was sustained: over 8 million bottles in 1941, 6.5 million in 1942, nearly 8 million in 1943 and nearly 4 million in the few months of 1944 before Cognac was liberated (although the Cognacais now say that much of the 'tribute' was paid not in true cognac but in alcohol made from beetroots). The French market had soared to nearly 30 million bottles in 1941, a far higher figure than the pre-war record of 22 million bottles in 1935. Obviously, ordinary exports, which had been running at just under 15 million bottles during the pre-war years, dropped – to a mere couple of million by 1944 – but the region's financial and commercial structure remained intact, as the Germans paid handsomely for their purchases.

Maurice Hennessy had acted, nominally, as president of the town's Chamber of Commerce. He found a partner, Pierre Verneuil, among the growers. Together they used two mechanisms: the Comités d'Organisation pour Produits Alimentaires, designed to share out scarce foodstuffs, and the Bureau de Répartition, established to organize sales to the Germans. As in Champagne and Bordeaux, wartime hardships produced a new feeling of communal warmth between growers and merchants, last seen in Cognac in the equally hard times that had followed the phylloxera (Hennessy's partner was the son of the grower who had done so much to re-establish the Cognac vineyards). Although some of the greedier, or more pro-German, merchants wanted to sell more than their quota, the mechanism worked smoothly enough. In Hennessy's words: 'Thanks to the prevailing spirit of mutual understanding, if the merchants' stocks suffered considerably, those in the hands of the growers expanded so much that at the end of the war the working capital that the region had at its dispoal to take up its place in the world again was bigger, and indeed more usable, than that available in 1939.'

14 · Recovery

Physically Cognac was largely untouched by the war. The only air raids were aimed at the airfield at Châteaubernard to the south of the town, which was used by the *Luftwaffe*'s bombers attacking Allied convoys. Liberation – by the French themselves – came quickly and quietly in September 1944. It brought with it reprisals against those who were thought to have collaborated. These included members of the Jules Robin family. The once magnificent firm finally collapsed a few years later with the success of the Communist revolution in China and the loss of the firm's single most important market. It was taken over by Martell, a purchase that enabled Martell to round out its properties in the middle of the town. It now has its own 'compound', a jumble of distilleries, offices and *chais* between the town's main square (named after an earlier Martell) and the river.

But the day of Germany's surrender, 8 May 1945, was not one of undiluted rejoicing. That night there was a disastrous, unprecedentedly late frost, which reduced that year's crop to a mere 24,000 hectolitres, a quarter of even the reduced wartime level and one-fifth of the pre-war average of 120,000 hectolitres. Sales immediately soared once the war was over: whereas only 9 million bottles had been exported in 1945, 21 million bottles were sent abroad in 1946. Of these, 5.5 million went to the United States, nearly 4 million to Britain (and its still extensive empire) and a couple of million to Belgium, leaving only 8 million for the French themselves. Inevitably, the merchants had to draw on their stocks: by the end of 1946 they held only 260,000 hectolitres, three-quarters of their pre-war level. But because growers' stocks had doubled the total was virtually the same as in 1939. For the first time since the phylloxera era, the growers were able to finance stocks and were not forced to sell their spirit to the merchants as soon as it was distilled. The occupation had provided them with capital and hence confidence. This did not entirely suit Maurice Hennessy. As he wrote after the war: 'The risk [and, he implied, the profits] of stocking is one that is inherent in our trade'.

The growers' boldest move came in 1947 with the creation of the Prince Hubert de Polignac trademark. The Coopérative de Cognac had been set up in 1929 to resist the downward pressure on prices, and two years later the growers formed a business they called Unicoop to sell cognacs directly to buyers at home and abroad. Traditionally, the co-operatives had been confined to the outskirts of the Cognac region; they had been marginal. In the nineteenth century the growers had relied on the names of their general managers, M. Salignac and then M. Monnet, to sell their cognacs, and inevitably the firms had drifted away from the co-operative ideal. The use of the name of one of France's most distinguished families was a declaration that they were now in the mainstream. The Polignac brand name has enjoyed some success (especially in France), and the co-operatives are now the biggest single suppliers of 'buyers' own brands' for powerful clients like supermarkets.

The change in their fortunes gave the growers the confidence to maintain their war-time co-operation with the merchants, a link symbolized by the foundation of the Bureau National Interprofessionel de Cognac, the spirit's ruling body. Like similar bodies in Champagne and Bordeaux, it was the product of the initiative of a single merchant working with the growers more systematically, more closely and more personally than ever before. In Champagne Maurice Hennessy's role had been played by 'Bob' de Vogüe of Moët & Chandon, the initiator of what became the Comité Interprofessionel des Vins de Champagne (CIVC). Fernand Ginestet played a similar role in founding the CIVB in Bordeaux.

Like them, the BNIC could trace its origins back to an earlier, voluntary body without much power or influence – the Union de la Viticulture et du Commerce, founded in 1921. The Bureau National de Répartition had provided a much better model: it included two members each from the growers and the merchants and four nominated by central government. For eighteen months at the end of the war the fledgling BNIC was directly controlled by the Ministry of Agriculture, but it gained its independence in July 1946. It is an unusual animal, for, unlike its brethren elsewhere in France, it has official powers normally vested in central government officials.

Nevertheless, it was nearly still-born. The Cognacais voted to abolish the Bureau de Répartition, which had been responsible for disciplining the market, but a single voice rose up at the meeting saying simply that this move was ridiculous, that some other body would have to be found to do the same job. So the Cognacais became involved in the BNIC's creation, which owed a great deal to a former civil servant, Henri Coquillaud, then an Inspecteur Principal des Contributions Indirectes and therefore responsible for supervising the movement and taxation of cognac.[1]

Coquillaud could rely on the wartime team of Hennessy, Pierre Verneuil and Gaston Briand, two growers with tremendous authority over their thousands of individualistic peasant followers. The final constitution gave growers and merchants the real power: the central government's representatives have acted as observers rather than exercising the behind-the-scenes control usual in France. The Bureau was even endowed with its own source of finance, a 1 per cent levy on all sales. One maverick merchant mounted a lengthy delaying action over the Bureau's legal status. It was only confirmed in 1975.

The Bureau shares overall control with the Administration Fiscale, which polices the *appellation* and the quantities of brandy distilled by the *bouilleurs de cru*, and with the Inspecteurs des Fraudes, who test the qualities of the cognacs on sale. The Bureau itself is responsible for guaranteeing the age of the cognacs on offer (a demanding enough task for the Bureau de Contrôle et Interventions, which has only four inspectors to supervise nearly 3,000 *bouilleurs de cru*). Many of the home distillers have *alembics* of a mere couple of hectolitres, but if they want to modify their *chaudières*, they have to satisfy not only the BNIC and the Inspecteur des Fraudes but also the local representative of the Institut National des Appellations d'Origine, the otherwise all-powerful body that supervises all France's Appellation d'Origine Contrôllées (AOC). For the Bureau involves itself in everything connected with cognac: it supervises the labelling of cognacs, pays for the Station Viticole and runs excellent statistical and publicity departments.

Because the BNIC represented both growers and merchants it was a natural arbiter between the two in setting the prices to be paid for young cognacs. Martell and Hennessy's long-standing duopoly collapsed in 1954, and two years later the Bureau stepped in to try to establish a generally agreed price structure. Four years of squabbling ended only in 1960, when the Bureau was given

[1] His predecessor and the first director of the Bureau National, M. Louis-Miron, was originally a civil servant, an Inspecteur des Fraudes. It naturally suited the administration to have someone whom they could trust running such an unusual body.

wider powers. The result was a scale of *comptes*, from o and oo[1] for cognacs that had been made during the current distillation season up to Compte 5, brandies that were effectively five and a half years old because cognac's official year, the *Campagne*, starts on 1 September, five months after most distillation has been completed. Martell and Hennessy did not like the system but, like much of Cognac's new rule book, it merely confirmed ancient practice, including the price gap of 5–10 per cent between cognacs from the Grande Champagne, the Petite Champagne and the Borderies (normally priced together) and the different categories of Bois. By 1960 a marked distinction had emerged between the Champagnes and the Borderies, where the *bouilleurs de cru* distilled over half of the total, the Fins Bois, where they represented only one-quarter, and the lesser Bois where the co-operatives were dominant and individual *bouilleurs de cru* accounted for only one-tenth. Overall they were distilling only one-third of the total as against two-fifths at the end of the war. It took the BNIC until 1964 to confirm another usage: that Cognac should not include more than two parts per thousand of colouring matter and 2 per cent added sugar. With this amount of sugar in it the spirit is reduced to 38 per cent.

Although the age-grading system was extended in 1978 to include a Compte 6, it does not cover old cognacs. This enabled the BNIC to quash any pretence that a brand was a specific age; there were to be no more of those '100-year-old cognacs' beloved of the unscrupulous. But this still does not prevent the same merchants from making sometimes exaggerated claims for their pricier brands, often giving the impression that their contents come from casks kept for generations in ancestral vaults. To the BNIC the same rule implied that cognacs from a single year could not be sold to the public. This placed Cognac at something of a disadvantage by comparison with Armagnac, which benefits from a slightly less rigid system of control and can continue to sell single-vintage bottles. It also met with profound objections from those English merchants, and their traditional suppliers (such as Hine and Delamain), who were used to storing single-vintage cognacs for decades and selling them as such. (They can continue to do so but only in Britain.)

Martell and Hennessy had split seven years before their duopoly was broken. The corporate 'marriage' had always been personal, based on the mutual trust and affection binding one generation of both families. But Maurice Hennessy's closest friend, Maurice Firino-Martell (father of the present chairman, René Firino-Martell), had died. Maurice Hennessy was not willing or able to impose his policies on the younger cousins, like Killian Hennessy, waiting to take over, let alone on the even younger nephews, Gerald de Geoffre and Alain de Pracomtal, who were to guide the company through to the 1970s. So the agreement was not renewed at the end of its term in 1947 and the two were free to compete.[2]

Of course, the division had never been absolute: just before the war Maurice packed off his cousin, the Honourable Freddie,[3] to England to organize a more aggressive sales stance. Freddie

[1] Compte oo applies only to the small quantity of cognac distilled after 31 March in any given year. These late-distilled cognacs lose a year.

[2] Students of monopoly practices should note that the two companies have enjoyed much the same share of the world market, around 40 per cent, whether they have competed or not.

[3] He was more English than French. After the death of his grandfather, Richard Hennessy, his grandmother (herself born a Hennessy) had married Lord James Douglas-Hamilton, taking the children, George and Richard, with her to Scotland. George went into politics, became a Member of Parliament and was ennobled as Lord Windlesham.

proved a worthy scion of the family, shrewd and amiable, and his efforts were part of a process that ended Martell's dominance of what was still cognac's biggest single market. After the war Martell enjoyed an unbelievable 80 per cent share there. It is now nearer 30 per cent, lower than Hennessy's stake in the now much larger American market.

In Cognac, as in most of the rest of the world, the outlook immediately after the war seemed grey, for no one foresaw the prosperity of the 1950s and 1960s. Even Maurice Hennessy was a prisoner of the past. The 1945 frost, he wrote, had 'negated a four-year effort which had succeeded in considerably increasing the reserves of cognac sleeping in our *chais*'. Even when these had been reconstituted, the outlook was bleak. He believed that the immediate post-war surge in the demand for cognac came partly from the markets deprived of scotch, which would return to the pre-war allegiance as soon as they could. In France itself the retail price, inflated by taxes as well as the distribution process, was double that paid to the merchants. Hennessy was mortally afraid of such inflation. His dearest wish had always been that cognac should be regarded as an everyday drink of moderate price and not reserved for a few well-heeled connoisseurs. 'But the cost of cultivating an hectare of vines has risen so high because of the inflation of the past few years that we must fear for the future of our outlets.' Hennessy was thinking largely of the United States, once a major market, buying 200,000 cases in 1914. Prohibition killed all that, and the recovery was aborted by the war. And, indeed, in the 1950s it

Maurice Hennessy, niece Catherine and grandson Jack

was scotch, not cognac, that took the fancy of the average American. Cognac's sales remained limited to well-heeled connoisseurs, although this limitation did not matter for a generation after the war as the traditional clientele prospered. But Hennessy's pessimism was unfounded: sales even in the United States more than doubled in the 1950s, and their value nearly quadrupled. The Cognacais hired a New York public relations outfit headed by Edward Gottlieb, a pilot effort for the Cognac Bureaux later established in a number of major markets. Gottlieb's efforts were imaginative and far-reaching. He lobbied groups of potential buyers, like the Physicians' Wine Appreciation Society; he published three booklets on cooking in which cognac featured prominently; he produced an embarassingly named but indubitably successful promotional film, *Fun at the Chafing Dish*; and he ensured that the drink was frequently mentioned in the smarter magazines – orthodox enough public relations techniques but markedly more sophisticated than the efforts of any other French exporters at the time. In the long term the combination of price and his campaigns preserved cognac's up-market image, which was to to serve it well in the 1970s when most scotch became a mere commodity.

By then cognac was coming to the end of twenty-five years of almost continuous boom. The first fifteen years after the war were devoted largely to the reconquest of traditional markets. Britain (where sales trebled) and the United States took 40 per cent of a total that doubled in the late 1940s and 1950s. but there was clearly scope in non-traditional markets: in 1958–9 Denmark still took more than West Germany and Ireland took more than Italy or the Netherlands. Within France itself cognac made steady progress. It was still a luxury drink, so the steady reduction in the sale of spirits in bars – which permanently reduced the sale of rum – was more than counterbalanced by the natural rise in demand as the country grew more prosperous. The Cognacais were also helped by the gradual suppression of the rights of the *bouilleurs de cru*. Until the 1950s millions of them were allowed to distil up to 10 hectolitres of alcohol, ostensibly for their own use. In reality half their production – up to 40 million bottles annually – trickled out to families, to friends and to small cafés all over the country. These home brews had been major competitors to the cheaper cognacs.

The biggest beneficiary from the controls imposed on the *bouilleurs de cru* was Courvoisier. Its surge in the 1950s was inspired by Christian Braastad, from a talented Norwegian family that had settled in Jarnac. (One of the family married a Mademoiselle Delamain: their son, Alain, runs the firm today.) Braastad continued to promote the firm's connection with Napoleon (complete with a new type of frosted bottle) but otherwise broke completely with tradition. He promoted exports vigorously, but not to the detriment of the French market – where the firm is still number two to Martell. They are the only two brands seen in virtually every retail outlet in France. Above all, he did not hold much stock. He bought as and when required, often using brokers, the *courtiers* so famous in Bordeaux but largely ignored in Cognac because of the historical direct links between growers and merchants. Braastad's strategy worked brilliantly – for a time. But then the success, not only of his own firm but of the region as a whole, caught up with him. World sales had risen to 58 million bottles annually, and production simply could not keep pace. In 1946 stocks had represented six years' sales. By the end of the 1950s they were down to less than four years' requirements. By the early 1960s Courvoisier was caught with its stocks down, desperately needing a substantial injection of capital to build them up. In the past such a crisis had inevitably spelled the end of such a challenge to Martell and Hennessy. But new players from all over the world were eager to participate in such a healthily-growing business.

15 · Greed

Rémy Martin was the first house to express an interest in Courvoisier. But in 1963 the Simons' heirs sold the firm to the Canadian liquor group, Hiram Walker. The takeover was logical, for in the 1960s Cognac seemed a desirable place for investment. The decade saw an explosion of demand unprecedented since the golden days of Napoleon III and based on markets far wider than those of a century earlier. Sales in all cognac's traditional markets, including France, doubled without any dilution of its reputation for quality, and a new group of countries emerged as major markets.

The reduction of duties that followed the Treaty of Rome had an immediate effect. By the end of the 1960s the five other countries of the original Common Market accounted for nearly half Cognac's exports, a 10 per cent increase in market share during a decade when sales everywhere else were also rising. Sales in Germany, a mere 2.3 million bottles in the late 1950s, had jumped more than threefold in the decade. (These figures did not include half as much again of the young cognacs used to fortify local spirits.) By 1970 Germany had temporarily replaced the United States as Cognac's biggest market.

But the biggest surprise came in the East. Sales to Hong Kong rose nearly five times; by 1970 the Chinese there had become by far the biggest consumers of cognac per head in the world. Japan tried hard to keep cognac out by imposing duties of more than 200 per cent; but nevertheless it was almost as good a market as Hong Kong. But there was a difference between the two markets. The 'overseas Chinese' – those in Singapore, Malaysia and, later, Thailand as well as in Hong Kong – were interested only in the best cognacs. They allegedly thought of them as aphrodisiacs (whereas scotch, it was said, was supposed to induce impotence). They treated cognac as a drink to be taken not in sips after meals but in decent-sized glasses with their food. Rémy Martin had a head-start because of Otto Quien's pioneering efforts, but other houses were not far behind. By 1970 cognac was France's single biggest export to Singapore.

The Japanese were more cautious: they bought mostly bulk cognac. But this was an exception. Only a few other markets (mainly the Scandanavian state monopolies) retained the habit of buying in bulk. Their purchases had represented one-third of total exports in 1950 but accounted for only one-fifth twenty years later. A vicious price war broke out, in which the co-operatives were largely victorious, so houses such as Hardy and Tiffon, which had relied on selling brandy in bulk, were forced to sell under their own names, sometimes for the first time and inevitably at a major disadvantage compared with better-known rivals.

But there were opportunities to grow fast. Because the Japanese, in particular, were allowed to import 3 litres of spirits duty-free, a substantial proportion of sales in the Far East were made through the duty-free shops. This gave a major opportunity to Camus, 'la Grande Marque', an old firm which had nearly gone out of business just after the war, so that its owner, Michel Camus, had to start effectively from scratch. He was both clever and lucky. In 1961, two young American graduates of the hotel school at Cornell University foresaw that duty-free sales would be a growing market. Their firm, Duty Free Shoppers, acquired the concessions for virtually every airport in the Pacific Basin. Originally they were aiming at American servicemen returning from tours of duty in the Pacific. The major houses refused them credit, but Michel Camus, anxious to rebuild his firm, agreed to let them pay when they could. The result was an enormously successful partnership as the number of Japanese travelling abroad multiplied. Camus devised his own brands for the market, notably 'Célébration', launched in 1963. This was largely composed of three- to ten-year-old cognacs from the Bois but was promoted as superior to the average Three-Star (he later reinforced the image with a Napoleon).

Most of the many bids for cognac firms involved total takeovers by major liquor groups. These increasingly felt obliged to establish themselves wherever spirits were produced. Hiram Walker's arrival was a signal that Cognac was no longer a backwater but was about to become one of the battlegrounds on which the world's liquor giants were fighting. The Courvoisier precedent looked promising enough: although the extra capital from Hiram Walker enabled the firm to build up excess stocks at the wrong time when the market broke in the early 1970s, the connection had helped Courvoisier to maintain its sales momentum throughout the 1960s, as did the formation of a distribution company in England, J. R. Philips, owned jointly by two of Britain's biggest brewery groups, Allied Breweries and Whitbread. By the early 1970s Courvoisier was almost as big as Martell in Britain and in 1973 actually sold more bottles wordwide than anyone else in Cognac.

Many local firms welcomed outside help. They required more capital or – the classic reason for a takeover in France – there was an *indivision de famille*: French inheritance laws ensure that, over the generations, shares in a family property fall into the hands of many heirs, who may be totally uninterested in the business. The bidders came from all over the world. Some of them made quiet, small-scale investments: Martini & Rossi bought Barriasson, Gaston de Lagrange and a substantial stake in Otard; Jean Monnet's family firm was bought by the German firm Scharlachberg; the apéritif firm Berger bought Gauthier; Bénédictine bought Comandon and Denis Mounié (which it subsequently resold); and the Spanish sherry house of Domecq did the same with Lucien-Foucauld.

But some of the newcomers made a bigger splash. In 1967 the heirs to M. Laporte-Dubouché sold Bisquit to Pernod-Ricard. M. Ricard, who had built up his fame and fortune selling *pastis*, confidently indulged in by far the biggest single piece of capital investment since the Martells had constructed their mighty 'brandy factory' in the 1880s. He bought the Château de Lignières, an enormous property in the Fins Bois north-east of Rouillac and turned it into a magnificent sight: hillsides of uniformly regimented vines on a scale unique in the region. At the Château he built Cognac's first, and to this date only, industrial-sized distillery, with 56 stills in gleaming rows. Aiming at another blow at tradition, he then transferred Bisquit's stocks from their traditional resting place by the river at Jarnac and lodged them in the newly built warehouses on the same site. He was confident that he could sell the increased production through his firm's incomparable domestic sales force and by aggressive selling abroad. By the early 1970s Bisquit, like Courvoisier, was a major force in the Three-Star market.

Sam Bronfman, the former bootlegger who had built Seagram's into the world's biggest hard-liquor business, adopted an altogether subtler approach. In the 1960s he had revolutionized the world's scotch whisky market with Chivas Regal. He had bought and stored a wide range of excellent scotches for ten or more years and then blended them into a new 'de luxe blend'. Chivas was an instant and lasting success. So it was natural for Bronfman to try and repeat the trick with cognac. Having failed in his attempts to buy Martell, Courvoisier and Bisquit, he turned to the natural vehicle for his scheme, Augier, the oldest firm in Cognac. The partnership was an unlikely one: Jacques de Varenne of Augier is related to the Hennessys (and is one of Maurice Hennessy's closest friends), a descendent of most of the leading names in the town's history, a delightful, wry, aristocratic figure. Bronfman was a brilliant thug. They got on like a house on fire. Bronfman wanted quality; Augier was happy to sell control of his firm and to spend five years buying enough old cognacs to be ready to launch the cognac equivalent to Chivas Regal, which might have had as beneficial an effect on the whole cognac market in the 1970s as Chivas had on scotch in the 1960s. But, sadly, 'Mr. Sam' died in 1972, before the launch, and his sons did not want to pursue their late father's ideas. The stocks were dispersed, and while Seagram kept Augier, it has apparently lost interest in the firm, and its sales have remained minimal. (Seagram has preferred to launch a cognac bearing the name of Mumm, a leading champagne firm it owns).

The fashion was catching, and in 1971 Distillers, the world's largest scotch distillers, bought the family house of Hine. For a few years Hine drifted but has now regained its former high reputation, largely because the cousins, Jacques and Bernard Hine, stayed on, and Bernard still supervises the buying and blending.

The takeovers inevitably forced Hennessy and Martell to think about their future. Martell decided it could remain independent. But the shareholdings within the Hennessy family were more dispersed, and the two oldsters, Kilian and Maurice Hennessy, did not feel there were enough members of the younger generation available to run the company. A natural partner was Moët & Chandon, another family-owned business in the luxury drinks business, which was already quoted on the Paris Bourse; the merger enabled those members of the Hennessy family who wanted to sell to do so.

These capitalist manoeuvres merely compounded the pressure from the trade, through the BNIC, for increased plantings. In France, especially in regions governed by the AOC regulations, any additional acreage is a matter for prolonged argument, since the *droit de plantation* (right to plant) is a valuable asset. For several generations cognac had been a relatively unprofitable business; as a result, the area planted with vines had remained virtually stationary, at just over 60,000 hectares, between 1940 and 1959. That year 2,000 additional hectares were authorized, another 11,000 in 1962, a further 10,000 in 1970 and the same acreage two years later. By 1971 the area actually under vines had jumped by over one-third to 86,000, and much more had been authorized. Production in the 1970s was bound to rise substantially, after the new vines of three years old and more had began to contribute to the production of cognac.

Production rose even faster than acreage. Better clones of St-Émilion vines, better cultivation, more fertilizer, better insecticides, meant that yields rose from an average of 50 hectolitres of wine per hectare in the late 1950s to 90 ten years later. (The peaks were 124 hectolitres per hectare in 1970 and 149 three years later. At that level each hectare was producing enough cognac to fill nearly 1,000 bottles).

The average quality was also increasing, for growers in the lesser *crus* could transfer their rights to plant. Between 1965 and 1972 the Bons Bois and Bois Ordinaires transferred an extra 1,700 hectares to the nobler *crus*, on top of the new plantings. Despite the apparent generosity of the allocations, the BNIC was under considerable pressure. It had to be seen to be fair to the existing growers, but the average age in the countryside was increasing rapidly, so it naturally wanted to encourage *jeunes agriculteurs*. It also had to try to find some land for the *pieds noir*, the French settlers returning from newly independent North African countries bringing with them some capital and much more expertise in wine making.

The authorities were unable to change the structure of the region. Holdings continued to be tiny – only 3,500 out of 30,000 were larger than 5 hectares. Even in the late 1970s two-thirds of the cognac vineyard belonged to growers owning between 3 and 15 hectares of vines. The BNIC also had to allow for the market projections indicating an increased demand for better cognacs. As a result, the Fin Bois (which received half the new acreage) and the Petite Champagne (which received one-fifth) benefited most. Nevertheless, everyone was left unsatisfied. Another complication was that by 1970 over three-fifths of the cultivable land within the Grande Champagne and the Borderies was covered with white wine grapes. Inevitably, some of the new plantations were in unsuitable soils. In the Grande Champagne vines were planted in the clayey flood plain of the Charente, a stretch that peasant wisdom had kept vine-free through the ages. In the Petite Champagne some magnificent chestnut woods growing on stony clays were uprooted to make way for yet more vines. Seeing the spread of vines to unsuitable soils within the Grande Champagne, the growers from the Archiac area, famously the best in the Petite Champagne, appealed to the INAO for re-classification. The INAO was not unwilling to help, but local pressure prevented any revision of boundaries.

The surge in production left a great many growers heavily indebted. They all wanted to continue to distil the vastly increased quantities of wines they were producing – indeed, the capacity of the *chaudières* owned by the *bouilleurs de cru* jumped by a half between 1966 and 1973, although only to 13 hectolitres, and many of them were buying second-hand. An ambitious grower (and there were many) could spend FF80,000 on an *alembic* holding 15 hectolitres; a tractor and its attachments cost FF70,000; and vats and equipment cost another FF80,000. At the same time many of the growers were converting their *alembics* to gas, another heavy capital expenditure. At the time the investments seemed profitable enough, for incomes were rising as never before. The cash yield per hectare of vines tripled to nearly FF23,000 between 1959 and 1973, with the Fins Bois doing almost as well as the nobler *crus*.

With prosperity came greed. In the words of Gerald de Geoffre, who succeeded his uncle, Maurice Hennessy, as the merchants' chief representative on the BNIC, 'Inevitably, between 1965 and 1973 the growers got into the habit of assuming that everything they produced would go for distillation at steadily rising prices. Although production in those years never actually fell below consumption, prices were rising more than they were paying in interest to the Crédit Agricole, so they were naturally unwilling to sell to us.' The Bureau National reckoned that prices rose only 10 per cent annually through the late 1960s, but, as a study by the Banque de France showed, cognacs kept during the crucial years from 1967 to 1973 could double or triple in value.

Nevertheless, the stock level had stabilized. Courvoisier's crisis marked the low point: in 1961–2 stocks were less than three and a half years' sales. During the rest of the decade they struggled upwards to stay at a little over four years'. The *bouilleurs de cru* managed to hang on to the advantage they had gained during the war. Together with the co-operatives (whose stocks attained prominence only in the late 1960s), they still held over one-third of the total in 1970 (a fall of only 3 per cent since 1946 and a rise of 300,000 hectolitres to 473,000 hectolitres, enough to fill 67 million bottles). But stocks were dangerously concentrated on younger spirits. Stocks of cognacs more than five years old increased less than one-fifth between 1948 (when they represented nearly half the total) and 1972 (when they constituted a mere one-sixth). Not surprisingly, pressure continued for even more acreage to be planted. The BNIC's apparently sober forecasts showed no real improvement in stock levels through most of the 1970s.

The peaceful prosperity of the late 1960s was broken by the 'cognac war', a farcical enough affair but one with extensive repercussions within the Cognac community. It originated in the sales policy of that maverick insider Rémy Martin, selling, then as now, only cognacs from the Champagnes and, until recently, nothing under a VSOP. Rémy's rise had been stunningly swift. It dates from the end of the war, when André Renaud[1] was joined by his elder son-in-law, André Hériard-Dubreuil, a *polytechnicien* and thus the first member of the French intellectual élite ever to be involved in the cognac business. Rénaud's younger daughter – who inherited just under 50 per cent of the shares when her father died in 1965 – had married M. Max Cointreau, of the family liqueur firm. Even before the marriage the friendship between the two families ensured that Rémy Martin was able to use the Cointreaus' international distribution network. But the Hériard-Dubreuils have never allowed the minority shareholders any say in running the business, and the Cointreaus' resentment has led to a lengthy legal war between the in-laws. In the 1960s Rémy became a cult both in traditional markets and in the Far East, thanks to the pioneering efforts of Otto Quien and a later, equally legendary salesman, Nik Schuman, a Dutchman who was as lean and weather-beaten as a first mate out of Conrad. In the 1960s Hériard-Dubreuil had naturally pressed the case for the growers in the Champagnes to be allocated a greater acreage of the new plantings. He had also paid substantially more for their cognacs than had Martell or Hennessy, always worried by any shift in the balance of power towards the growers.

The Rémy threat was not only commercial, for Martell and Hennessy had founded their fame and fortune on two rather distinct types of cognac, the basic Three-Star, and superior brandies, like Hennessy's XO and the Cordon Bleu that Martell introduced between the wars. To them the whole idea of VSOP was inevitably an unhappy compromise. Moreover, because they knew and appreciated the Borderies, they were extremely reluctant to sell any cognac (apart from the very oldest) purely from the Champagnes. So in late 1970 Martell, Hennessy and Courvoisier took the offensive: they decided to omit the words 'Fine Champagne' from their labels, claiming that the quality of cognacs from the Champagnes had greatly deteriorated. Rémy Martin had always featured Fine Champagne on virtually all its labels, from its VSOP up to its XO, and the decision provided Hériard-Dubreuil with an immediate and unrivalled opportunity to emphasize the superiority of the name. He resigned as president of the Syndicat des Exportateurs which included the eleven most important firms in the business, and was followed by Otard and two lesser houses, Boulestin and Gaston de la Grange. His act, he explained, was 'to protest against the efforts of the Big Three to disgrace and to standardize their unique product. Cognac's policy ought to be to increase the product's value in order to reward the growers.' To emphasize his point, the three firms set up their own group, Syndicat Tradition et Qualité. This was music to the ears of the growers in the Champagnes, afraid of domination by the permanent majority enjoyed within the growers' 'college' by the lesser breeds from the Bois (two years earlier the Champenois had set up a joint company, Champaco, to hold stocks of their precious cognacs).

[1] He himself was also a son-in-law. He had married Mademoiselle Frapin and thus had access to her family's magnificent stocks of cognacs from the family's estate, the largest in the Grande Champagne. The Frapin firm (and its stocks) are now owned by Madame Cointreau.

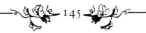

*André Hériard-
Dubreuil and family*

The newspapers seized on the *guerre de cognac* with great glee. Poor Coquillaud, the director of the BNIC who had tacitly encouraged the reformers, made matters worse with a bland declaration: 'There is no cognac war and one is inconceivable ... What they are trying to say is that there is only one good cognac, Fine Champagne. That's ridiculous and could even become dangerous.' The mayors of the canton of Segonzac, the heart of the Grande Champagne, immediately protested, and the 3,750 growers from the Champagnes walked out of the growers' Federation. Individual growers went even further; they assumed the whole thing was a plot, with the BNIC in league with Martell, Hennessy and Courvoisier. To them it was no accident that the BNIC had awarded a prize to a detective thriller in which the author used the word *alcool* to describe the word cognac.

The three major firms counter-attacked, writing to the papers to refute suspiciously similar articles that all represented Rémy's point of view. Their only weapons were facts: that the words 'Fine Champagne' provided absolutely no guarantee of quality; that Rémy represented under 5 per cent of the total sales of cognac; and that the 'Big Three' far from despising or neglecting Champagne cognacs, had the first choice among them and regularly bought 70 per cent of the total. Their protest was in vain: even the normally level-headed *l'Exprés* painted the contrast as 'on one side industry, on the other craftmanship, art indeed'.

The association with the art form of cognac was even more useful for Otard, which did not enjoy the same worldwide reputation for quality as Rémy Martin. It seized the opportunity to

launch its own Fine Champagne, Baron Otard. Rémy Martin and Otard, said its export director loftily in an interview with a Canadian paper, 'refuse to degrade their cognacs. We believe in a certain code of quality and honour. The good name of France itself is at stake, and the house of Otard, which honours this name in fifty-four countries, will not lower its flag of high quality.'

The war was clear evidence of a breakdown in the consensus that had governed Cognac since the war. It was partly a matter of generations. Hennessy and Verneuil had retired without leaving successors who enjoyed the same moral authority. The only local political figure with enough stature to act as mediator, Felix Gaillard, a former Prime Minister, had died in the mid-1960s. The gap remained unfilled, and relations between different classes of growers (and between them and the merchants, themselves now divided into three groups) were strained even before the crisis of the 1970s. In the short term the war was clearly too damaging to the image of cognac to be allowed to continue – in public anyway. Within a few months a truce was declared. Both sides promised to keep mum, and the major firms abandoned their original idea and kept Fine Champagne on their labels where appropriate. Since sales were rising at about 20 per cent annually at the time, no one felt that the episode had done any permanent harm. But it had: greed had weakened the unity forged in slump and war. As Claude Belot, a radical local professor, wrote in 1973: 'It is undeniable that in the last few years something has changed in this region of ours, which was so cautious for so long.'[1]

[1] In *Norois*, 1973.

16 · Nemesis

Maurice Hennessy had always worried that cognac was considered a luxury, and one that had proved only too dispensable in earlier slumps: hence the hope he expressed just after the war that cognac would be regarded as a normal article of consumption for ordinary people. His hopes seemed ridiculous, his fears groundless, in the euphoria of the 1960s. They seemed painfully relevant during the decade after the first oil shock of 1973.

The warning signs were already visible. Between 1971 and 1973 exports remained virtually stationary at around 90 million bottles, a level they did not reach again for five years. It was no consolation that all purveyors of alcohol were in much the same predicament; that in the 1970s much of the world's disposable income was diverted to teetotal Muslims. In fact, cognac did proportionately better than most other spirits: the volume of exports did rise, albeit only by one-quarter, in the eight years after the first oil shock, and inflation ensured that they more than doubled in value. The problem, as elsewhere, was that expectations had been aroused and production and stocks geared to a more buoyant rhythm. Inevitably, the decade was one of crisis, economic and social. And because of the forces let loose in the previous years, the Cognacais could not face their new problems with the same solidarity they had found when invaded by phylloxera or the Germans.

With declining sales came increased competition. The home market encapsulated all the problems. Taxes quadrupled between 1973 and 1983 to reach 28 francs a bottle, four times the cost of the wine required to make the cognac itself. Not surprisingly, sales have never regained the level of 18 million bottles reached in 1971 – ten years later they were down by over 25 per cent. They have suffered, like those of every other spirit, from the ravages made by scotch, whose sales trebled in the same period. The French market has always been fragmented. The two leaders are still Martell and Courvoisier, but they share only one-quarter of it. Hennessy had benefited from the link-up with Moët & Chandon, and Bisquit from Pernod's hard sell. The supermarkets now all have their own brands – which are sometimes more profitable for suppliers because the shops often use the better-known brands as barely profitable promotional items.

Modern marketing does not vary a great deal from country to country, so, not surprisingly, the French situation found a number of echoes in Britain, where sales bobbed around, depending on the state of the economy. A particular British twist came with a reversion to an old habit – the search for a cheaper substitute. In the nineteenth century British brandy had provided the alternative: in the 1970s French grape brandy, usually sold by one of the major cognac houses, was the threat. Brandies as a whole kept their share of the spirits market, but grape brandies took one-third of the total. Despite continuous promotional efforts, the market remained stratified in its historic pattern: Martell was favoured among the elderly and in the Midlands; Hennessy was strong in the north of England; and Rémy Martin was well established among the young and in London and the south-east of England. Characteristically, Courvoisier, which does not aim to be number one in any individual market, is number two over virtually the whole country.

The same rhythm applied in all the other markets so carefully nurtured during the previous generation. Virtually everywhere in Europe sales peaked in the early 1970s and drifted, gently but increasingly unprofitably, afterwards. Martell, Hennessy, Courvoisier and Rémy Martin waged a worldwide war which left none of the profitable little niches formerly available for ambitious smaller firms. There are still a few quirks. The lower end of the Dutch market is dominated by the local firm, Joseph Guy, a subsidiary of Bols. But then the Dutch have curious habits. They drink a great deal of a lethal-sounding liquid called Vieux, a spirit of varying origins by no means made necessarily from wine. Greek *eau-de-vie* is a major constituent of a drink that the Dutch called 'cognac' until the EEC stopped them.

During the 1970s Cognac was saved from collapse largely by the steady growth in the American market, which nearly trebled to over 70 million bottles, half as much again as the quantity sold in Britain or France. Until the 1970s the cognac habit had been confined largely to the East Coast. It steadily 'went national' during the decade, although New York continued to take nearly one-tenth of the total. A major, and still unexplained, boost came with vastly increased consumption by the black community – in 1980 the depressed, but largely black city of Detroit, one-quarter the size of New York, drank two-thirds as much cognac. This ethnic predisposition to brandy attracted all sorts of explanations. The most vivid, libellous and unreliable vignette is of black – not white – drug dealers carrying half-bottles in their hip-pockets to make 'black-smack', cognac and cocaine.

Inevitably, marketing efforts were concentrated on the United States. Rémy Martin even introduced a VS quality both in Britain and in the United States.[1] It spent lavishly, up to $2 a bottle, on advertising. Martell was originally reluctant to lay out the vast sums required but, to its great benefit, was eventually persuaded to do so by its importers, another respected, family-owned spirits business, Brown-Forman, famous for Jack Daniel. Nevertheless, Hennessy actually increased its traditional lead. The family had established agents in Boston, Philadelphia and New Orleans before the end of the eighteenth century and had spread the cognac message up the Mississippi in the 1860s. Before 1914 it had half the market and has since managed to recover that position. It had the same agent, Schieffelin, from the beginning; and the advantage of size was evident when in 1981 Moët-Hennessy took over Schieffelin.

Inevitably, the Cognacais were vulnerable to the waves of protectionism induced by the slump. In the 1960s they had merely been annoyed when the famous 'chicken war', between the Americans and the Common Market resulted in discriminatory tariffs. The increase in duties imposed as part of President Nixon's austerity package in August 1971 hit them much harder. For they were helpless in the face of international trends, even after François Mitterrand, son of a local vinegar maker (his sister is a *bouilleur de cru*), was elected President in 1981. That same year their most profitable and thirstiest market, Hong Kong, dealt them another blow. The watch makers of the Jura were in danger of extinction, partly because of cheap imports from Hong Kong. When the French imposed import restrictions, some of the leaders of the Chinese community in Hong Kong tried to persuade their countrymen to forswear cognac. In the end the boycott failed, but the political traumas of the next year led to an alarming temporary slump all the same.

Not surprisingly, the Cognacais follow every wrinkle of the debate over Hong Kong's future,

[1] The star system had become so devalued – Salignac even had a Five-Star – that the Cognacais substituted the VS label to try to associate their cheaper brandies with the VSOP quality.

for the 'overseas Chinese' now account for a quarter of world sales and Japan for another 5 per cent. The capitalist economies of the Far East have survived successive oil shocks better than the Europeans and have been able to continue to indulge their taste for the better things in life. But all these markets are divided up between the Big Four, Martell, Hennessy, Rémy Martin and Courvoisier. The only outlet where an outsider has a major position is in the duty-free trade, where Camus has retained its importance.

Japan is the only market where bulk sales still matter.[1] The sensible Orientals concentrate on better-class spirits, as do the million or more Japanese who swarm into Hong Kong's duty-free shops. This helps Rémy, which has nearly half the Japanese 'quality' market, and works against Hennessy, which dominates the Three-Star market and was slow to introduce better cognacs into the Far East in the 1970s. It is now making something of a comeback, thanks to its XO – a particularly good seller in that intriguing new market, Communist China. Firms now create new brands, like Martell's Cordon Noir and Exshaw's Age d'Or, purely for Hong Kong. Martell even had to produce a Napoleon for the oriental duty-free market.

All this talk about international trends, new brands and market shares was a far remove from Hériard-Dubreuil's presentation of his firm's cognac as an 'art form', but it was the logical consequence of the corporate activities of the 1960s. Cognac was now largely (though never merely) one aspect of the international spirits business, which itself was increasingly polarized between a handful of international giants and a few highly respected specialists. This brought some advantages for a company like Hine, which could rely on the agents that distributed brands like Johnny Walker, also owned by Distillers. Courvoisier was less lucky. It found that it was stronger than its parent in many markets. Pernod-Ricard was not big enough to play in the same league. Moët-Hennessy could compete; so could Martell and Rémy Martin, although they had to go it alone, relying on their names, their products and an increasing ruthlessness with their distribution arrangements. In some countries they have their own subsidiaries; in others they have arrangements hallowed through the years, like Martell's association with Matthew Clark in Britain. Rémy Martin was always prepared to be rougher. In Germany, where it was number one, it nevertheless abandoned a long-standing relationship with a local importer and established a wholly-owned subsidiary. All four followed corporate fashion and diversified. Moët-Hennessy led the way. By now it is a star in the French multinational firmament, investing in a major winery project in California and in roses to add to Dior perfumes (a development that could help enormously in producing better clones of vines). Martell, typically was more cautious. But it is now quoted on the Paris Bourse and thus open to external pressures. It too bought a perfume company, as well as Janneau, one of the leading brands of Armagnac. Rémy Martin set up a successful vineyard, Château Rémy, in Australia. In France it bought control of De Luze, a leading Bordeaux shipper, Krug, which enjoyed an even better reputation in Champagne than Rémy did in Cognac, and Nicolas, most famous of Parisian wine merchants. In California it has an ambitious joint venture making double-distilled 'alembic brandy' – mostly from the Colombard grape – in conjunction with Schramsberg, makers of California's best sparkling wines.

The growers naturally looked askance at these corporate manoeuvrings. As they saw it, the Big Four were no longer concerned primarily to sell their products. Their own opinion, that they needed these new weapons to help sell cognac, was not going to cut any ice with the growers. Yet

[1] These are still falling as a proportion of total sales. Only Japan and Germany take any real quantities. Anti-alcohol campaigners have further restricted the traditional Scandinavian markets.

the Big Four controlled 80 per cent of cognac's total sales and thus decided the livelihoods not only of 6,000 direct employees but of 29,000 growers and their families as well. But the growers were caught in a web of increasing financial commitments, and in any case the 'cognac war' had divided them.

So they were helpless. All the merchants had to retrench, and the easiest way was to reduce their commitments to the *bouilleurs de cru*. Hennessy and Martell merely cut down the amounts they took from 'their' growers, but other firms (notably Bisquit) had to cancel some of their contracts, and by the end of the decade even the *bouilleurs'* old friend Rémy Martin had let them down. For five years it had comfortably bucked the general trend; exports multiplied over four times between 1974 and 1982 to reach FF646 million, 95 per cent of total turnover. So Rémy Martin had continued to increase purchases of wines or brandies by up to 20 per cent every year. The inevitable slow-down was made more abrupt because of the family problem. The minority shareholders, M. and Mme Cointreau, were clearly not going to subscribe to a capital increase while they were denied any say in the running of the company. So Rémy, like the growers, had to rely increasingly on expensive bank borrowings.

These were inevitable as stocks accumulated with frightening rapidity – from just over four years' sales in 1973 to over seven years' four years later. The trade managed to shift the burden to the growers (who enjoyed relatively cheap loans through the Crédit Agricole). Between 1973 and 1982 total stocks rose by just over one-third to over 2.75 million hectolitres. In the late 1970s, for the first time in a century, the growers actually had more cognac in stock than the trade.

The problem was worst in the Fins Bois, which alone had over one-third of all the stocks in growers' hands – moreover, these may turn out to be particularly unsaleable, since the growers do not have the same tradition of reserving their best brandies for themselves as their fellows in the Champagnes. All over Cognac, as the stocks got bigger, their average age increased. Of the extra 1 million hectolitres accumulated between 1973 and 1982, 700,000 hectolitres were over five years old. Many of the growers are merely holding on to thousands of casks of mediocre spirit that was never very saleable and is never going to improve greatly.

They received some help from ORECO, Coquillaud's idea of a co-operative organization to stock surplus brandies. He had founded it while still director of the BNIC, but no funds were available. However, it now stores 28,000 hectolitres, bought from 12,000 growers. These stocks are financed at special rates through the Banque de France and stored in buildings all over Cognac (including the Maison de la Gabelle in the rue Saulnier). Coquillaud has also launched SIDECO, which provides finance for buying and selling cognacs on extended terms. The merchants did not escape the burden: they now have to buy 10 per cent more stock than they sell in the course of a year – an obligation that obviously weighs particularly heavy on the smaller concerns. The same sort of pressure was being felt by the *bouilleurs de profession*, subject to a squeeze by the bigger firms.

But these two measures were merely palliatives in the 1970s. It took some time for the depth of the crisis to sink in: 'In the beginning they thought the crisis was merely a passing hiccup,' said one sympathetic official, 'so they took temporary measures. Now they realize that its an extensive one.' In 1975 they started the long trek backwards. New plantations were forbidden until at least the end of 1986, and by the end of the 1970s the taxpayers of the whole Common Market were stumping up substantial funds to rescue the growers from the results of their own greed. European Community premiums were being given to growers prepared to dig up their vines, although they could replant within eight years if conditions permitted. Production on the reduced acreage was severely restricted. Only a certain amount of alcohol could be distilled as cognac; the surplus was carted off to be distilled as industrial alcohol, again with the help of Community funds. Growers were allowed to load only a proportion of even their limited crop on the market. By 1982–3 they could sell immediately only about half their production, 4.5 hectolitres for every hectare of vines; the rest had to be stocked at their expense. Over the last couple of years these Draconian measures have had some effect – production in the outer areas is now only half the record levels of the early 1970s.

Desperation has bred some promising initiatives. The most bizarre is the attempt by the BNIC to exploit Cognac's name by starting a film festival devoted exclusively to detective films. This has now become a small, exclusive but widely recognized event in the festival calendar. More directly, the Cognacais have made a systematic attempt to entice young drinkers to the joys of cognac. In France sales per head to the under-thirty-fives had gone down by nearly 20 per cent in the later 1970s, so the Cognacais resurrected the old *fine à l'eau* trade in a rather more sophisticated guise. During the smug, fat years they had neglected to exploit their brandy's advantages as a base for mixed drinks. Because it is made from grapes, it is eminently suitable for cocktails that will not react too violently with wine drunk later in the evening.[1]

All these initiatives have been in the hands either of the BNIC or of individual firms, for the region lacks any real tradition of direct sales by the growers. Most private clients – the base of any direct sales network – are not going to buy cognac in the quantity that they purchase, say, champagne. And although in the past many growers used their stocks as a foundation for their transformation into merchants, the tradition of blending, of drawing supplies from a wide range of vineyards and vintages, has always been dominant. In the 1960s and 1970s the Champenois had showed the way; individual growers and co-operatives had come to dominate the home market. Even in Cognac one or two growers, notably Marcel Ragnaud in the Grande Champagne, had been selling their own single-vintage cognacs for a generation or more, as had some of the growers and co-operatives in the tourist region near and on the coast. The growers on the islands, in particular, can still rely on the tourists' undiscriminating summer thirsts and until recently had largely escaped the effects of the slump.

In the 1970s a few dozen others, in both Champagne and even in the Fins Bois, ventured forth. Not many have made any impact abroad: the Ragnaud family has split, with both halves providing superior cognacs, and the Lhéraud family in the Petite Champagne, on the border of the Grande Champagne, is doing well in Britain (notably with their VSOP, one of the finest on the market). A couple of dozen others have established themselves with private buyers all over France, always looking for wines or spirits from personal suppliers. But only a dozen or so out of a couple of hundred *vendeurs directs* can rely exclusively on private sales for a living. Even Guy Lhéraud has to spend much of the year selling at France's innumerable fairs. For the complications are endless: any quality cognac depends on age, which itself assumes a very special inheritance. Most cognacs, including those from private growers, are a blend; and if a grower needs even a tiny percentage of someone else's brandy to balance his own product he has to get a merchant's licence.

[1] The old wives told the right tale. Grain and grape really do not mix. Their warning rings hideously true to this writer the next morning if he has taken even the smallest tincture of whisky before drinking wine in any quantity. Cognac-based cocktails really are healthier.

On a more modest level, some growers are exploiting the tourist market more systematically by offering not only cognacs but their own brand of Pineau des Charentes as well. Pineau is a refreshing local apéritif, greatly resembling the light port that is such a favourite with the French. Indeed, it is made in the same way: the fermentation of local grapes is stopped by the addition of local brandy. To be legally entitled to the name Pineau des Charentes, the result must contain between 16 and 22 per cent alcohol and has to be stored in wood for a year before it is sold. It was merely a cottage industry when the regulations were being drawn up, so Pineau can be brewed only by co-operatives, *bouilleurs de cru* and *bouilleurs de profession* (and they can use only their own grapes). Inevitably, until recently it was sold to individuals, and those mostly tourists. Camus was the pioneer with its Plessis brand, and in the past decade Unicoop has exploited its advantages by launching Reynac. Like many drinks first brought home by holidaymakers, Pineau has spread. In the early 1980s it mopped up the equivalent of 21,000 hectolitres of pure alcohol, an increase of over 11,000 in five years and enough to fill 7 million bottles of cognac. Another growing market, brandy destined for liqueurs based on cognac and fruits soaked in the stuff, absorbed the same amount, double their previous average; but neither outlet was ever going to be more than a safety valve. The growers also exploited their ability to mass-produce large quantities of decent, if unexciting, dry white wine from their grapes, but the competition is ferocious.

Within the trade the new mood of gritty realism is personified by Michel Coste. An accountant by training, he was drawn to Cognac in the early 1960s because his beloved yacht was moored at Arcachon, west of Bordeaux. For a decade or more he worked for Otard, rising to become managing director. Then in the mid-1970s he made his bid for independence. With the help of a substantial credit line from the local branch of the Société Générale, he set up a holding company, CCG (Compagnie Commerciale de Guyenne) and proceeded to buy up a number of the many houses left stranded by the slump. With Meukow came some stocks of old cognac; with Lucien-Foucauld (bought from Domecq) came an even better-known name, together with spacious premises in the middle of Cognac itself; with Richard Frères a well equipped warehouse and bottling complex at St-Jean-d'Angely. Coste is now one of the major suppliers to French supermarkets (his major rival is Unicoop), which rely on him for technical advice as well as supplies. Abroad he simply looks for niches – employing the legendary Nik Schuman, for instance, to sell a new Meukow, VRXO, in his old stamping ground in the Far East. Otard uses the venerable name of Exshaw, a firm it took over in 1975, in the same markets.

Exshaw and Meukow may have changed hands, but at least they still adorn the name of up-market cognacs. A worse fate befell Denis Mounié. It had been the favourite cognac of that noted imbiber, King Edward VII. As a result Denis Mounié was given the first royal warrant ever awarded to a cognac firm, which responded by naming their best Grande Champagne after their royal client. But the firm fell on hard times, and the name was acquired by Bénédictine, which sold it in 1982 to Hine, its successor in royal favour which now proposes to use the name as a secondary brand. Poor Jules Robin has suffered an even worse fate. It is now merely a grape brandy.

But all these manoeuvrings cannot alter the fundamental shape of the new cognac landscape. Michel Coste sees the future bleakly: 'There's only room for the four biggest firms. There won't be any more. Rémy Martin caught the last train.' And he is suiting his actions to his words, relying for growth on Armagnac rather than his many brands of cognac. The figures back him up. In the 1982–3 *Campagne* the Cognacais exported enough brandy to fill just over 106 million bottles, 2.3 per cent fewer than the previous year. Martell and Hennessy accounted for their historic 40 per cent of the total. Rémy Martin and Courvoisier shared another 28 per cent and Camus, Unicoop, Bisquit and Renault-Castillon a further 12.5 per cent (the latter mostly bulk cognacs). So Cognac's couple of hundred other companies were left scrabbling for a mere fifth of the market. Only a few firms – such as Hine and Bisquit with their powerful parents, Delamain with its magical name or the few growers, like Ragnaud or Lhéraud, with worthwhile names – seem able to escape from the clutches of the only other outlets available to the mass of the Cognacais: the sharp-witted buyers for European supermarkets or Japanese blenders. Is there no way out?

Conclusion · Only the Best is Good Enough

In the 1960s the Cognacais lost their way. They caught the prevailing disease of gigantomania and are still suffering from the consequences. They forgot their manifest destiny – to be the producers of limited quantities of the world's finest brandy, as they had been for two centuries or more. Mere quantity does not preclude high standards: yet, ironically, it was Jean Martell himself, founder of the town's biggest business, who wrote that he was 'less ambitious to do things on a large scale than to do them little and well'. His words remain to this day a suitable motto for the town.

Of course all the major houses – and many of the minor ones as well – produce especially fine cognacs, of XO quality and above, but only a few of the smaller ones rely on sales of these for a substantial part of their income. Inevitably, however, XOs and the like form only a small proportion of the sales of major houses, so their reputation is bound up with their lesser offerings.

A handful of firms are trying to escape this straitjacket. The Rothschilds of Lafite are using the Château's name for a special cognac: the mighty house of Seagram is attaching the name of one subsidiary, the champagne house of Mumm, to cognacs blended by its previously inactive cognac house, the venerable Augier. Smaller firms have also seized the point that exclusivity can be highly profitable. Individuality plus high quality is, of course, the key to the success of some of the growers – like the two branches of the Ragnaud family – who sell their own cognacs. Among the smaller merchants Alain Royer took advantage of the stocks of fine cognac accumulated by the family firm of Louis Royer to sell speciality cognacs under the name of Jules Duret – a friend of Manet's who had to sell his firm to the Royer family: and the new management of Moyet is doing the same with its stocks of old cognacs.

But these are very much exceptions. Most of Cognac is having to live with the hangover generated by the over-expansion of the late 1960s and early 1970s. This has, inevitably, bred a kind of desperation. Most dangerous to the image of cognac is a desperate attempt to sell the stuff in whatever guise. Cognac provides the most suitable base for brandy sours, or Pineau de Charentes, or those jars of preserved fruits bought in desperation just before Christmas as stop-gap presents. It offers a deeper taste and a better base than lesser spirits. But the cognacs used for these semi-industrial purposes, or for VS cognacs (or some firms' VSOPs and Napoleons) are not worthy upholders of the name. As I showed in chapter 11, they lack one of the crucial dimensions required in true cognac, for they are not aged and cannot be improved by age. Inevitably, they are by no means inimitable. Recently an international firm specializing in the creation of artificial substitutes for natural tastes concocted an *ersatz* cognac and smuggled it into one of the routine tastings conducted by the BNIC. It was duly approved. By no means outstanding, said the tasters, but perfectly acceptable.

This is an awful warning to the Cognacais. Unless they tighten up the regulations surrounding the use of their precious name, the world will not long continue to accept its uniqueness. The remedy is in their hands. They have to recognize that only a proportion of the present Cognac area is capable of producing great cognac and divide the region accordingly. They have to follow the logic that guided the merchants and growers who made their name famous in the first place. For the whole idea of *terroir* enshrined in Cognac, as in the names of other fine products of French agriculture, is not confined to an area's soil and subsoil, its geology, its drainage and its weather. It also embodies the historic judgment of the market and, through that commercial link, the considered judgment of generations of connoisseurs.

Yet when they were defining their boundaries legally the Cognacais yielded to temptation. Boundaries were drawn rather slackly for a host of reasons, among them an easy life (Hell hath no fury like a de-classified wine maker) and administrative convenience (always a disastrous excuse). For historical reasons, and to appease the tens of thousands of growers in the Charente Maritime (and the merchants who sold their wares), the blessed name was extended to the coast – and beyond. Even more reprehensibly, the boundaries of the Champagnes followed administrative rather than geographical boundaries. So, as we have seen, the superb products of the chalky slopes of Archiac are denied the *appellation* available to the likes of Gensac-la-Pallue, a name that exudes a certain muddiness. (It is, in fact, one of the communes in the flood plain of the Charente planted only in the 1960s).

This is not my opinion alone. The INAO has been excluded from any interference with the *appellation* because of the many changes that, it was feared, would result from any scientific analysis of the boundaries of the various *crus*. As Patrick Daniou, a leading geographer, put it recently: 'Consequently, it seems eminently desirable, in order to defend the quality of cognac's brandies, to take greater account of *terroir* in a new definition of the cognac *appellation*, which should be based on scientific criteria and on boundaries that should not necessarily be administrative ones.'[1]

The problem seems rather more complicated to me. Any attempt to relaunch cognac must be preceded by two steps: first, to separate out those limited portions of the present *appellation* capable of producing 'true' cognacs; second, to redefine even this inner core so that its boundaries correspond more precisely with the qualities historically associated with the idea of Grande and Petite Champagne, of Borderies and of the Bois. The products of the outer zone would be entitled merely to the name of cognac *tout court*, with none of the present distinctions between different types of Bois – a name that means virtually nothing to the cognac-buying public in any case. Only the outer areas – the islands off the coast and the marginal Bois communs – need lose their precious *appellation*.

The inner zone would include most of the present Champagnes, the Borderies (whose boundaries are generally accepted), and a semi-circular swathe of the Fins Bois to the north, east and south of the Champagnes. As the map on page 157 shows, these would then be divided into four familiar names: Grande and Petite Champagne, Borderies and Fins Bois. The whole would have to given a new name, easily recognizable and pronounceable everywhere cognac is drunk, from Manhattan to Kowloon: 'Cognac Classique', perhaps, or 'Grande Cognac', or 'Fine Cognac'.

The exercise is aimed at preserving historic reality – not upsetting the judgment of ages but reflecting it more accurately and thus providing buyers with the qualities they perceive as being those of Cognac's various *crus*. The actual boundaries are less easy to define, although the French

[1] *Annales GREH*, 1983.

Cognac:
a new appellation

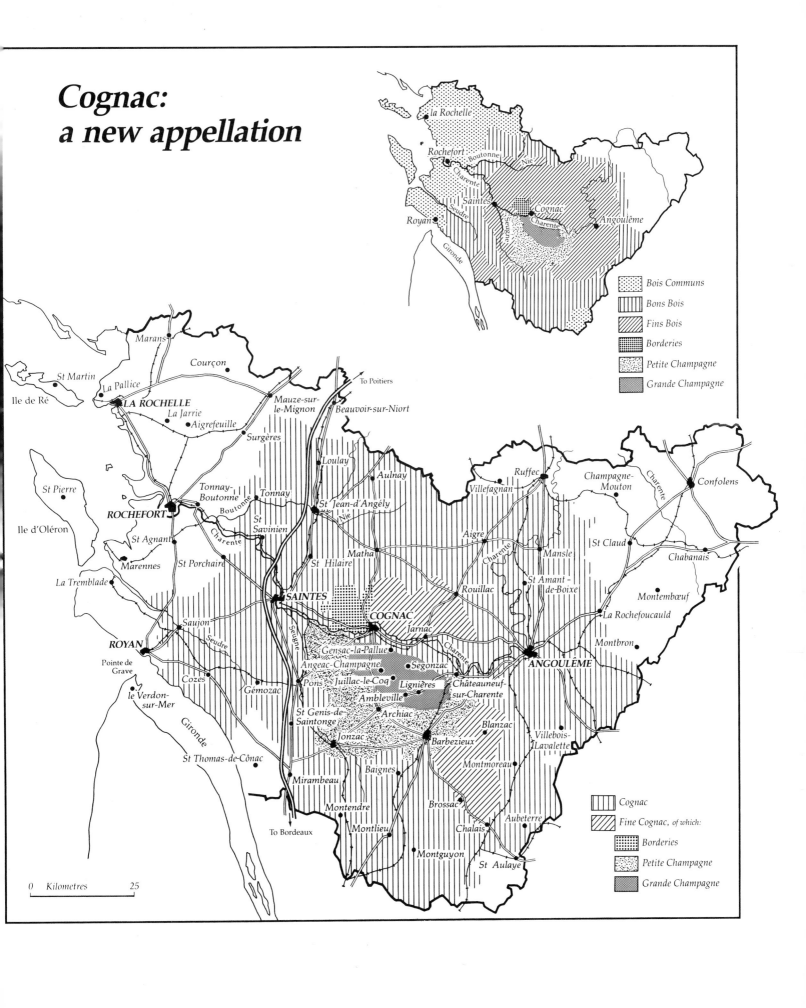

Bois Communs

Bons Bois

Fins Bois

Borderies

Petite Champagne

Grande Champagne

la Rochelle
Rochefort
Boutonne
Nie
Charente
Saintes
Seudre
Royan
Cognac
Charente
Angoulême
Seugne
Gironde

Marans

St Martin
Ile de Ré
St Pierre
Ile d'Oléron
La Tremblade

Courçon

La Pallice
LA ROCHELLE
La Jarrie
Aigrefeuille
Surgères

Mauze-sur-le-Mignon
Beauvoir-sur-Niort
To Poitiers

Loulay
Aulnay

Tonnay-Boutonne
Tonnay
Boutonne
St Jean-d'Angély
ROCHEFORT
St Savinien
Nie
St Agnant
Charente
St Hilaire
Matha
Marennes
St Porchaire
SAINTES

Ruffec
Champagne-Mouton
Confolens
Villefagnan
Charente
Aigre
St Claud
Mansle
Chabanais
St Amant-de-Boixe
Rouillac
Montembœuf
COGNAC
Jarnac
La Rochefoucauld

Saujon
Seudre
Gensac-la-Pallue
Angeac-Champagne
Segonzac
Charente
Montbron
ROYAN
Seugne
Pons
Juillac-le-Coq
Lignières
Châteauneuf-sur-Charente
ANGOULÊME
Pointe de Grave
Cozes
Gémozac
Ambleville
le Verdon-sur-Mer
St Genis-de-Saintonge
Archiac
Blanzac
Villebois-Lavalette
Gironde
Jonzac
Barbezieux
Montmoreau
St Thomas-de-Cônac
Baignes

Mirambeau
Brossac
Aubeterre
Montendre
Montlieu
Chalais
To Bordeaux
Montguyon
St Aulaye

Cognac

Fine Cognac, *of which:*

Borderies

Petite Champagne

Grande Champagne

0   Kilometres   25

Geological Service publishes excellent maps. The physical characteristics of the area have been analysed by geographers like M. Daniou, and my map is based on their boundaries. But I have also taken into account the results of discussions with the buyers of Cognac's most reputable firms. They, even more than the map makers, are the guardians of cognac's quality. They alone know the wrinkles attached to every corner of the region. For two centuries they have been choosing and blending the cognacs which act as the very definition of the area.

For, inevitably, only cognac can convey the essence of cognac. Words certainly cannot do justice to its complexity. Perhaps every copy of this book ought to be accompanied by a sample of some of Cognac's finest creations: one of M. Tesseron's older cognacs to celebrate the glories of the past; an XO from Hennessy or a Cordon Bleu from Martell to demonstrate that size does not preclude quality; a sample from Hine or Delamain to celebrate the English taste; and a single-vineyard Grande Champagne from Madame Ragnaud to remind us that cognac made its name before blending was possible.

All that then remains is to take the advice of the Abbé Talleyrand, as recalled in arguably the most famous anecdote about cognac:

At the end of a sumptuous supper, one of the guests tossed down his glass of Fine Champagne in one gulp in the Russian manner. Talleyrand took the liberty of advising his friend quite quietly: 'That is not how you should drink cognac. You take your glass in the hollow of the hand, you warm it, you rotate it with a circular movement so that the spirit gives off its aroma. Then you carry it to your nostrils and inhale ... and then, my dear sir, you put down your glass and talk about it.

APPENDICES

A Compendium of Cognac

1 · Cognac Houses

There are over 200 'merchants' in the Cognac region. I have confined myself to providing basic information about the leading firms and any other marques that the reader is likely to come across.

The information on companies' products is provided by them and should not be taken as tasting notes. The numbers denote the claimed age of the cognacs in the blend.

† Indicates that the firm sells only cognacs which it has distilled itself.

Visits. I have mentioned only those firms where an appointment is not necessary. It is possible to visit most of the other firms in working hours (except during the holiday period) if you ring up in advance.

Sources. Apart from the firms themselves and the books listed in the general notes, I have also used extensively the 'Cognac Producers Directory' in Harrod's *Book of Brandies*, published by *Decanter* magazine.

AUGIER

Place de la Salle Verte, 16102 Cognac
Tel: (45) 82 00 01

Mumm VSOP

The oldest house in Cognac, founded in 1643 and for a long time one of the most important. It is still situated between Martell and Hennessy. It was sold to Seagram's in 1968. A mere shell for many years. Now blends cognac for Mumm, a fellow-subsidiary of Seagram.

BISQUIT

Société Ricard, Domaine de Lignières, 16170 Rouillac
Tel: (45) 96 55 11

*** 2–5
VSOP 8–10
Napoléon about 20
Extra Vieille Or around 40

Visits: Every day between 1 July and 15 September, from 10 a.m. to 3 p.m.

Founded by Alexandre Bisquit in 1819 when he was only nineteen. A staunch Republican, he became mayor of Jarnac in 1849. His daughter married Adrien Dubouché, and their daughter married Maurice Laporte, who became a Senator but also pushed sales, especially in the Far East. But in 1967 the firm was sold to Pernod-Ricard, which also bought the estate of Château Lignières in the Fins Bois, about 20 miles north-east of Cognac. There it built Cognac's most modern and spectacular distillery surrounded by the company's 200 hectares of vineyards, the largest estate in the region.

BOUTELLEAU

Formerly owned by the family of the writer Jacques Chardonne; now owned by TIFFON.

J. R. BRILLET†

J. R. Brillet, Les Aireaux-Graves, 16120 Châteauneuf
Tel: (45) 97 05 06

Petite Champagne Selection 4
Petite Champagne Grande Réserve 8
Petite Champagne 15
Grande Champagne Napoléon 10
Très Rare Cognac Héritage 30

Visits: Every day, 9 a.m. to 7 p.m.

The Brillets have owned vines in the Cognac region since 1684. Brillet remains a family-owned firm, run by Jean and Patrick Brillet. One-third of its 100 hectares of vines are in the Grande Champagne, two-thirds in the Petite Champagne.

BRUGEROLLE

Cognac Brugerolle, 17160 Matha
Tel: (46) 58 50 60

Brugerolle 3
Luxe 4
VSOP 6
Napoléon Aigle Rouge 10
Napoléon Aigle d'Or 25–30
Très Vieux Cognac Réserve Spéciale XO

Visits: Monday to Friday, 2 to 4 p.m.; closed in August

CAMUS

Camus La Grande Marque, 29 rue Marguérite de Navarre, BP 19, 16101 Cognac
Tel: (45) 32 28 28

Célébration
Camus Grand VSOP
Camus Napoléon
Camus XO

Visits: In the summer from 2.30 to 4 p.m.; by appointment the rest of the year

Founded by Jean-Baptiste Camus, a grower and distiller living in the Borderies, with the help of a number of other local growers. His son Gaston built an enormous business in Russia. (The firm still has the exclusive agency for the trade in wines and spirits between France and Russia.) After the war Gaston's son, Michel, rescued what had become a moribund concern largely by exploiting the duty-free market in the Far East with the Célébration cognac. Camus is now the largest privately owned company in Cognac and is the fifth largest exporter. It has two important Armagnac brands, Chabot and Marquis de Puységur, and its Pineau (named Plessis after one of the family's properties) is a leading brand.

CASTILLON RENAULT

See RENAULT.

GOURRY DE CHADEVILLE†

SARL Gourry de Chadeville, 16130 Segonzac
Tel: (45) 83 40 54

VSOP 5
Napoléon 10–12
Très Vieux 18–20

Visits: Every day except Sundays and festivals

The domaine of Chadeville in the heart of the Grande Champagne has been in the Gourry family since 1619.

PASCAL COMBEAU

Société Gemace, 28 rue des Ponts, 16140 Aigre
Tel: (45) 96 10 02

Pascal Combeau
Normandin
Girard
de Laage

COMPAGNIE COMMERCIALE DE GUYENNE (CCG)

26 rue Pascal Combeau, Cognac

Founded in 1976 by Michel Coste, formerly managing director of OTARD. Owns a number of brands, including MEUKOW and LUCIEN-FOUCAULD.

GILLES COSSON†

SARL La Grange Neuve, Guimps, 16300 Barbezieux
Tel: (45) 78 90 37

Cognac Sélection Petite Champagne 4
VSOP Fine Champagne 15
Très Vieille Réserve Fine Champagne 25

The Cosson family has been established in Cognac for six generations. It now owns 46 hectares, one-third in the Grande Champagne, the rest in the Petite Champagne.

COUPRIÉ†

Ets Couprié, La Roumade, 16300 Ambleville/Barbezieux
Tel: (45) 83 54 69

VSOP 8
Napoléon 14
XO Très Vieille Réserve 20
Très Vieux Cognac Hors d'Age 42

Made from 22 hectares of vines in the Grande Champagne.

COURVOISIER

Courvoisier SA, place du Château, 16200 Jarnac
Tel: (46) 81 04 11

*** 5–8
VSOP 8–15
Napoléon 15–25
Extra Vieille 50–60

Visits: Monday to Friday, 8.30 to 11.30, 2 to 5. Advance appointments advisable off-season. Small charge but free miniature supplied

The founder, Emmanuel Courvoisier, supplied wine and spirits to Napoleon I. In 1835 Félix Joseph Courvoisier set up in Jarnac. In 1860 the firm became supplier to Napoleon III. Courvoisier was bought by Guy and Georges Simon in 1909. They adopted the slogan 'The Brandy of Napoleon', which has served the company well ever since (it also pioneered the use of frosted glass bottles). Loyal employees preserved the British-owned concern during the war. After 1945, under Christian Braastad, Courvoisier became one of the most important in the business but was caught short of stock and in 1964 was sold to Hiram Walker. The biggest seller of cognacs in the mid-1970s.

CROIZET

Cognac Croizet, BP3, 16720 St-Même-les-Carrières
Tel: (45) 81 90 11

*** Fine Cognac
VSOP
Napoléon
Bonaparte
Age Inconnu
Réserve Royale

CRYSTAL DRY†

Castel Sablons, St-Maigrin, 17520 Archiac
Tel: (46) 70 00 30

Crystal Dry 3 ('a colourless cognac, very light, for use in long drinks and cocktails')
VSOP 8
Napoléon 15

One of the rare direct sellers in the Fins Bois.

DE LAAGE

Subsidiary of Pascal Combeau

DELAMAIN

Delamain & Co, BP 16, 16200 Jarnac
Tel: (45) 81 08 24

Pale and Dry Grande Champagne
Vesper Grande Champagne
Très Vieux Grande Champagne
Réserve de la Famille, Grande Champagne

Founded in the seventeenth century. In 1763 James Delamain joined his father-in-law, Isaac Ranson, in the firm of Ranson and Delamain. The Delamains are related to virtually every major Cognac family, but they themselves have always been interested as much in science and history as in business. Henry Delamain was a distinguished entomologist and his son, Philippe, an equally distinguished archaeologist. Jacques and Maurice Delamain were noted literary figures in pre-war Paris. The best history of Cognac was written by Robert Delamain, grandfather of the present chairman, Alain Braastad. Under his scrupulous direction Delamain Pale and Dry is generally recognized as the best of the standard 'English-style' cognacs.

JULES DURET

Founded by a friend of Manet's who painted him. Now owned by LOUIS ROYER.

Fine Champagne
Grande Champagne
Collectors' series

EXSHAW

Cognac Exshaw SA, 127 boulevard Denfert-Rochereau, 16100 Cognac
Tel: (45) 82 40 00

Exshaw No. 1
Exshaw Age d'Or

Once famous among the British aristocracy. Firm bought by OTARD in 1975.

JEAN FILLIOUX†

Fillioux Fils, La Pouyade, Juillac-le-Coq, 16130 Segonzac
Tel: (45) 83 47 01

Coq 3–4
Napoléon 8–10
Cep d'Or 15
Très Vieux 20
Réserve Familiale over 45

A family firm owning 16 hectares in the Grande Champagne, founded in the last century by an independent-minded member of the Fillioux family, which normally works for HENNESSY.

FOUCAULD

See LUCIEN-FOUCAULD.

FRAPIN

***
VSOP Fine Champagne
Domaine Frapin: Vieille Grande Fine Champagne
Grande Champagne Très Vieille Reserve
Grande Champagne Château de Fontpinot
Grande Champagne Napoléon

A family firm, the only one with premises in Segonzac, the heart of the Grande Champagne. Owns some of the biggest estates in the Grande Champagne, including Les Gabloteaux and the Château de Fontpinot. Now owned by Mme Max Cointreau, younger daughter of André Renaud of RÉMY MARTIN, who married a Mlle Frapin.

GAUTIER

Cognac Gautier, 28 rue des Ponts, 16140 Aigre
Tel: (45) 96 10 02

***
VSOP
Napoléon
XO (also marked in flasks shaped like a lantern and a ship's wheel)

For 270 years after its foundation in 1700 this was one of the most distinguished family firms in Cognac. It is now owned by the Berger *pastis* group.

GIRARD

Founded in 1884; now a subsidiary of PASCAL COMBEAU.

JEAN GUERBÉ†

Maison Guerbé et Cie, Hameau de l'Echalotte, Juillac-le-Coq, 16130 Segonzac
Tel: (45) 83 47 27

Logis 5
Spécial 7
VSOP 9
Napoléon 15
Grande Réserve 25

The firm owns 34 hectares in the Grande Champagne.

GODET

Godet Frères, 1 rue du Duc, 17000 La Rochelle
Tel: (46) 41 10 66

*** Fins Bois 2
VSOP Fine Champagne Gastronome 7–9
Napoléon
Grande Fine Champagne Extra Vieille

The Godet family was of Dutch origin and settled in the area around 1600. They originally shipped their cognacs in cask and started using their own name in 1838.

L. GOURMEL

L. Gourmel, BP 194, 16106 Cognac
Tel: (45) 82 07 29

L'Age des Fleurs 12
L'Age des Épices 15
Quintessence

One of the rare producers of cognacs exclusively from the Fins Bois and from a single year. According to the firm, 'They tend to be very pure, not very woody, and to mature quite quickly.' The firm is run by Pierre and Michèle Voisin and their daughter, Caroline.

A. HARDY

A. Hardy, BP 27, 147 rue Basse, de Croun, 16100 Cognac
Tel: (45) 82 59 55

Red Corner *** 3
VSOP 5 +
Noces d'Or Fine Champagne 50

The Hardys were major local distillers, probably of English descent. Antoine Hardy was a broker on behalf of English buyers who founded his own firm in 1863. He specialized in sales to Russia, even producing a special 'Cognac de l'Alliance' to celebrate the Franco-Russian alliance. Sales to Britain slumped so badly after duty increases that the Hardys shut their London office. Antoine's son, Valéri, developed such a loathing of all things British that he sent his son, Armand, to study in Germany and concentrated on Central European rather than Anglo-Saxon markets. The six sons of Armand Hardy took over, but one died in a car crash; another, Francis, was more involved in politics than commerce (he is Deputy and mayor of Cognac). The Crédit Commercial de France now owns a third of the firm. Nevertheless, it is still run by the family.

HENNESSY

Société Jas Hennessy & Co, 1 rue de la Richonne, 16101 Cognac
Tel: (45) 82 52 22

VS
VSOP Fine Champagne
XO
Paradis

Visits (to Hennessy's unique cooperage museum as well as to its cellars): 1 September to 30 June, Monday to Friday, 8.30 to 11 a.m., 1.45 to 4.30 p.m.; July and August: 8.30 a.m. to 4.45 p.m.

Founded in 1765 by Richard Hennessy, an army officer of Irish descent. For nearly 200 years it has been one of the two leaders of the cognac business, sometimes in partnership with, more often as a rival to, the Martells. For six generations the Hennessys have relied heavily on the Fillioux family, whose members have been buyers and tasters. In 1971 Hennessy merged with Moët & Chandon to form one of France's biggest drinks groups. The combined group controls Parfums Dior and has recently invested heavily in rose breeding and other biotechnological businesses. Outside France it invested in Domaine Chandon, making sparkling wines in California, and in 1981 took over the Schieffelin Corporation, which had handled sales of the company's cognacs since the eighteenth century. Hennessy still owns a number of properties, 450 hectares of oak in the Limousin and 470 hectares of vineyards, but these provide only one-twentieth of the company's requirements. It owns 28 distilleries and has contracts with 2,300 growers exclusively in the Champagnes, the Borderies and the Fins Bois. Its stocks would fill 87 million bottles. Hennessy is still run by Alain de Pracomtal and Gerald de Geoffre, both descendants of the founder.

HINE

Cognac Hine SA, 16 quai de L'Orangerie, 16200 Jarnac
Tel: (45) 81 11 38

*** VS 6
VSOP Fine Champagne 10
Napoléon 20 (also sold in a porcelain flask modelled on the Arc de Triomphe)
Antique 25
Old Vintage 30–5
Triomphe 40
Family Reserve ('a vintage Cognac')

Visits: Monday to Friday, 8.30 to 11.30 a.m.; 1.30 to 4.30 p.m.

Founded by an Englishman, Thomas Hine, who settled in Jarnac at the end of the eighteenth century, married into the Delamain family and became a partner. Hine specialized in selling cognac to be aged and bottled in Britain and only reluctantly adopted a trademark (the famous stag may be a pun, a hind being, of course, a female deer). Later in the century Hine became a major supplier to the British aristocracy and gentry. Indeed, its Three-Star was introduced only after the Second World War. Since 1962 Hine has been royal warrant holder to Her Majesty Queen Elizabeth II. It was bought by the Distillers' Company in 1971, but the cousins Jacques and Bernard Hine, great-great-greatgrandsons of Thomas Hine, are still active directors.

DE LAAGE

Founded in 1856. Now subsidiary of PASCAL COMBEAU.

LAFITE ROTHSCHILD

Grancru sa, 33250 Pauillac
Très vieille Réserve

A blend of old cognacs from the Borderies marketed by the Rothschilds who own Château Lafite.

GASTON DE LAGRANGE

Rue de la Pierre Levée, Château Bernard, 16100 Cognac
Tel: (45) 82 18 17

*** 3
VSOP 8–10
Napoléon 12
XO 30

Owned by Martini & Rossi.

F. LATOUR & CIE

SARL Cognac Beausoleil, 34 rue de Segonzac, 16104 Cognac
Tel: (45) 32 10 25

*** 3
Napoléon 6
Extra 15

Visits: July and August, 1.30 p.m. to 5 p.m.

Founded in 1872 by François Latour. In 1946 it was bought by the Guignard family, the present owners.

LHÉRAUD

Cognac Lhéraud Domaine de Lasdoux Angeac, 16120 Châteauneuf
Tel: (45) 97 12 33

*** 3
VSOP
La Réserve du Templier Fine Champagne 10
Single-vineyard cognacs from a fine estate on the border between the Petite and Grande Champagne.

LUCIEN-FOUCAULD

***
VSOP

Formerly a family firm that won a number of awards at the turn of the century. Now part of the COMPAGNIE COMMERCIALE DE GUYENNE.

MARTELL

Martell & Co., BP 21, place Martell, 16100 Cognac
Tel: (45) 82 44 44

*** VS
Médaillon VSOP
Cordon Bleu
Cordon Argent Extra
Cordon Noir

So strong is Martell's commitment to blending and its confidence in its quality that none of its cognacs is a Fine Champagne.

Visits: Monday to Friday, 9 a.m. to 12.30 p.m.; 2.30 to 5 p.m.

Founded in 1715 by Jean Martell, a native of Jersey, then a major centre for smuggling brandy into Britain. He married daughters of two Cognac merchants, his second wife being Rachel Lallemand, from one of the most distinguished Cognac families. After her husband's death she carried on the business under the name Veuve Martell-Lallemand, taking her sons, Jean and Frederick, into partnership. The firm became the leading firm in Cognac during the French Revolutionary period and has never lost its position for more than a few years. It remains a family business through the Firino family, who married into the Martells during the nineteenth century and subsequently called themselves Firino-Martell. Martell was a pioneer in establishing subsidiaries abroad to distribute its cognacs, starting with Mexico in 1949. After the war it bought Jules Robin. In the 1970s it issued some of its shares to the public and has diversified, owning Janneau Armagnac, Jacomo scents and taking a stake in Noilly Prat, but remains firmly family-controlled. Since the 1890s the Martell installations have been almost a town within a town, with sixteen bottling lines and a great sprawl of warehouses and offices. Its stocks are valued at over 1 billion francs. It has 21 distilleries of its own and 18 more under contract.

MENARD†

J.-P. Menard et Fils, 16720 St-Même-les Carrières
Tel: (45) 81 90 26

Sélection des Domaines 3–5
Réserve Familiale 10

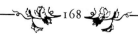

Tradition Impériale 20–5
Vieille Réserve Extra 35
Grande Fine Ancestrale 45

Established in 1815; owns 80 hectares of vines in the Grande Champagne.

MEUKOW

VSOP
Napoléon
XO (Grande Champagne)
NPU (Nec Plus Ultra) – VRXO (Grande Champagne)
Rarissime (70 years old)

Originally German-owned. Confiscated in 1914 and now owned by COMPAGNIE COMMERCIALE DE GUYENNE.

MONNET

J. G. Monnet & Co., BP 22, 52 ave P. F. Martell, 16101 Cognac
Tel: (45) 82 57 11

Tradition
VSOP
Napoléon & Josephine Grande Reserve
Anniversaire Très Ancienne Sélection
XO
Extra Belle Réserve

Founded in 1838; in the later nineteenth century acted as sales representative for the growers. Jean Monnet, 'the father of Europe' and Cognac's most distinguished son, was the son of J. G. Monnet. In the 1960s the firm was bought by the German firm Scharlachberg.

LOGIS DE LA MONTAGNE†

Paul Bonnin, Logis de la Montagne, Challignac, 16300 Barbezieux
Tel: (45) 78 55 65 / 78 52 71

*** 4
VSOP 8
Vieille Réserve 15
Extra Hors d'Age 20

A family company that has been making its own cognacs in the Fins Bois for four generations. Owns 30 hectares.

DENIS MOUNIÉ

Denis Mounié SA, BP 14, 16200 Jarnac
Tel: (45) 81 05 38

***
VSOP
VSOP Fine Champagne
Edouard VII Grande Réserve Fine Champagne
Napoléon
Grande Champagne Extra

Founded in 1838 by Justin Denis and Henri Mounié. In 1908 it received the royal warrant from Edward VII. Bought by Bénédictine (which also owned Comandon) and recently resold to HINE.

MOYET

62 Rue de l'Industrie,
16104 Cognac
Tel: (45) 82 04 53

Founded in 1864. Quiescent for 20 years: until 1980 since when it has been offering a series of single lots of old cognacs.

NORMANDIN

Founded in 1844. Now a subsidiary of PASCAL COMBEAU.

NORMANDIN-MERCIER

Cognac J. Normandin-Mercier, Château de la Peraudière, 17139 Dompierre
Tel: (46) 34 28 11

Vieille Fine Champagne 15
Petite Champagne 55° 19
Grande Champagne 50° 21
Grande Champagne Réserve 30
Tres Vieille Grande Champagne over 70

Founded in 1872 by Jules Normandin, who bought the Château de la Peraudière in 1885 and has always specialized in Champagne cognacs.

OTARD

Otard SA, Château de Cognac, BP 3, 16101 Cognac
Tel: (45) 82 40 00

*** VS
Baron Otard VSOP Fine Champagne 8
Princes de Cognac 15
Napoléon XO 35
Extra over 50

Visits: Every day from 1 April to 30 September, 10 a.m. to 5 p.m.; 1 October to 31 March, Monday to Friday, 10 a.m. to 5 p.m.

The Otards were a leading Scottish family devoted to the failing fortunes of the House of Stuart, whom they followed into exile in France. James Otard de la Grange, indeed, received a barony for his bravery in serving Louis XIV. They subsequently became landowners. The firm was founded by Jean-Antoine Otard de la Grange, who had narrowly escaped death during the Terror of 1792, being rescued only at the last minute by locals loyal to him. In 1795 he went into partnership with Jean Dupuy and quickly became one of the town's leading merchants (his former town house is now the Town Hall). Together they bought the Château des Valois in Cognac, which has served as the firm's cellars ever since. But the family became 'more interested in public and social life than in business', according to the present chairman, and 'when their competitors began to sell their brandies in bottles under their own names, they declared, "We are not grocers."' In 1930 control passed to the de Ramefort family, which now shares it with Martini through St-Raphaël. Bought EXSHAW in 1975.

CHATEAU-PAULET

Chateau Paulet SA, route de Segonzac, BP 24, 16101 Cognac
Tel: (45) 32 07 00

Écusson Rouge ***
VSOP Réserve
Napoléon
XO
Very Rare Age Inconnu
Borderies Très Vieilles

Founded at the end of the last century by Jean-Maurice Lacroux, who owned Château Paulet. Now owned by Cusenier.

PRINCE HUBERT DE POLIGNAC

Unicoop, 49 rue Lohmeyer, 16102 Cognac
Tel: (45) 82 45 77

***
Couronne
VSOP Fine Champagne
Napoléon Fine Champagne
XO Fine Champagne
Dynastie Grande Champagne

Visits to warehouses at Le Laubaret, on RN 141 between Cognac and Jarnac: all year round

The brand name of the Union des Viticulteurs Charentais (Unicoop). It was founded in 1931 under the guidance of Pierre-Lucien Lucquand and now brings together 3,500 growers owning 5,200 hectares and producing 40,000 hectolitres in 127 *alembics*, half in the Fins Bois, and one-third in the Bons Bois. It bought from the family the right to use the Polignac name, one of the oldest in France, in 1947. Also a major producer of 'own-brand' cognacs and the leader in the Pineau des Charentes market with its Reynac brand.

PRUNIER

Maison Prunier SA, 16102 Cognac
Tel: (45) 82 01 36

VS
VSOP
Fine Champagne
Napoléon
Family Reserve

The Prunier family has been shipping cognac since 1700. In 1918 the widow of Alphonse Prunier called in her nephew, Jean Burnez, to run the company, and his son Claude now runs what remains a family-owned business.

RAGNAUD SABOURIN†

SA Ragnaud Sabourin, Domaine de la Voûte, Ambleville, 16300 Barbezieux
Tel: (45) 83 54 61

Grande Champagne 1er Cru de Cognac 4
Grande Champagne VSOP 10
Grande Champagne Réserve Spéciale 20
Grande Champagne Fontvieille 35
Grande Champagne Héritage Gaston Briand, 1925
Héritage Gaston Briand la Paradis about 90
Héritage Mme Paul Ragnaud 1903

Gaston Briand, the president of the Cognac growers, started to sell his own cognacs about forty years ago. His daughter, Denise, and Marcel Ragnaud, his son-in-law, took over the business, which is now run by their daughter Annie and her husband Paul Sabourin.

RAYMOND RAGNAUD†

Madame Raymond Ragnaud, Le Château Ambleville, 16300 Barbezieux
Tel: (45) 83 54 57

Haute Roche Fine Petite Champagne Réserve
Château Ambleville Grande Fine Champagne Vieille Réserve
Château Ambleville Grande Fine Champagne Réserve Extra
Château Ambleville Grande Fine Champagne Hors d'Age

One of the first, and still one of the best, family firms selling its own cognacs direct. Half the 36 hectares of vines are in the Grande Champagne, the other half in the Petite Champagne.

RÉMY MARTIN

E. Rémy Martin & Co., 20 rue de la Société Vinicole, BP 37, 16102 Cognac
Tel: (45) 35 16 16

Petite Fine Champagne VS 3
Fine Champagne VSOP 7
Fine Champagne Centaure Napoléon 15–17
Fine Champagne Centaure XO 22–5
Fine Champagne Centaure Extra 27–30
Grande Champagne Louis XIII over 50 (sold in a special Baccarat crystal flask modelled on a flask
    discovered on the site of the Battle of Jarnac)

Founded in 1724; remained a family firm for nearly 200 years. It was saved after the phylloxera crisis by André Renaud, a grower with ample stocks who later took over the firm. He insisted on selling only cognacs from the Champagnes and ensured that all the wines were distilled on their lees in relatively small vats. His elder son-in-law, André Hériard-Dubreuil, took over on Renaud's death in 1965 and expanded sales enormously, especially in the United States and the Far East. M. Max Cointreau, who married Renaud's younger daughter, owns a substantial minority stake but is not allowed any part in running the firm. Rémy's turnover is over 1 billion francs a year. It owns the biggest coopers in France, selling casks all over the world. Rémy owns the major Bordeaux house of de Luze, controls Krug Champagne and Nicolas, France's biggest specialized wine merchants. Outside France it has joint ventures producing wine in Australia (Château Rémy), and China (Tian Jin) and, in partnership with Schramsberg, produces RMS 'alembic brandy' in California.

RENAULT

Castillon Renault SA, 23 rue du Port, 16101 Cognac
Tel: (45) 82 52 88

Carte Noire Extra 12–15
OVB (Old Vintage Blend) 12–15
XO 20–5
Age Unknown, in Crystal carafe 40 +

Founded in Jean Antonin Renault in 1835, the firm was one of the first to export cognac in bottle. Merged with Castillon in 1963. Now sells only under Renault name. Controlled by a major French bank.

JULES ROBIN

Once one of the biggest firms in Cognac. The family was accused of collaboration, lost its markets in China after the war and was taken over by MARTELL, which uses the name for marketing grape brandy and specialized liqueurs.

ROULLET

Roullet et Fils 16200, Le Goulet de Foussignac
Tel: (45) 81 14 58

Amber Gold VS
VSOP Réserve
Grande Réserve
Extra Grande Champagne
XO

A family vineyard since 1760. Now 50 per cent owned by the English brewers, Greene King.

ROY RENÉ†

Roy René, Le Mas, Juillac-le-Coq, 16130 Segonzac
Tel: (45) 83 47 09

*** 5
VSOP 8
Napoléon 15

A family business owning 30 hectares in the Grande Champagne.

ROUYER

Rouyer Guillet SA, Château de la Roche, 17100 Saintes
Tel: (46) 93 15 26 / 93 01 41

Brevet Royal 4
Damoisel VSOP 15
Rois de France 30
Philippe Guillet Grande Fine Champagne 80

Founded in 1701 by Philippe Guillet. Has had an office in London since 1860. Run by Mme Marie-Suzanne Rouyer Guillet.

LOUIS ROYER

Cognac Louis Royer, BP 12, 16200 Jarnac
Tel: (45) 81 02 72

***
VSOP Fine Champagne
Grande Réserve Extra Vieille Fine Champagne
Grande Fine Champagne Extra
XO Réserve

A family firm, founded in the last century by Louis Royer, which specialized in supplying bulk cognacs. It has recently taken a number of interesting initiatives in packaging its better cognacs and in supplying special 'cooking cognacs'.

SALIGNAC

L. de Salignac & Cie SA, Domaine de Breuil, rue Robert Daugas, 16100 Cognac
Tel: (45) 81 04 11

*** 5
VSOP 10–12
Napoléon 15–20
Très Vieille Grande Réserve 50+

Founded in 1809 by Antoine de Salignac. In the 1830s it became the spearhead for direct sales by the growers under the name of the United Vineyard Proprietors. Under the founder's grandson it became a more orthodox company and is now a subsidiary of COURVOISIER.

M. TIFFON

Ets M. Tiffon, BP 15, 16200 Jarnac
Tel: (45) 81 08 31

***
Extra
VSOP

Established by Méderic Tiffon in 1875. It has long specialized in selling to the state monopolies in Scandinavia. It also owns BOUTELLEAU.

UNICOGNAC

BP No 2 17500 Jonzac
Tel: (46) 48 10 99

Roi des Rois
Napoléon Fine Champagne Corónation
Mona Lisa (in Limoges porcelain decanter)

Coopérative formed in 1959. Brings together 3,000 growers owning 5,000 hectares.

2 · Cognac and the Law

The Cognacais are governed by three authorities: the Direction générale des Impôts, which regulates the quantity distilled; the Direction de la Consommation et de la Repression des Fraudes, which polices the quality of the spirit; and the BNIC, which, among other tasks, issues the *certificats d'âge* stating the age of the cognac being sold.*

The basic legislation covering the use of the word 'cognac' is the Decree of 15 May 1936, which further amplified the definitions of *terroirs délimitées (sub-zone: terroir* or *crus)* first set out in the Decree of 1 May 1909 and amplified by the law of 6 May 1919. All three provided that the term 'cognac' (and also *eau-de-vie de Cognac* and *eau-de-vie des Charentes*) could be used only for spirits produced and distilled in the region illustrated on the map on pages 19 and 157.

The *sous-appellations*, Grande Champagne, Petite Champagne, Borderies, Fins Bois and Bons Bois, on the same map were defined in a series of decrees, the first issued on 13 January 1938, the latest dated 16 February 1978.

The word 'Fine' can be attached to any *sous-appellation* (sub-Appellation), as in 'Fine Borderies'. But 'Fine Champagne cognacs' have to contain at least 50 per cent spirit from the Grande Champagne, with the rest coming from the Petite Champagne. The word 'Grande' is reserved for cognacs from the Grande Champagne. There is some confusion concerning the use of words such as *cru, clos, château*, etc. In theory they can be used only when all the spirits involved come from a specific plot of land, but merchants have been allowed to use the term for *châteaux* that do not produce all the spirit in the bottle. Nevertheless, the BNIC exercises strict control over labels, ensuring, among other things, that the addresses given on labels are those of the merchants' or growers' actual establishments and not merely post boxes.

Permitted grape varieties are divided into two categories. The 'principal' varieties are the Folle Blanche, the Ugni Blanc (also called St-Émilion-des-Charentes) and the Colombard. In addition Sémillon, Blanc Ramé, Jurançon Blanc, Montils and Sélect can be used in up to 10 per cent of the total.

Wine making must be conducted according to local custom. The use of continuous 'Archimedes' presses is specifically forbidden. In the Charente itself no sugar can be added to the must. In the Charente Maritime and Deux-Sèvres sugar can, in theory, be added but only to musts destined to provide table or sparkling wines. Growers have to declare the acreage of vines and quantities of wine produced (including wines set aside for home consumption). Growers also have to declare the quantities of each variety. These declarations must be completed before any *titre de mouvement* is issued, and this alone allows the cognac to be transported on a public highway.

Article 443 of the Tax Code (Code Général des Impôts) forbids the movement of any wines or spirits without the appropriate documentation. Each certificate must include details of the quantity, the type and the *appellation* demanded. All cognac carried on the public highway has to be accompanied by an *acquit jaune d'or*, the famous golden-coloured permit used by no other drink and first authorized in 1929.

Distillation

To call itself cognac the spirit has to be double-distilled, to a strength not exceeding 72°. Continuous distillation is expressly forbidden. The *alembic charentais* consists essentially of a still heated by a naked flame, with a *chapiteau (head)* (with or without a *chauffe-vin* – wine-warmer) and a cooling coil'. The alembic

*The sources for the following information are the BNIC and Marguerite Landrau, *Le Cognac devant la loi*, Cognac, L'Ile d'Or, 1981.

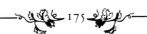

used for the second distillation must not hold more than 30 hectolitres, nor be loaded with more than 25 hectolitres. Bigger *alembics* (pot stills), holding up to 140 hectolitres, are allowed for the *première chauffe*. The cognac should be aged in casks made of oak from either the Troncais or the Limousin.

There are three classes of distillers: the co-operatives, the *bouilleurs de profession* (including the Cognac merchants), who buy the wine from the growers, and the *bouilleurs de cru*, who can distil only their own wine and only if they produce more than 50 hectolitres of pure alcohol. The use, purchase, sale or repair of the *alembics* are subject to supervision by the local tax office, whom the *bouilleur de cru* has to inform when he wants to start distillation. Manufacturers and salesmen of alembics have to maintain a register providing details of all *alembics* bought, manufactured, repaired or sold.

Before sale cognac has to be reduced to between 40 and 45 per cent alcohol through the addition of distilled water or weaker spirit (which must also come from the Cognac region). Additives are restricted to caramel, oak chippings and sugar. Sugar, limited to 2 per cent of the total volume, can be in the form of either syrup or sugar soaked in spirit of a strength of between 20 and 30 per cent. Such additions may reduce the strength of the cognac to 38°. Colouring matter is limited to two parts in 1,000.

Ageing

All cognacs are registered by age, and the certificates giving the age of any parcel of cognac are an indispensable adjunct to the *acquit jaune d'or*. The age classification is as follows (ageing starts officially only on 31 March each year):

oo is for cognacs distilled between the harvest and the following 31 March, at which point they turn into o cognacs. Brandies distilled after 1 April retain their oo designation until the following 31 March.
1 is for cognacs more than one year old on 1 April of any given year.
2, 3, 4 and 5 cover cognacs from two to five years old on 1 April.
6, introduced in 1979, covers all cognacs more than six years old.

The youngest cognac that can be sold must be at least thirty months old (i.e. Compte 2). It can be called only VS or ***.

To be called Réserve, VO or VSOP, the youngest cognac in the blend must be at least four and a half years old (i.e. Compte 4).

To be labelled Extra, Napoléon, Vieux, Vieille Réserve and the like, the youngest *eau-de-vie* in the blend must be at least Compte 6.

There are no official regulations covering cognacs older than Compte 6.

In addition, many countries have special requirements, and most demand a *certificat d'âge*. For some countries – including Britain, Ireland, Malaysia, Hong Kong, South Korea, Nigeria, New Zealand and Singapore – the cognac must be at least three years old. Argentina requires that 'superior qualities' must be at least four years old.

Allied Products

Esprit de cognac is a tripled-distilled cognac, of between 80° and 85°, used when making sparkling wines.

Pineau des Charentes consists only of wine from the Cognac region fortified during fermentation, once only, with cognac, to give a beverage of between 16 and 22°.

In *fruits au cognac* only cognac can be used. If it is *à base de cognac*, then at least 51 per cent of the total liquid content must be cognac.

For a *liqueur au Cognac* the minimum content is 30 per cent.

Vins vinés of up to 24 per cent alcohol, mostly for export to Germany, are also covered by German law, which now correspond to French regulations.

Le Bureau National Interprofessionel du Cognac (BNIC)

The BNIC is a quasi-administrative joint board, with specific legal rights and financial autonomy.

It comprises forty-eight members: two 'eminent persons', one representing viticulture, the other commercial interests; nineteen delegates representing growers and co-operatives; a similar number representing the merchant houses and professional distillers (*bouilleurs de profession*); one delegate from the syndicate of fortified wines (*vins vinés*); one from the producers of Pineau des Charentes; and one each from the various professions involved in producing or selling cognac – brokers, allied industries, industrial and agricultural workers, technicians, etc.

The state is represented by a Commissaire du Gouvernement, who can either agree the decisions taken by the BNIC or refer them to the Minister of Agriculture or the Minister of Finance. An Ingénieur Général de l'Agriculture presides over the work of the Bureau, and a Contrôleur d'État from the Ministry of Finance is charged with verifying all the Bureau's financial operations and ensuring that they are approved by the relevant Ministries.

The functions of the BNIC are to study and prepare all the regulations covering the buying, distillation, stockage and sale of wines and *eaux-de-vie* produced in the Cognac area; to supervise the preservation of the historic methods of making cognac; to control the quantity of cognac produced or allowed to be sold and to promote any measures likely to improve the production or sale of cognac.

The General Assembly of the BNIC controls its policies. The decisions at which it arrives are submitted to the Commissioner representing the Government. In certain cases the decisions are confirmed by official decree.

The BNIC is financed by a quasi-fiscal levy that covers its administration and promotional activities.

Recent Restrictions

Over the past decade a number of restrictions have been introduced to reduce the growing surplus of cognac. Since 1975 there have been limitations on the alcoholic yield of 1 hectare of vines and separate quotas covering the quantity that can be distilled and (a lower amount still) the quantity that can be sold. As a result of EEC regulations, in 1982–3 only 100 hectolitres of wine could be produced per hectare under Cognac's own restrictions; only 4.5 hectolitres of spirit could be sold freely; 1 hectolitre could be stored; a further 3 hectolitres could be kept or sold under certain conditions; and any surplus spirit could not be kept or sold as cognac. In 1980 further plantings of vines were forbidden until 30 November 1986, and a bonus of 13,500 francs per hectare was provided for growers who pulled up their vines

3 Size of Vineyard and Total Production, 1878–1981

Year	Area of Vineyard (hectares)	Total production (million bottles)
1878	285,150	107.6
1879	n/a	29.8
1880	233,110	43.7
1881	201,219	63.3
1882	171,001	42.6
1883	153,623	50.0
1884	116,217	63.0
1885	85,240	28.9
1886	75,061	26.6
1887	65,399	26.6
1888	65,390	22.2
1889	60,518	16.4
1890	53,963	18.7
1891–1900	46,589*	22.2
1901–10	62,088*	32.2
1911–20	73,854*	31.0
1921–30	76,540*	39.9
1931–40	69,051*	38.4
1941–50	59,843*	29.7
1951–60	63,041*	49.0
1961–70	77,666*	126.5
1971	78,411	150.6
1972	79,948	145.2
1973	84,765	264.3
1974	89,995	194.4
1975	102,460	257.1
1976	107,613	159.7
1977	107,727	126.6
1978	106,761	179.6
1979	106,328	234.0
1980	104,208	161.3
1981	100,622	145.5
1982	98,250	194.9
1983	96,113	157.9
1984	93,495	154.7
1985	91,887	N/A

Note: *Figures represent the average for the decade.
Source: BNIC.

4 Sales of Cognac, 1947–82

Year	France	Export (million bottles)	Total
1947	7.16	15.6	22.7
1948	10.86	21.1	32.0
1949	6.4	21.6	28.0
1950	8.6	27.4	36.0
1951	11.6	32.3	44.9
1952	9.6	26.4	36.0
1953	11.8	28.5	40.2
1954	11.4	31.5	42.9
1955	9.6	31.8	41.4
1956	10.9	38.2	49.0
1957	11.8	36.3	48.1
1958	9.6	31.1	40.7
1959	8.6	36.4	45.0
1960	11.4	41.5	52.9
1961	13.3	44.2	57.5
1962	14.8	48.4	63.2
1963	15.6	54.5	70.1
1964	16.3	55.2	71.5
1965	16.2	56.2	72.3
1966	18.0	59.9	77.9
1967	19.3	62.2	81.6
1968	21.0	68.2	89.2
1969	21.3	71.1	92.4
1970	22.6	80.5	103.1
1971	26.1	94.5	120.3
1972	24.4	99.5	123.9
1973	24.2	95.0	119.3
1974	22.0	76.0	97.9
1975	27.7	76.0	103.7
1976	27.0	90.5	117.5
1977	27.3	88.4	115.7
1978	30.6	105.4	136.0
1979	31.1	120.6	151.6
1980	27.8	117.3	145.1
1981	31.2	120.1	151.3
1982	30.5	110.1	140.65
1983	29.3	114.5	143.8
1984	23.7	118.5	142.2

Source: BNIC.

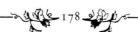

5 Cognac's Major Foreign Markets *Export sales, 1949–84 (in millions of bottles)*

	USA	UK	W. Germany	Belgium and Holland	'Chinese overseas markets'*	Scandinavia†	Japan
1949	1.6	6.0	0.01	0.8	1.4	3.8	0.2
1959	5.3	6.3	3.2	1.3	2.7	4.8	0.1
1969	9.2	10.4	9.4	5.2	6.0	8.6	0.9
1974	9.1	18.0	6.4	6.4	5.3	7.5	1.8
1979	20.3	20.5	11.9	11.8	15.1	6.9	5.1
1982	25.1	14.8	10.3	8.9	13.9	4.6	7.6
1983	25.8	15.7	9.6	9.1	15.7	6.6	9.9
1984	29.5	14.9	10.9	9.9	15.6	5.3	9.8

Notes: *Hong Kong, Malaysia, Thailand, Singapore.   †Denmark, Norway, Sweden, Finland.
Source: BNIC.

6 The top twenty export markets, 1984

	Volume (million bottles)		Value (millions FF)
USA	29.5	USA	1,337.6
UK	14.9	UK	611.8
W. Germany	10.9	Hong Kong	582.5
Japan	9.8	Japan	385.7
Hong Kong	8.4	W. Germany	372.3
Belgium & Luxembourg	5.1	Singapore	217.5
Netherlands	5.0	Malaysia	196.2
Canada	4.0	Netherlands	151.8
Malaysia	3.0	Belgium & Luxembourg	140.9
Singapore	2.9	Canada	131.5
Eire	2.3	Taiwan	98.6
Finland	2.1	Thailand	92.0
Italy	1.7	Eire	82.4
Switzerland	1.5	Italy	70.9
Denmark	1.5	Denmark	68.5
Thailand	1.4	Switzerland	47.9
Taiwan	1.3	Finland	43.2
Sweden	1.0	South Korea	35.5
E. Germany	1.0	Austria	27.9
Austria	0.7	Sweden	27.2

Source: BNIC.

7 Per capita consumption of cognac

	Population ('000)	Per capita consumption (in bottles)
Hong Kong	5,000	15.2
Singapore	3,000	8.2
Ireland	3,400	6.3
Belgium & Luxembourg	10,226	4.9
Finland	4,800	4.1
Netherlands	14,246	3.1
UK	56,010	2.6
Switzerland	6,398	2.4
Denmark	5,125	2.4
W. Germany	61,670	1.7
Malaysia	13,300	1.7
Canada	24,210	1.3
Norway	4,100	1.2
USA	229,810	1.1
Sweden	8,324	1.1
Austria	7,510	0.7
Japan	117,650	0.6
Taiwan	15,000	0.5
E. Germany	16,740	0.5
Thailand	47,000	0.3
Italy	57,200	0.3

Source: BNIC.

8 · Weights and Measures

Cognac has always had its own peculiarities when measuring its products.* Even today production and sales are measured by the quantity of pure alcohol produced. Cognac is sold in bottles holding 70 centilitres with a strength of 40°, so 1 hectolitre of pure alcohol (1 hl AP) = 357 bottles.

Before the French Revolution the *barrique de Cognac* or *barrique de Charente* held 27 *veltes*, the Dutch measure, or between 195 and 205 litres. The *tierçon* was 2 *barriques*, about 404 litres (a *tonneau* of wine was 4 *barriques*).

Around 1900 the *barrique* held 275 litres; now it holds 350 litres. A *pipe* of cognac holds 600 litres.

Before 1789 the *pinte* was a very varied measure, holding 93 millilitres at Cognac, 1.86 litres at Châteauneuf and 1.55 litres at Segonzac. The *velte* (effectively 1 Imperial gallon) represented 8 *pintes de Paris* or 6 *pintes d'Angoulême*.

Before the Revolution the *journal* corresponded roughly to 1 acre, while the *pied* and the *pouce* were a little longer than the foot and the inch respectively.

Finally, the *picotin* represented the amount of grain that a horse could eat in one day.

*The sources of the following information are Jacques Taransaud, *Le Livre du tonnelier*, Paris, La Roue à Livres Diffusion, 1968, and Gaston Gregor, 'Mesures au XVIIIe siècle', *Annales GREH*, 1982.

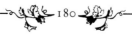

Glossary

For legal definitions of types of cognac, etc. see page 176.

ACQUIT Administrative paper required by every load of wine or spirit transported on the public highway.

ACQUIT JAUNE D'OR Special ACQUIT introduced in 1928 especially for Cognac.

ALEMBIC CHARENTAIS (originally CUCURBITE and also known as CHAUDIÈRE D'EAU-DE-VIE) Literally a spirit boiler. The pot still, the vat used for distilling cognac.

APPELLATION D'ORIGINE CONTROLÉE (AOC) Legally enforced guarantee that a wine or spirit conforms with certain provisions as to its geographical origin, the manner of its production, the grapes from which it is made, the maximum yield of the vines, etc. Awarded to France's finest wine and spirits regions and to a lot of Corsican products as well.

ARRONDISSEMENT Old name for a CANTON. Not to be confused with the Parisian variety.

ASSIGNATS Rapidly depreciating monetary certificates issued by the early revolutionary governments after 1789.

BAN DES VENDANGES Official starting date for the wine harvest. Before the Revolution a feudal right that ensured that the gentry's grapes were picked before those of the peasantry. Now an administrative formality.

BARRIQUE DE COGNAC Wooden cask, which formerly held between 195 and 205 litres. It now holds 350 litres.

BASSIOT Basin, bucket or other receptacle used to catch the newly distilled spirit as it emerges from the still.

BNIC see BUREAU NATIONAL DE COGNAC.

BOIS Wooded areas surrounding the Champagnes and producing less distinguished cognacs. Now legally divided into three: Fins Bois (354,200 hectares); Bons Bois (386,000 hectares); Bois Ordinaires (274,000 hectares). Before these were legally defined, a mass of names were used to distinguish different areas, including Premiers Fins Bois, Deuxièmes Bois, Bois Ordinaires, Bois Communs, etc.

BONBONNE Glass jar, holding approximately 25 litres, used to store old cognacs.

BONNE CHAUFFE Second distillation, which produces the cognac itself.

BORDERIES Small rectangular area north of Cognac that produces fine, nutty, cognacs.

BOUILLEUR Distiller.

BOUILLEUR DE CRU Grower allowed to distil only his own wine.

BOUILLEUR DE PROFESSION Professional distiller allowed to distil other people's wines.

BRANDEWIJN, BRANDVIN, BRANDYWIJN Literally 'burnt wine'. Dutch word for brandy.

BROUILLIS Half-strength spirit produced by the first distillation.

BRULERIE Literally 'burning house'. In reality the vat house, distillery.

BUREAU NATIONAL DE COGNAC (BNIC) Cognac's ruling body supervising the production and sale of the spirit. Set up in 1946 (for details see page 177).

BUYERS' OWN BRANDS (BOB) Cognacs bottled under their own names for major buyers, state liquor monopolies, supermarkets and the like.

CAMPAGNE The cognac year. Runs from 1 September to 31 August.

CAMPANIAN (Fr. *Campanien*) A type of chalky soil found exclusively in the Grande Champagne.

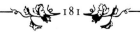

CANTON   Administrative district (formerly called an ARRONDISSEMENT). Several *cantons* make a Département.

CHAI   Any warehouse used for storing cognac.

CHAMPAGNES   Name derived from the Roman *Campania* describing the fertile chalky slopes south and east of Cognac, which produce the finest brandies. *Grande Champagne*: the inner semi-circle just south of the town (35,700 hectares); *Petite Champagne*: a larger arc of land (68,400 hectares) surrounding the Grande Champagne; *Fine Champagne*: a mixture of cognacs from the two Champagnes, with not less than a half coming from the Grande Champagne.

CHAPELET   The white circular head formed by newly distilled cognac when poured into a glass.

CHAPITEAU   Literally a circus tent, the 'big top'. Small round container that traps the alcoholic vapours emanating from the ALEMBIC below.

CHAUDIÈRE D'EAU-DE-VIE   See ALEMBIC.

CHAUFFE   Literally 'heating'. Used for a single pass through the still. Cognac is made from two *chauffes*, *la première* and *la bonne*.

CHAUFFE-VIN   Apparatus used to heat the wine before distillation by passing it through the cooling chamber attached to the vat.

CHLOROSIS (Fr. *Chlorose*)   Malady in which the vines are choked by an excess of chalk in the soil.

COL   The neck of the still.

COL DE CYGNE   Literally 'swan's neck'. The modern shape of the COL (see also TÊTE DE MAURE).

COLOMBARD (or COLOMBAR or COLOMBAT or FRENCH COLOMBARD)   Grape variety formerly planted in the BORDERIES to produce sweet wines, later used to provide a particularly aromatic cognac.

COMPTES   Term used to describe the age of cognacs (for details see page 176).

COURTIERS   Cognac brokers.

CRU   In Cognac the term is used to indicate the six subdivisions of the Cognac APPELLATION (Grande and Petite CHAMPAGNE, BORDERIES, Fins and Bons BOIS and BOIS Ordinaires).

CUCURBITE   See ALEMBIC.

EARLY-LANDED   Cognacs shipped young in cask, mostly to Britain, and traditionally matured in dock-side warehouses.

EAU-DE-VIE   Any spirit distilled from fruit.

ESPRIT-DE-VIN   Eighteenth-century term describing the strong spirit (approximately 67 per cent alcohol) resulting from the second CHAUFFE.

FINE   French colloquial expression for any brandy.

FINE A L'EAU   Brandy and water.

FINE CHAMPAGNE   See CHAMPAGNE.

FOLLE BLANCHE (also known as FOLLE)   Grape variety that dominated the Cognac region from the eighteenth century until the onset of PHYLLOXERA.

FUREUR DE PLANTER   Mania for planting vines that swept south-west France in the early eighteenth century.

GABARE   Barge used to ship cognac down the Charente.

GABELLE   Salt tax levied from the Middle Ages until 1789.

GOUT DE TERROIR   A disagreeable earthy flavour found in many cognacs made in the west of the region.

GROIES   Special type of clayey soil found only in the BORDERIES.

LEES   The detritus, leaves, twigs, skins and other solids left in the vat after fermentation.

LIMOUSIN   One of the two types of oak used for cognac casks (see also TRONCAIS).

MAITRE DE CHAI   Cellar master responsible for the care, blending and dilution of the cognac.

MALOLACTIC FERMENTATION (LE MALO)   Secondary fermentation, during which the malic acid in the wine is transformed into lactic acid.

MONOPOLE SAULNIER   Monopoly right that entitled the Cognacais to offload any cargo of salt passing the town.

MOUT   Must, grape juice.

MOUT NEUTRE   Neutral MOUT with no defects.

NAPOLÉON   Name applied to a particular quality of cognac, above VSOP, below XO.

OIDIUM   Fungoid disease that afflicted the vineyards during the 1850s.

PARADIS   Chai used for storing old cognacs.

PART DES ANGES   'The angels' share'. Local term for spirit lost through evaporation.

PETITES EAUX   Mixture of brandy and water used when reducing the strength of cognac before it is sold.

PHYLLOXERA VASTATRIX   'Wine louse' that devastated the Charente in the early 1870s.

PINEAU DES CHARENTES   Local apéritif made by adding spirit to the fermenting MOUT. Pineau must be between 16 and 22 per cent alcohol and has to be aged in wood for a year.

PRESSOIR   Press house used for making wine.

PREUVE   Strength of spirits. *Preuve de Cognac*: about 60 per cent alcohol; *Preuve d'Hollande*: about 49 per cent alcohol; *Preuve de Londres*: about 58 per cent alcohol.

QUART DE SEL   Medieval tax of 25 per cent paid whenever salt changed hands.

QUEUES   The end of a run of cognac through the still.

QUINT   Alternative to the QUART DE SEL; a single tax of 20 per cent on salt.

RANCIO CHARENTAIS   Rich cheesy flavour developed by the best cognac after fifteen years or more in cask.

RIMÉ   A cognac that has overheated in the still and has a disagreeably burned flavour.

ST-ÉMILION (also known as UGNI BLANC)   Grape variety, now virtually the only one used in Cognac.

SAINTONIAN (Fr. *Saintonien*)   Type of chalky soil found only in the CHAMPAGNES.

SECONDES   The later emanations from the still, which are not allowed to be included into the final spirit.

SERPENTIN   The cooling coil attached to the still.

TERROIR   Umbrella term covering the geological, physical and chemical composition of a vineyard's soil, its aspect and its weather.

TÊTE   The 'head' of the cognac, the first trickle to emerge. Not included in the final product.

TÊTE DE MAURE   Old-fashioned type of COL, supposedly shaped like a Moor's head complete with turban.

TIERÇON   Cask holding about 500 litres.

TONNEAU   In Cognac, any large cask.

TONNELIER   Cooper.

TONNELLERIE   Wood-working shop where casks are made.

TORULA COMPNIACENSIS RICHON   Fungus that lives off cognac fumes and darkens the roofs of CHAIS.

THREE-STAR   The basic quality of cognac.

TRONCAIS   One of the two types of oak used for casks (see also LIMOUSIN).

UGNI BLANC   See ST-ÉMILION.

VELTE   Dutch measure of volume – about 7 litres.

VINS VINÉS   Fortified wines often exported to Germany.

VS   Very Special. Has replaced THREE-STAR to describe basic-quality cognacs.

VSOP   Very Superior Old Pale.

WIJNBRANDERS   Early distillers.

XO   Extra Old. Superior cognacs produced by a few major houses, generally comprising cognacs more than fifteen or twenty years old.

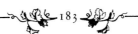

Bibliography

*, **, *** *indicate the relative importance of the source.*

Books

*Arcère, Père, *Histoire de La Rochelle*, 2 vols., La Rochelle, 1753

Baudoin, A., *Les faux eaux-de-vie et la fabrication de Cognac*, Cognac, 1893

*Baudy, Guy, *Le marché du Cognac*, thesis, Bordeaux, 1962

*Belanger, X., *La Charente sous le Second Empire*, Angoulême, 1974

*Berrault, *Annuaires: Cognac 1880–1898*

*Berry, Charles Walter, *In Search of Wine*, London, Constable, 1935

*'Bertall' (Charles Albert d'Arnoux), *La vigne*, Paris, 1878 (Reprint, Bruno Sepulchre 1981)

**Boraud, Henri, *De l'usage commercial du nom de Cognac*, Bordeaux, 1904

La Charente, pays du Cognac, Paris, ACE, 1984

*Coquand, H., *Description physique*, Paris, 1858

Corlieu, J., *Receuil en forme d'histoire* (reprint), Marseilles, Jeanne Laffitte, 1976

***Delamain, Robert, *Histoire du Cognac*, Paris, Stock, 1935

*Demachy, Jean, *L'Art du distillateur des eaux-fortes*, Paris, 1773

*Denizet, Jean, *La famille et la maison Hennessy au XVIIIe* (Ms Hennessy)

**Firino, Roger, *La famille Martell*, Paris, Libraire Ancienne Edouard Champion, 1924

*Forbes, A., *History of Distillation*, Leiden, 1970

**Gervais, Jean, *Mémoire sur l'angoumois* (reprint), SAHC, 1964

Healy, Maurice, *Stay Me with Flagons*, London, Michael Joseph, 1949

***Julien-Labruyère, François, *Paysans charentais*, La Rochelle, Rupella, 1982

**Lafon, R., Lafon, J., and Coquillaud, P., *Le cognac, sa distillation*, Paris, J. B. Baillière et Fils, 1964

*Landrau, Marguerite, *Le Cognac devant la loi*, Cognac, l'Ile d'Or, 1981

Layton, T. A., *Cognac and Other Brandies*, London, Harper Trade Journals, 1968

*Long, James, *The Century Companion to Cognac and Other Brandies*, London, Century, 1983

**Lys, Jean, *Le commerce du Cognac*, Bordeaux, 1929

**Monnet, Jean, *Mémoires*, Paris, Fayard, 1976

**Munier, Étienne, *L'Angoumois à la fin de l'Ancien Régime*, Paris, Bruno Sepulchre, 1977

**Munier, Étienne, *Sur la manière de brûler ou de distiller les vins*, Paris, Bruno Sepulchre, 1981

**Neau, Maurice, *De la crise viticole en Charente*, Paris, 1907

Prioton, M., *L culture de la vigne dans les Charentes*, Paris, 1929

*Quenot, J.-P., *Statistique du Departement de la Charente*, Paris, 1818

**Ravaz, Louis, and Vivier, Albert, *Le pays du Cognac*, Angoulême, 1900

*Ray, Cyril, *Cognac*, London, Heinemann, 1985

Rozier, Abbé, *De la fermentation des vins*, Lyon, 1776

**Savary, Abbé P. L., *Dictionnaire universel du commerce*, Paris, 1823

**Sepulchre, Bruno, *Le livre du Cognac: trois siècles d'histoire*, Paris, Hubschmidt & Bouret, 1983

**Taransaud, Jean, *Le livre de la tonnellerie*, Paris, La Roue à Livres Diffusion, 1968

Tesseron, G., *La Charente sous Louis XIV*, Angoulême, 1958

Tesseron, G., *La Charente au XVIIIe*, Angoulême, 1967

***Tovey, Charles, *British and Foreign Spirits*, London, Whittaker, 1864

*Vandyke Price, Pamela, *The Penguin Book of Spirits and Liqueurs*, Harmondsworth, Penguin, 1979

Periodicals and Articles

**Annales GREH: Annales du Groups de Recherches et d'Études Historiques de Segonzac* (1979–81), *de la Charente Saintongeaise* (1982–   )

****Annales GREH*, special issue on cognac, December 1983

**Bulletin SAHC: Bulletin de la Société Archéologique et Historique de la Charente*

***Bureau National: statistics and regularly updated information sheets

**Revue Périodique Mensuelle*, Paris, 1892

**Station Viticole, *Elaboration de Cognac*

**Station Viticole, *Notes pratiques sur la distillation charentaise*

*Belot, Claude, 'Vers une nouvelle géographie du vignoble charentais', Norois, 1974

*Burès, Maurice, 'Le type saintongeais', *La Science Sociale*, vol. 23, Paris, 1908

***Caumeil, Michel, 'Le cognac', *Pour la Science*, December, 1983

*Cullen, L. M., and Butel, Pierre, *Négoce et industrie en France et en Irlande aux XVIIIe et XIXe siecles*, CNRS, 1980

**Delafosse, Marcel, 'Le port de La Rochelle au XVIIIe', *Revue Touristique du Pays de l'Ouest*, 1945

*Martin-Civat, Pierre, 'La monopole des eaux-de-vie sous Henri IV', *100e Congrès Nationale des Sociétés Savantes*, Paris, 1975

*Pairault, François, 'Les expeditions d'eau-de-vie du Cognac', *Revue de la Saintonge et de l' Aunis*, tome II, 1976

Index